Part IV Supplement

Custom Edition

Albright

Australia • Brazil • Japan • Korea • Mexico • Singapore • Spain • United Kingdom • United States

Part IV Supplement

Data Analysis Decision Making
ALBRIGHT | WINSTON | ZAPPE

© 2011 Cengage Learning. All rights reserved.

Executive Editors:
Maureen Staudt
Michael Stranz

Senior Project Development Manager:
Linda deStefano

Marketing Specialist:
Courtney Sheldon

Senior Production/Manufacturing Manager:
Donna M. Brown

Production Editorial Manager:
Kim Fry

Sr. Rights Acquisition Account Manager:
Todd Osborne

For product information and technology assistance, contact us at
Cengage Learning Customer & Sales Support, 1-800-354-9706

For permission to use material from this text or product,
submit all requests online at **cengage.com/permissions**
Further permissions questions can be emailed to
permissionrequest@cengage.com

This book contains select works from existing Cengage Learning resources and was produced by Cengage Learning Custom Solutions for collegiate use. As such, those adopting and/or contributing to this work are responsible for editorial content accuracy, continuity and completeness.

Compilation © 2012 Cengage Learning
ISBN-13: 978-1-285-13067-5

ISBN-10: 1-285-13067-7

Cengage Learning
5191 Natorp Boulevard
Mason, Ohio 45040
USA
Cengage Learning is a leading provider of customized learning solutions with office locations around the globe, including Singapore, the United Kingdom, Australia, Mexico, Brazil, and Japan. Locate your local office at:
international.cengage.com/region.

Cengage Learning products are represented in Canada by Nelson Education, Ltd.
For your lifelong learning solutions, visit **www.cengage.com/custom.**
Visit our corporate website at **www.cengage.com.**

Printed in the United States of America

Brief Contents

Chapter 10 Regression Analysis: Estimating Relationships..............................529

Chapter 11 Regression Analysis: Statistical Inference 601

Chapter 12 Time Series Analysis and Forecasting 669

PART

4

Regression Analysis and Time Series Forecasting

CHAPTER 10
Regression Analysis: Estimating Relationships

CHAPTER 11
Regression Analysis: Statistical Inference

CHAPTER 12
Time Series Analysis and Forecasting

Regression Analysis: Estimating Relationships

© Denkyw/Dreamstime.com

SITE LOCATION OF LA QUINTA MOTOR INNS

Regression analysis is an extremely flexible tool that can aid decision making in many areas. Kimes and Fitzsimmons (1990) describe how it has been used by La Quinta Motor Inns, a moderately priced hotel chain oriented toward serving the business traveler, to help make site location decisions. Location is one of the most important decisions for a lodging firm. All hotel chains search for ideal locations and often compete against each other for the same sites. A hotel chain that can select good sites more accurately and quickly than its competition has a distinct competitive advantage.

Kimes and Fitzsimmons, academics hired by La Quinta to model its site location decision process, used regression analysis. They collected data on 57 mature inns belonging to La Quinta during a three-year business cycle. The data included profitability for each inn (defined as operating margin percentage—profit plus depreciation and interest expenses, divided by the total revenue), as well as a number of potential explanatory variables that could be used to predict profitability. These explanatory variables fell into five categories: competitive characteristics (such as number of hotel rooms in the vicinity and average room rates); demand generators (such as hospitals and office buildings within a 4-mile radius that might attract customers to the area); demographic characteristics (such as local population, unemployment rate, and median family income); market awareness (such as years the inn has been open and state population per inn); and physical considerations (such as accessibility, distance to downtown, and sign visibility).

The analysts then determined which of these potential explanatory variables were most highly correlated (positively or negatively) with profitability and entered these variables into a regression equation for profitability. The estimated regression equation was

$$\text{Predicted Profitability} = 39.05 - 5.41\text{StatePop} + 5.81\text{Price}$$
$$-3.09\sqrt{\text{MedIncome}} + 1.75\text{ColStudents}$$

where *StatePop* is the state population (in 1000s) per inn, *Price* is the room rate for the inn, *MedIncome* is the median income (in $1000s) of the area, *ColStudents* is the number of college students (in 1000s) within four miles, and all variables in this equation are standardized to have mean 0 and standard deviation 1. This equation predicts that profitability will increase when room rate and the number of college students *increase* and when state population and median income *decrease*. The R^2 value (to be discussed in this chapter) was a respectable 0.51, indicating a reasonable predictive ability. Using good statistical practice, the analysts validated this equation by feeding it explanatory variable data on a set of *different* inns, attempting to predict profitability for these new inns. The validation was a success—the regression equation predicted profitability fairly accurately for this new set of inns.

La Quinta management, however, was not as interested in predicting the exact profitability of inns as in predicting which would be profitable and which would be unprofitable. A cutoff value of 35% for operating margin was used to divide the profitable inns from the unprofitable inns. (Approximately 60% of the inns in the original sample were profitable by this definition.) The analysts were still able to use the regression equation they had developed. For any prospective site, they used the regression equation to predict profitability, and if the predicted value was sufficiently high, they predicted that site would be profitable. They selected a decision rule—that is, how high was "sufficiently high"—from considerations of the two potential types of errors. One type of error, a false positive, was predicting that a site would be profitable when in fact it was headed for unprofitability. The opposite type of error, a false negative, was predicting that a site would be unprofitable (and rejecting the site) when in fact it would have been profitable. La Quinta management was more concerned about false positives, so it was willing to be conservative in its decision rule and miss a few potential opportunities for profitable sites.

Since the time of the study, La Quinta has implemented the regression model in spreadsheet form. For each potential site, it collects data on the relevant explanatory variables, uses the regression equation to predict the site's profitability, and applies the decision rule on whether to build. Of course, the model's recommendation is only that—a recommendation. Top management has the ultimate say on whether any site is used. As Sam Barshop, then chairman of the board and president of La Quinta Motor Inns stated, "We currently use the model to help us in our site-screening process and have found that it has raised the 'red flag' on several sites we had under consideration. We plan to continue using and updating the model in the future in our attempt to make La Quinta a leader in the business hotel market." ■

10.1 INTRODUCTION

Regression analysis is the study of relationships between variables. It is one of the most useful tools for a business analyst because it applies to so many situations. Some potential uses of regression analysis in business include the following:

- How do wages of employees depend on years of experience, years of education, and gender?
- How does the current price of a stock depend on its own past values, as well as the current and past values of a market index?
- How does a company's current sales level depend on its current and past advertising levels, the advertising levels of its competitors, the company's own past sales levels, and the general level of the market?
- How does the total cost of producing a batch of items depend on the total quantity of items that have been produced?
- How does the selling price of a house depend on such factors as the appraised value of the house, the square footage of the house, the number of bedrooms in the house, and perhaps others?

Each of these questions asks how a single variable, such as selling price or employee wages, depends on other relevant variables. If we can estimate this relationship, then we can not only better understand how the world operates, but we can also do a better job of predicting the variable in question. For example, we can not only understand how a company's sales are affected by its advertising, but we can also use the company's records of current and past advertising levels to predict future sales.

The branch of statistics that studies such relationships is called **regression analysis**, and it is the subject of this chapter and the next. Because of its generality and applicability, regression analysis is one of the most pervasive of all statistical methods in the business world. There are several ways to categorize regression analysis. One categorization is based on the overall purpose of the analysis. As suggested previously, there are two potential objectives of regression analysis: to understand how the world operates and to make predictions. Either of these objectives could be paramount in any particular application. If the variable in question is employee salary and we are using variables such as years of experience, level of education, and gender to explain salary levels, then the purpose of the analysis is probably to understand how the world operates—that is, to explain how the variables combine in any given company to determine salaries. More specifically, the purpose of the analysis might be to discover whether there is any gender discrimination in salaries, after allowing for differences in work experience and education level.

Regression can be used to understand how the world operates, and it can be used for prediction.

On the other hand, the primary objective of the analysis might be prediction. A good example of this is when the variable in question is company sales, and variables such as advertising and past sales levels are used as explanatory variables. In this case it is certainly important for the company to know how the relevant variables impact its sales. But the company's primary objective is probably to predict *future* sales levels, given current and past values of the explanatory variables. A company could even use a regression model for a what-if analysis, where it predicts future sales for many conceivable patterns of advertising and then selects its advertising level on the basis of these predictions.

Fortunately, the same regression analysis enables us to solve both problems simultaneously. That is, it indicates how the world operates and it enables us to make predictions. So although the objectives of regression studies might differ, the same basic analysis always applies.

A second categorization of regression analysis is based on the type of data being analyzed. There are two basic types: cross-sectional data and time series data. *Cross-sectional data* are usually data gathered from approximately the same period of time from a population. The housing and wage examples mentioned previously are typical cross-sectional studies. The first concerns a sample of houses, presumably sold during a short period of time, such as houses sold in Florida during the first couple of months of 2010. The second concerns a sample of employees observed at a particular point in time, such as a sample of automobile workers observed at the beginning of 2011.

In contrast, *time series data* involve one or more variables that are observed at several, usually equally spaced, points in time. The stock price example mentioned previously fits this description. We observe the price of a particular stock and possibly the price of a market index at the beginning of every week, say, and then try to explain the movement of the stock's price through time.

Regression can be used to analyze cross-sectional data or time series data.

Regression analysis can be applied equally well to cross-sectional and time series data. However, there are technical reasons for treating time series data somewhat differently. The primary reason is that time series variables are usually related to their own past values. This property of many time series variables is called *autocorrelation*, and it adds complications to the analysis that we will discuss briefly.

A third categorization of regression analysis involves the number of explanatory variables in the analysis. First, we need to introduce some terms. In every regression study there is a single variable that we are trying to explain or predict, called the **dependent** variable (also called the **response** variable or the **target** variable). To help explain or predict the dependent variable, we use one or more **explanatory** variables (also called **independent** variables or **predictor** variables).[1] If there is a single explanatory variable, the analysis is called **simple regression**. If there are several explanatory variables, it is called **multiple regression**.

> The **dependent** (or **response** or **target**) variable is the single variable being explained by the regression. The **explanatory** (or **independent** or **predictor**) variables are used to explain the dependent variable.

There are important differences between simple and multiple regression. The primary difference, as the name implies, is that simple regression is simpler. The calculations are simpler, the interpretation of output is somewhat simpler, and fewer complications can occur. We will begin with a simple regression example to introduce the ideas of regression. But simple regression is really just a special case of multiple regression, and there is little need to single it out for separate discussion—especially when computer software is available to perform the calculations in either case.

> A **simple** regression analysis includes a single explanatory variable, whereas **multiple** regression can include any number of explanatory variables.

"Linear" regression allows you to estimate linear relationships as well as some nonlinear relationships.

A final categorization of regression analysis is of linear versus nonlinear models. The only type of regression analysis we study here is *linear* regression. Generally, this means that the relationships between variables are *straight-line* relationships, whereas the term *nonlinear* implies curved relationships. By focusing on linear regression, it might appear

[1]The traditional terms used in regression are *dependent* and *independent* variables. However, because these terms can cause confusion with probabilistic independence, a completely different concept, there has been an increasing use of the terms *response* and *explanatory* (or *predictor*) variables. We tend to prefer the terms *dependent* and *explanatory*, but this is largely a matter of taste.

that we are ignoring the many nonlinear relationships that exist in the business world. Fortunately, linear regression can often be used to estimate nonlinear relationships. As you will see, the term *linear regression* is more general than it appears. Admittedly, many of the relationships we study can be explained adequately by straight lines. But it is also true that many nonlinear relationships can be linearized by suitable mathematical transformations. Therefore, the only relationships we are ignoring in this book are those—and there are some—that cannot be transformed to linear. Such relationships can be studied, but only by advanced methods beyond the level of this book.

In this chapter we focus on line-fitting and curve-fitting; that is, on estimating equations that describe relationships between variables. We also discuss the interpretation of these equations, and we provide numerical measures that indicate the goodness of fit of the estimated equations. In the next chapter we extend the analysis to statistical inference of regression output.

10.2 SCATTERPLOTS: GRAPHING RELATIONSHIPS

A good way to begin any regression analysis is to draw one or more scatterplots. As discussed in Chapter 3, a scatterplot is a graphical plot of two variables, an *X* and a *Y*. If there is any relationship between the two variables, it is usually apparent from the scatterplot.

The following example, which we will continue through the chapter, illustrates the usefulness of scatterplots. It is a typical example of cross-sectional data.

EXAMPLE | **10.1 SALES VERSUS PROMOTIONS AT PHARMEX**

Pharmex is a chain of drugstores that operate around the country. To see how effective its advertising and other promotional activities are, the company has collected data from 50 randomly selected metropolitan regions. In each region it has compared its own promotional expenditures and sales to those of the leading competitor in the region over the past year. There are two variables:

■ Promote: Pharmex's promotional expenditures as a percentage of those of the leading competitor

■ Sales: Pharmex's sales as a percentage of those of the leading competitor

Note that each of these variables is an *index*, not a dollar amount. For example, if Promote equals 95 for some region, this tells us only that Pharmex's promotional expenditures in that region are 95% as large as those for the leading competitor in that region. The company expects that there is a positive relationship between these two variables, so that regions with relatively larger expenditures have relatively larger sales. However, it is not clear what the nature of this relationship is. The data are listed in the file Drugstore Sales.xlsx. (See Figure 10.1 for a partial listing of the data.) What type of relationship, if any, is apparent from a scatterplot?

Objective To use a scatterplot to examine the relationship between promotional expenses and sales at Pharmex.

Solution

First, recall from Chapter 3 that there are two ways to create a scatterplot in Excel. You can use Excel's Chart Wizard to create an X–Y chart, or you can use StatTools's Scatterplot

Figure 10.1

Data for Drugstore
Example

	A	B	C	D	E	F	G	H
1	Region	Promote	Sales					
2	1	77	85					
3	2	110	103					
4	3	110	102		Each value is a percentage of what			
5	4	93	109		the leading competitor did.			
6	5	90	85					
7	6	95	103					
8	7	100	110					
9	8	85	86					
10	9	96	92					
11	10	83	87					

procedure. The advantages of the latter are that it is slightly easier to implement and it provides automatic formatting of the chart.

Which variable should be on the horizontal axis? It is customary to put the explanatory variable on the horizontal axis and the dependent variable on the vertical axis. In this example the store believes large promotional expenditures tend to "cause" larger values of sales, so Sales is on the vertical axis and Promote is on the horizontal axis. The resulting scatterplot appears in Figure 10.2.

Figure 10.2

Scatterplot of Sales
Versus Promote

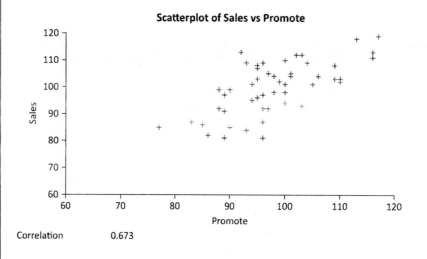

Correlation   0.673

Remember that a
StatTools chart is
really just an Excel
chart. So you can
manipulate it using
Excel tools. For this
scatterplot, we
changed the scales of
the axes so that the
scatter filled up more
of the chart area.

This scatterplot indicates that there is indeed a positive relationship between Promote and Sales—the points tend to rise from bottom left to top right—but the relationship is not perfect. If it were perfect, a given value of Promote would prescribe the value of Sales exactly. Clearly, this is not the case. For example, there are five regions with promotional values of 96 but all of them have different sales values. So the scatterplot indicates that while the variable Promote is helpful for predicting Sales, it does not lead to perfect predictions.

Note the correlation of 0.673 shown at the bottom of Figure 10.2. StatTools inserts this value automatically (if you request it) to indicate the strength of the linear relationship between the two variables. For now, just note that it is positive and its magnitude is moderately large. We will say more about correlations in the next section.

Finally, we briefly discuss causation. There is a tendency for an analyst (such as a drugstore manager) to say that larger promotional expenses *cause* larger sales values. However, unless the data are obtained in a carefully controlled experiment—which is certainly not the case here—you can never be absolutely sure about causation. One reason is that you can't always be sure which direction the causation goes. Does *X* cause *Y*, or does *Y* cause *X*? Another reason is that you can almost never rule out the possibility that some other variable is causing the variation in *both* of the observed variables. Although this is unlikely in this drugstore example, it is still a possibility. ▪

The following example uses time series data to illustrate several other features of scatterplots. We will follow this example throughout the chapter as well.

EXAMPLE | 10.2 EXPLAINING OVERHEAD COSTS AT BENDRIX

The Bendrix Company manufactures various types of parts for automobiles. The manager of the factory wants to get a better understanding of overhead costs. These overhead costs include supervision, indirect labor, supplies, payroll taxes, overtime premiums, depreciation, and a number of miscellaneous items such as insurance, utilities, and janitorial and maintenance expenses. Some of these overhead costs are *fixed* in the sense that they do not vary appreciably with the volume of work being done, whereas others are *variable* and do vary directly with the volume of work. The fixed overhead costs tend to come from the supervision, depreciation, and miscellaneous categories, whereas the variable overhead costs tend to come from the indirect labor, supplies, payroll taxes, and overtime categories. However, it is not easy to draw a clear line between the fixed and variable overhead components.

The Bendrix manager has tracked total overhead costs for the past 36 months. To help explain these, he has also collected data on two variables that are related to the amount of work done at the factory. These variables are:

▪ MachHrs: number of machine hours used during the month

▪ ProdRuns: the number of separate production runs during the month

The first of these is a direct measure of the amount of work being done. To understand the second, we note that Bendrix manufactures parts in large batches. Each batch corresponds to a production run. Once a production run is completed, the factory must set up for the next production run. During this setup there is typically some downtime while the machinery is reconfigured for the part type scheduled for production in the next batch. Therefore, the manager believes that both of these variables could be responsible (in different ways) for variations in overhead costs. Do scatterplots support this belief?

Objective To use scatterplots to examine the relationships among overhead, machine hours, and production runs at Bendrix.

Solution

The data appear in Figure 10.3. (See the Overhead Costs.xlsx file.) Each observation (row) corresponds to a single month. The goal is to find possible relationships between the

Figure 10.3

Data for Bendrix Overhead Example

	A	B	C	D
1	Month	MachHrs	ProdRuns	Overhead
2	1	1539	31	99798
3	2	1284	29	87804
4	3	1490	27	93681
5	4	1355	22	82262
6	5	1500	35	106968
7	6	1777	30	107925
8	7	1716	41	117287
9	8	1045	29	76868
10	9	1364	47	106001
11	10	1516	21	88738
35	34	1723	35	107828
36	35	1413	30	88032
37	36	1390	54	117943

Overhead variable and the MachHrs and ProdRuns variables, but because these are time series variables, you should also be on the lookout for any relationships between these variables and the Month variable. That is, you should also investigate any time series behavior in these variables.

This data set illustrates, even with a modest number of variables, how the number of potentially useful scatterplots can grow quickly. At the very least, you should examine the scatterplot between each potential explanatory variable (MachHrs and ProdRuns) and the dependent variable (Overhead). These appear in Figures 10.4 and 10.5. You can see

Figure 10.4

Scatterplot of Overhead Versus Machine Hours

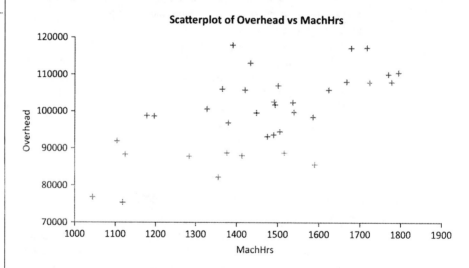

that Overhead tends to increase as either MachHrs increases or ProdRuns increases. However, both relationships are far from perfect.

To check for possible time series patterns, you can also create a time series graph for any of the variables. One of these, the time series graph for Overhead, is shown in Figure 10.6. It indicates a fairly random pattern through time, with no apparent upward trend or other obvious time series pattern. You can check that time series graphs of the MachHrs and ProdRuns variables also indicate no obvious time series patterns.

Finally, when there are multiple explanatory variables, you should check for relationships among them. The scatterplot of MachHrs versus ProdRuns appears in Figure 10.7. (Either variable could be chosen for the vertical axis.) This "cloud" of points indicates no relationship worth pursuing.

This is precisely the role of scatterplots: to provide a visual representation of relationships or the lack of relationships between variables.

Figure 10.5

Scatterplot of Overhead Versus Production Runs

Scatterplot of Overhead vs ProdRuns

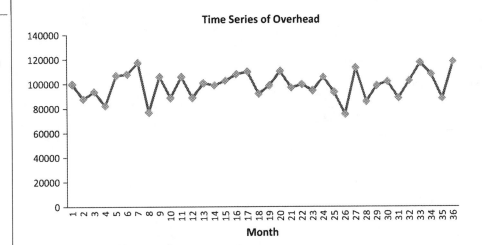

Figure 10.6

Time Series Graph of Overhead Versus Month

Time Series of Overhead

Figure 10.7

Scatterplot of Machine Hours Versus Production Runs

Scatterplot of MachHrs vs ProdRuns

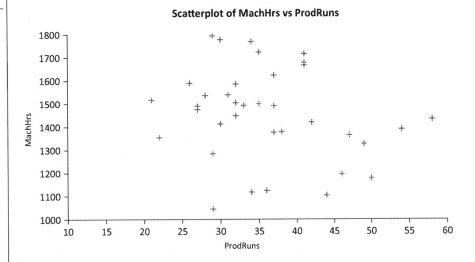

In summary, the Bendrix manager should continue to explore the positive relationship between Overhead and each of the MachHrs and ProdRuns variables. However, none of the variables appears to have any time series behavior, and the two potential explanatory variables do not appear to be related to each other. ∎

10.2.1 Linear Versus Nonlinear Relationships

Scatterplots are extremely useful for detecting behavior that might not be obvious otherwise. We illustrate some of these in the next few subsections. First, the typical relationship you hope to see is a straight-line, or *linear*, relationship. This doesn't mean that all points lie on a straight line—this is too much to expect in business data—but that the points tend to cluster around a straight line. The scatterplots in Figures 10.2, 10.4, and 10.5 all exhibit linear relationships. At least, there is no obvious curvature.

The scatterplot in Figure 10.8, on the other hand, illustrates a relationship that is clearly nonlinear. The data in this scatterplot are 1990 data on more than 100 countries. The variables listed are life expectancy (of newborns, based on current mortality conditions) and GNP per capita. The obvious curvature in the scatterplot can be explained as follows. For poor countries, a slight increase in GNP per capita has a large effect on life expectancy. However, this effect decreases for wealthier countries. A straight-line relationship is definitely not appropriate for these data. However, as discussed previously, *linear* regression—after an appropriate transformation of the data—might still be applicable.

Figure 10.8

Scatterplot of Life Expectancy Versus GNP per Capita

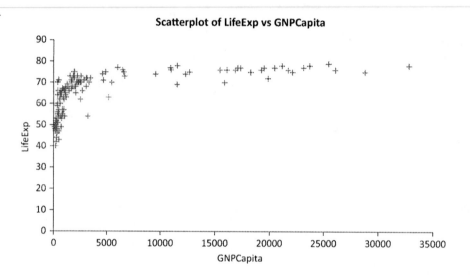

10.2.2 Outliers

Scatterplots are especially useful for identifying *outliers*, observations that lie outside the typical pattern of points. The scatterplot in Figure 10.9 shows annual salaries versus years of experience for a sample of employees at a particular company. There is a clear linear relationship between these two variables—for all employees except the point at the top right. Closer scrutiny of the data reveals that this one employee is the company CEO, whose salary is well above that of all the other employees.

> An **outlier** is an observation that falls outside of the general pattern of the rest of the observations.

Although scatterplots are good for detecting outliers, they do not necessarily indicate what you ought to do about any outliers you find. This depends entirely on the particular situation. If you are attempting to investigate the salary structure for typical employees at a company, then you should probably not include the company CEO. First, the CEO's salary is not determined in the same way as the salaries for typical employees. Second, if you do

Figure 10.9

Scatterplot of Salary
Versus Years of
Experience

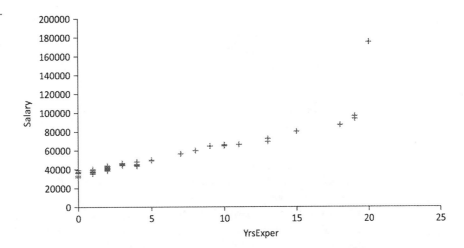

include the CEO in the analysis, it can greatly distort the results for the mass of typical employees. In other situations, however, it might *not* be appropriate to eliminate outliers just to make the analysis come out more nicely.

It is difficult to generalize about the treatment of outliers, but the following points are worth noting.

- If an outlier is clearly not a member of the population of interest, then it is probably best to delete it from the analysis. This is the case for the company CEO in Figure 10.9.

- If it isn't clear whether outliers are members of the relevant population, you can run the regression analysis with them and again without them. If the results are practically the same in both cases, then it is probably best to report the results with the outliers included. Otherwise, you can report both sets of results with a verbal explanation of the outliers.

10.2.3 Unequal Variance

Occasionally, there is a clear relationship between two variables, but the variance of the dependent variable depends on the value of the explanatory variable. Figure 10.10 illustrates a common example of this. It shows the amount spent at a mail-order company versus salary

Figure 10.10

Unequal Variance of
Dependent Variable
in a Scatterplot

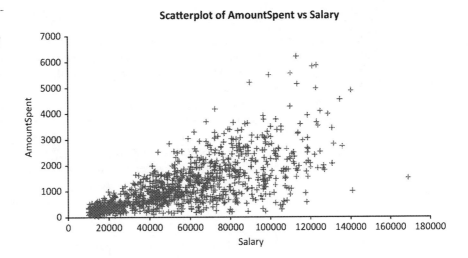

for the customers in the data set. There is a clear upward relationship, but the variability of amount spent increases as salary increases. This is evident from the *fan* shape. As you will see in the next chapter, this unequal variance violates one of the assumptions of linear regression analysis, and there are special techniques to deal with it.

10.2.4 No Relationship

A scatterplot can provide one other useful piece of information: It can indicate that there is *no* relationship between a pair of variables, at least none worth pursuing. This is usually the case when the scatterplot appears as a shapeless swarm of points, as illustrated in Figure 10.11. Here the variables are an employee performance score and the number of overtime hours worked in the previous month for a sample of employees. There is virtually no hint of a relationship between these two variables in this plot, and if these are the only two variables in the data set, the analysis can stop right here. Many people who use statistics evidently believe that a computer can perform magic on a set of numbers and find relationships that were completely hidden. Occasionally this is true, but when a scatterplot appears as in Figure 10.11, the variables are not related in any useful way, and that's all there is to it.

Figure 10.11

An Example of No Relationship

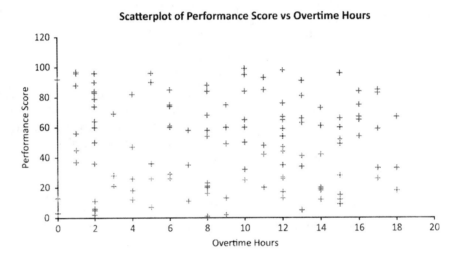

Scatterplot of Performance Score vs Overtime Hours

10.3 CORRELATIONS: INDICATORS OF LINEAR RELATIONSHIPS

Scatterplots provide graphical indications of relationships, whether they are linear, non-linear, or essentially nonexistent. **Correlations** are numerical summary measures that indicate the strength of linear relationships between pairs of variables.[2] A correlation between a pair of variables is a single number that summarizes the information in a scatterplot. A correlation can be very useful, but it has an important limitation: It measures the strength of *linear* relationships only. If there is a nonlinear relationship, as suggested by a scatterplot, the correlation can be completely misleading. With this important limitation in mind, let's look a bit more closely at correlations.

The usual notation for a correlation between two variables X and Y is r_{XY}. (The subscripts can be omitted if the variables are clear from the context.) The formula for r_{XY} is given by Equation (10.1). Note that it is a sum of products in the numerator, divided by the

[2]This section includes some material from Chapter 3 that we repeat here for convenience.

product $s_X s_Y$ of the sample standard deviations of X and Y. This requires a considerable amount of computation, so correlations are almost always computed by software packages.

Formula for Correlation

$$r_{XY} = \frac{\Sigma(X_i - \overline{X})(Y_i - \overline{Y})/(n - 1)}{s_X s_Y} \qquad (10.1)$$

The numerator of Equation (10.1) is also a measure of association between two variables X and Y, called the **covariance** between X and Y. Like a correlation, a covariance is a single number that measures the strength of the linear relationship between two variables. By looking at the sign of the covariance or correlation—plus or minus—you can tell whether the two variables are positively or negatively related. The drawback to a covariance, however, is that its magnitude depends on the units in which the variables are measured.

The magnitude of a covariance is difficult to interpret because it depends on the units of measurement.

To illustrate, the covariance between Overhead and MachHrs in the Bendrix manufacturing data set is 1,333,138. (It can be found with Excel's COVAR function or with StatTools.) However, if each overhead value is divided by 1000, so that overhead costs are expressed in thousands of dollars, and each value of MachHrs is divided by 100, so that machine hours are expressed in hundreds of hours, the covariance decreases by a factor of 100,000 to 13.33138. This is in spite of the fact that the basic relationship between these variables has not changed and the revised scatterplot has exactly the same shape. For this reason it is difficult to interpret the magnitude of a covariance, and we concentrate instead on correlations.

Unlike covariances, correlations have the attractive property that they are completely unaffected by the units of measurement. The rescaling described in the previous paragraph has absolutely no effect on the correlation between Overhead and MachHrs. In either case the correlation is 0.632. All correlations are between −1 and +1, inclusive. The sign of a correlation, plus or minus, determines whether the linear relationship between two variables is positive or negative. In this respect, a correlation is just like a covariance. However, the strength of the linear relationship between the variables is measured by the absolute value, or magnitude, of the correlation. The closer this magnitude is to 1, the stronger the linear relationship is.

A correlation close to −1 or +1 indicates a strong linear relationship. A correlation close to 0 indicates virtually no linear relationship.

A correlation equal to 0 or near 0 indicates practically no linear relationship. A correlation with magnitude close to 1, on the other hand, indicates a strong linear relationship. At the extreme, a correlation equal to −1 or +1 occurs only when the linear relationship is perfect—that is, when all points in the scatterplot lie on a single straight line. Although such extremes practically never occur in business applications, large correlations greater in magnitude than 0.9, say, are not at all uncommon.

Looking back at the scatterplots for the Pharmex drugstore data in Figure 10.2, you can see that the correlation between Sales and Promote is positive—as the upward-sloping scatter of points suggests—and is equal to 0.673. This is a moderately large correlation. It confirms the pattern in the scatterplot, namely, that the points increase linearly from left to right but with considerable variation around any particular straight line.

Similarly, the scatterplots for the Bendrix manufacturing data in Figures 10.4 and 10.5 indicate moderately large positive correlations, 0.632 and 0.521, between Overhead and MachHrs and between Overhead and ProdRuns. However, the correlation indicated in Figure 10.7 between MachHrs and ProdRuns, −0.229, is quite small and indicates almost no relationship between these two variables.

Correlations can be misleading when variables are related nonlinearly.

You must be careful when interpreting the correlations in Figures 10.8 and 10.9. The scatterplot between life expectancy and GNP per capita in Figure 10.8 is obviously nonlinear, and correlations are relevant descriptors only for *linear* relationships. If anything, the correlation of 0.616 in this example tends to underestimate the true strength of the relationship—the nonlinear one—between life expectancy and GNP per capita. In contrast, the correlation between salary and years of experience in Figure 10.9 is large, 0.894, but it is not nearly as large as it would be if the outlier were omitted. (It is then 0.992.) This example illustrates the considerable effect a single outlier can have on a correlation.

An obvious question is whether a given correlation is "large." This is a difficult question to answer directly. Clearly, a correlation such as 0.992 is quite large—the points tend to cluster very closely around a straight line. Similarly, a correlation of 0.034 is quite small—the points tend to be a shapeless swarm. But there is a continuum of in-between values, as exhibited in Figures 10.2, 10.4, and 10.5. We give a more definite answer to this question when we examine the *square* of the correlation later in this chapter.

As for calculating correlations, there are two possibilities in Excel. To calculate a *single* correlation r_{XY} between variables X and Y, you can use Excel's CORREL function in the form

$$=CORREL(Y\text{-range},Y\text{-range})$$

Alternatively, you can use StatTools to obtain a whole table of correlations between a set of variables.

Finally, we reiterate the important limitation of correlations (and covariances), namely, that they apply only to *linear* relationships. If a correlation is close to zero, you cannot automatically conclude that there is no relationship between the two variables. You should look at a scatterplot first. The chances are that the points are a shapeless swarm and that no relationship exists. But it is also possible that the points cluster around some curve. In this case the correlation is a misleading measure of the relationship.

10.4 SIMPLE LINEAR REGRESSION

Scatterplots and correlations are very useful for indicating linear relationships and the strengths of these relationships. But they do not actually *quantify* the relationships. For example, it is clear from the scatterplot of the Pharmex drugstore data that sales are related to promotional expenditures. But the scatterplot does not specify exactly what this relationship is. If the expenditure index for a given region is 95, what would you predict this region's sales index to be? Or if one region's expenditure index is 5 points higher than another's, how much larger would you predict sales of the former to be? To answer these questions, the relationship between the dependent variable Sales and the explanatory variable Promote must be quantified.

Remember that simple linear regression does not mean "easy"; it means only that there is a single explanatory variable.

In this section we answer these types of questions for simple linear regression, where there is a *single* explanatory variable. We do so by fitting a straight line through the scatterplot of the dependent variable Y versus the explanatory variable X and then basing the answers to the questions on the fitted straight line. But which straight line? We address this issue next.

10.4.1 Least Squares Estimation

The scatterplot between Sales and Promote, repeated in Figure 10.12, hints at a linear relationship between these two variables. It would not be difficult to draw a straight line through these points to produce a reasonably good fit. In fact, a possible linear fit is indicated in the graph. But we proceed more systematically than simply drawing lines freehand. Specifically, we choose the line that makes the vertical distances from the points to the line as small as possible, as explained next.

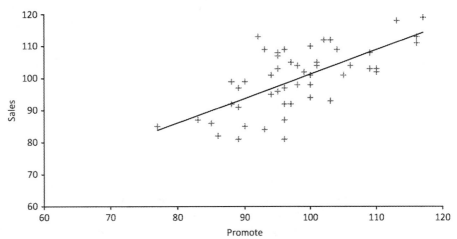

Figure 10.12

Scatterplot with Possible Linear Fit Superimposed

Consider the magnified graph in Figure 10.13. Several points in the scatterplot are shown, along with a line drawn through them. Note that the vertical distance from the horizontal axis to any point, which is just the value of Sales for that point, can be decomposed into two parts: the vertical distance from the horizontal axis to the line, and the vertical distance from the line to the point. The first of these is called the **fitted value**, and the second is called the **residual**. The idea is very simple. By using a straight line to reflect the relationship between Sales and Promote, you expect a given Sales to be at the height of the line above any particular value of Promote. That is, you expect Sales to equal the fitted value.

A **fitted value** is the predicted value of the dependent variable. Graphically, it is the height of the line above a given explanatory value. The corresponding **residual** is the difference between the actual and fitted values of the dependent variable.

Figure 10.13

Fitted Values and Residuals

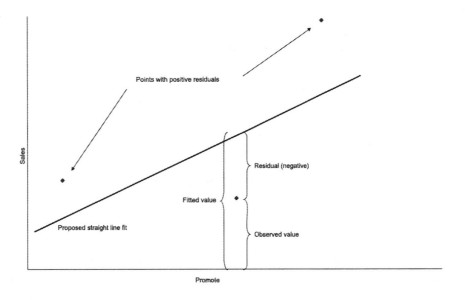

But the relationship is not perfect. Not all (perhaps not any) of the points lie exactly on the line. The differences are the residuals. They show how much the observed values differ from the fitted values. If a particular residual is positive, the corresponding point is above the line; if it is negative, the point is below the line. The only time a residual is zero is when the point lies directly on the line. The relationship between observed values, fitted values, and residuals is very general and is stated in Equation (10.2).

Fundamental Equation for Regression

$$\text{Observed Value} = \text{Fitted Value} + \text{Residual} \qquad \textbf{(10.2)}$$

We can now explain how to choose the best-fitting line through the points in the scatterplot. It is the line with the *smallest sum of squared residuals*. The resulting line is called the **least squares line**. Why do we use the sum of *squared* residuals? Why not minimize some other measure of the residuals? First, it is not appropriate to simply minimize the sum of the residuals. This is because the positive residuals would cancel the negative residuals. In fact, the least squares line has the property that the sum of the residuals is always exactly zero. To adjust for this, we could minimize the sum of the *absolute values* of the residuals, and this is a perfectly reasonable procedure. However, for technical and historical reasons, it is not the procedure usually chosen. The minimization of the sum of squared residuals is deeply rooted in statistical tradition, and it works well.

The **least squares line** is the line that minimizes the sum of the squared residuals. It is the line quoted in regression outputs.

The minimization problem itself is a calculus problem and is not discussed here. Virtually all statistical software packages perform this minimization automatically, so you do not need to be concerned with the technical details. However, we do provide the formulas for the least squares line.

Recall from basic algebra that the equation for any straight line can be written as

$$Y = a + bX$$

Here, a is the Y-intercept of the line, the value of Y when $X = 0$, and b is the slope of the line, the change in Y when X increases by one unit. Therefore, the least squares line is specified completely by its slope and intercept. These are given by equations (10.3) and (10.4).

Equation for Slope in Simple Linear Regression

$$b = \frac{\Sigma(X_i - \overline{X})(Y_i - \overline{Y})}{\Sigma(X_i - \overline{X})^2} = r_{XY}\frac{s_Y}{s_X} \qquad \textbf{(10.3)}$$

Equation for Intercept in Simple Linear Regression

$$a = \overline{Y} - b\overline{X} \qquad \textbf{(10.4)}$$

We have presented these formulas primarily for conceptual purposes, not for hand calculations—the software takes care of the calculations. From the right-hand formula for b, you can see that it is closely related to the correlation between X and Y. Specifically, if the standard deviations, s_X and s_Y, of X and Y are kept constant, then the slope b of the least squares line varies directly with the correlation between the two variables. The effect of the formula for a is not quite as interesting. It simply forces the least squares line to go through the point of sample means, $(\overline{X}, \overline{Y})$.

It is easy to obtain the least squares line in Excel with StatTools's Regression procedure. We illustrate this in the following continuations of Examples 10.1 and 10.2.

EXAMPLE | 10.1 SALES VERSUS PROMOTIONS AT PHARMEX (CONTINUED)

Find the least squares line for the Pharmex drugstore data, using Sales as the dependent variable and Promote as the explanatory variable.

Objective To use StatTools's Regression procedure to find the least squares line for sales as a function of promotional expenses at Pharmex.

Solution

To perform the analysis, select Regression from the StatTools Regression and Classification dropdown list. Then fill in the resulting dialog box as shown in Figure 10.14. Specifically, select Multiple as the Regression Type (this type is used for both single and multiple regression in StatTools), and select Promote as the single I variable and Sales as the single D variable, where I and D stand for independent and dependent. (There is always a *single D* variable, but in multiple regression there can be several I variables.) Note that there is an option to create several scatterplots involving the fitted values and residuals. We suggest checking the third option, as shown. Finally, there is an Include Prediction option. We will explain it in a later section. You can leave it unchecked for now.

Figure 10.14
Regression Dialog Box

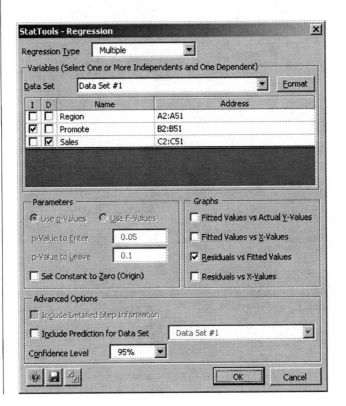

The regression output includes three parts. The first is the main regression output shown in Figure 10.15. The last two are a scatterplot of residuals and fitted values requested in the regression dialog box and a list of fitted values and residuals, a few of which are shown in Figure 10.16. (The list of fitted values and residuals is part of the output only if at least one of the optional scatterplots in the regression dialog box is selected.)

Figure 10.15

Regression Output for Drugstore Example

	A	B	C	D	E	F	G
7		Multiple R	R-Square	Adjusted R-Square	StErr of Estimate		
8	Summary						
9		0.6730	0.4529	0.4415	7.3947		
10							
11		Degrees of Freedom	Sum of Squares	Mean of Squares	F-Ratio	p-Value	
12	ANOVA Table						
13	Explained	1	2172.8804	2172.8804	39.7366	< 0.0001	
14	Unexplained	48	2624.7396	54.6821			
15							
16		Coefficient	Standard Error	t-Value	p-Value	Confidence Interval 95%	
17	Regression Table					Lower	Upper
18	Constant	25.1264	11.8826	2.1146	0.0397	1.2349	49.0180
19	Promote	0.7623	0.1209	6.3037	< 0.0001	0.5192	1.0054

Figure 10.16

Scatterplot and Partial List of Residuals Versus Fitted Values

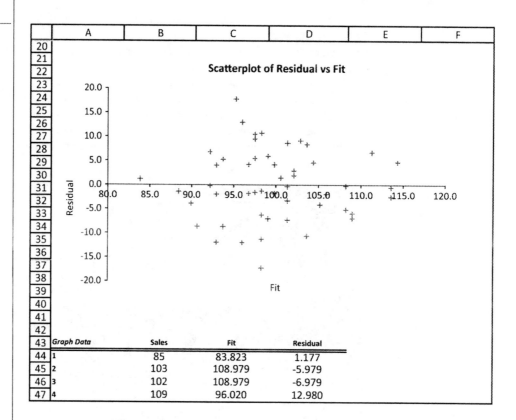

	A	B	C	D	E	F
43	Graph Data	Sales	Fit	Residual		
44	1	85	83.823	1.177		
45	2	103	108.979	-5.979		
46	3	102	108.979	-6.979		
47	4	109	96.020	12.980		

We will eventually interpret all of the output in Figure 10.15, but for now, we focus on only a small part of it. Specifically, the intercept and slope of the least squares line appear under the Coefficient label in cells B18 and B19. They imply that the equation for the least squares line is[3]

$$\text{Predicted Sales} = 25.1264 + 0.7623\text{Promote}$$

---

[3]We always report the left side of the estimated regression equation as the *predicted* value of the dependent variable. It is not the *actual* value of the dependent variable because the observations do not all lie on the estimated regression line.

Excel Tip *The Regression procedure for simple regression uses special StatTools functions to calculate all of the regression output. However, it can also be generated from several built-in statistical functions available in Excel. These include the CORREL, RSQ, STEYX, INTERCEPT, SLOPE, and LINEST functions. For example, the slope and intercept of the least squares line can be calculated directly with the formulas*

=SLOPE(Y-range,X-range)

and

=INTERCEPT(Y-range,X-range)

These formulas (with the appropriate X and Y ranges) can be entered anywhere in a spreadsheet to obtain the slope and intercept for a simple regression equation—no add-ins are necessary. The LINEST function can be used to find relevant output for a multiple regression. You can look up all of these functions in Excel's online help.

Excel Tip *As discussed in Chapter 3, you can also use superimpose a trendline on a scatterplot (by right-clicking on the chart and selecting the Trendline option). The line superimposed is indeed the least-squares regression line. In addition, you can ask for the equation of the trendline and its R^2 value (to be discussed shortly) to be added to the chart. However, this works only when there is a single X variable. There is no comparable trendline option for multiple regression.*

The regression equation for this example can be interpreted as follows. The slope, 0.7623, indicates that the sales index tends to increase by about 0.76 for each one-unit increase in the promotional expenses index. Alternatively, if two regions are compared, where the second region spends one unit more than the first region, the predicted sales index for the second region is 0.76 larger than the sales index for the first region. The interpretation of the intercept is less important. It is literally the predicted sales index for a region that does no promotions. However, no region in the sample has anywhere near a zero promotional value. Therefore, in a situation like this, where the range of observed values for the explanatory variable does not include zero, it is best to think of the intercept term as simply an "anchor" for the least squares line that enables predictions of *Y* values for the range of observed *X* values.

A useful graph in almost any regression analysis is a scatterplot of residuals (on the vertical axis) versus fitted values. This scatterplot for the Pharmex data appears in Figure 10.16 (along with a few of the residuals and fitted values used to create the chart). You typically examine such a scatterplot for any striking patterns. A good fit not only has small residuals, but it has residuals scattered *randomly* around zero with no apparent pattern. This appears to be the case for the Pharmex data. ✸

EXAMPLE | **10.2 EXPLAINING OVERHEAD COSTS AT BENDRIX (CONTINUED)**

The Bendrix manufacturing data set has two potential explanatory variables, MachHrs and ProdRuns. Eventually, we will estimate a regression equation with *both* of these variables included. However, if we include only one at a time, what do they tell us about overhead costs?

Objective To use StatTools's Regression procedure to regress overhead expenses at Bendrix against machine hours and then against production runs.

Solution

The regression output for Overhead with MachHrs as the single explanatory variable appears in Figure 10.17. The output when ProdRuns is the only explanatory variable appears in Figure 10.18. The two least squares lines are therefore

$$\text{Predicted Overhead} = 48621 + 34.7\text{MachHrs} \qquad \textbf{(10.5)}$$

and

$$\text{Predicted Overhead} = 75606 + 655.1\text{ProdRuns} \qquad \textbf{(10.6)}$$

Figure 10.17

Regression Output for Overhead versus MachHrs

	A	B	C	D	E	F	G
7		Multiple	R-Square	Adjusted	StErr of		
8	Summary	R		R-Square	Estimate		
9		0.6319	0.3993	0.3816	8584.739		
10							
11		Degrees of	Sum of	Mean of	F-Ratio	p-Value	
12	ANOVA Table	Freedom	Squares	Squares			
13	Explained	1	1665463368	1665463368	22.5986	< 0.0001	
14	Unexplained	34	2505723492	73697749.75			
15							
16		Coefficient	Standard	t-Value	p-Value	Confidence Interval 95%	
17	Regression Table		Error			Lower	Upper
18	Constant	48621.355	10725.333	4.5333	< 0.0001	26824.856	70417.853
19	MachHrs	34.702	7.300	4.7538	< 0.0001	19.867	49.537

Figure 10.18

Regression Output for Overhead versus ProdRuns

	A	B	C	D	E	F	G
7		Multiple	R-Square	Adjusted	StErr of		
8	Summary	R		R-Square	Estimate		
9		0.5205	0.2710	0.2495	9457.239		
10							
11		Degrees of	Sum of	Mean of	F-Ratio	p-Value	
12	ANOVA Table	Freedom	Squares	Squares			
13	Explained	1	1130247999	1130247999	12.6370	0.0011	
14	Unexplained	34	3040938861	89439378.26			
15							
16		Coefficient	Standard	t-Value	p-Value	Confidence Interval 95%	
17	Regression Table		Error			Lower	Upper
18	Constant	75605.516	6808.611	11.1044	< 0.0001	61768.754	89442.277
19	ProdRuns	655.071	184.275	3.5549	0.0011	280.579	1029.562

Clearly, these two equations are quite different, although each effectively breaks Overhead into a fixed component and a variable component. Equation (10.5) implies that the fixed component of overhead is about $48,621. Bendrix can expect to incur this amount even if zero machine hours are used. The variable component is the 34.7MachHrs term. It implies that the expected overhead increases by about $35 for each extra machine hour. Equation (10.6), on the other hand, breaks overhead down into a fixed component of $75,606 and a variable component of about $655 per each production run.

The difference between these two equations can be attributed to the fact that neither tells the whole story. If the manager's goal is to split overhead into a fixed component and a variable component, the variable component should include *both* of the measures of work activity (and maybe others) to give a more complete explanation of overhead. We will explain how to do this when this example is reanalyzed with *multiple regression*. ▪

10.4.2 Standard Error of Estimate

We now examine fitted values and residuals to see how they lead to a useful summary measure for a regression equation. In a typical simple regression model, the expression $a + bX$ is the fitted value of Y. Graphically, it is the height of the estimated line above the value X. The fitted value is often denoted as $\hat{Y}$ (pronounced Y-hat):[4]

$$\hat{Y} = a + bX$$

Then a typical residual, denoted by e, is the difference between the observed value Y and the fitted value $\hat{Y}$ [a restatement of Equation (10.2)]:

$$e = Y - \hat{Y}$$

Some of the fitted values and associated residuals for the Pharmex drugstore example are shown in Figure 10.19. (Recall that these columns are inserted automatically by StatTools's Regression procedure when you request the optional scatterplot of residuals versus fitted values.)

Figure 10.19

Fitted Values and Residuals for Pharmex Example

	A	B	C	D
43	Graph Data	Sales	Fit	Residual
44	1	85	83.823	1.177
45	2	103	108.979	-5.979
46	3	102	108.979	-6.979
47	4	109	96.020	12.980
48	5	85	93.733	-8.733
49	6	103	97.545	5.455
50	7	110	101.356	8.644
51	8	86	89.922	-3.922
52	9	92	98.307	-6.307
53	10	87	88.397	-1.397

The magnitudes of the residuals provide a good indication of how useful the regression line is for predicting Y values from X values. However, because there are numerous residuals, it is useful to summarize them with a single numerical measure. This measure, called the **standard error of estimate** and denoted s_e, is essentially the standard deviation of the residuals. It is given by Equation (10.7).

Formula for Standard Error of Estimate

$$s_e = \sqrt{\frac{\Sigma e_i^2}{n - 2}} \tag{10.7}$$

About two-thirds of the fitted Y values are typically within one standard error of the actual Y values. About 95% are within two standard errors.

Actually, because the average of the residuals from a least squares fit is always zero, this is identical to the standard deviation of the residuals except for the denominator $n - 2$, not the usual $n - 1$. As you will see in more generality later on, the rule is to subtract the number of parameters being estimated from the sample size n to obtain the denominator. Here there are two parameters being estimated: the intercept a and the slope b.

The usual empirical rules for standard deviations can be applied to the standard error of estimate. For example, about two-thirds of the residuals are typically within one

[4]We can also write Predicted Y instead of $\hat{Y}$, but the latter notation is common in the statistics literature.

standard error of their mean (which is zero). Stated another way, about two-thirds of the observed Y values are typically within one standard error of the corresponding fitted $\hat{Y}$ values. Similarly, about 95% of the observed Y values are typically within two standard errors of the corresponding fitted $\hat{Y}$ values.[5]

The standard error of estimate s_e is included in all StatTools regression outputs. Alternatively, it can be calculated directly with Excel's STEYX function (when there is only one X variable) in the form

=STEYX(Y-range,X-range)

In general, the standard error of estimate indicates the level of accuracy of predictions made from the regression equation. The smaller it is, the more accurate predictions tend to be.

The standard error for the Pharmex data appears in cell E9 of Figure 10.15. Its value, approximately 7.39, indicates the typical magnitude of error when using promotional expenses, via the regression equation, to predict sales. More specifically, if the regression equation is used to predict sales for many regions, about two-thirds of the predictions will be within 7.39 of the actual sales values, and about 95% of the predictions will be within two standard errors, or 14.78, of the actual sales values.

Is this level of accuracy good? One measure of comparison is the standard deviation of the sales variable, namely, 9.90. (This is obtained by the usual STDEV function applied to the observed sales values.) It can be interpreted as the standard deviation of the residuals around a *horizontal* line positioned at the mean value of Sales. This is the relevant regression line if there are no explanatory variables—that is, if Promote is ignored. In other words, it is a measure of the prediction error if the sample mean of Sales is used as the prediction for *every* region and Promote is ignored. Unfortunately, the standard error of estimate, 7.39, is not much less than 9.90. This means that the Promote variable adds a relatively small amount to prediction accuracy. Predictions with it are not much better than predictions without it. A standard error of estimate *well* below 9.90 would certainly be preferred.

The standard error of estimate can often be used to judge which of several potential regression equations is the most useful. In the Bendrix manufacturing example we estimated two regression lines, one using MachHrs and one using ProdRuns. From Figures 10.17 and 10.18, their standard errors are approximately $8585 and $9457. These imply that MachHrs is a slightly better predictor of overhead. The predictions based on MachHrs will tend to be slightly more accurate than those based on ProdRuns. Of course, the predictions based on *both* predictors should yield even more accurate predictions, as you will see when we discuss multiple regression for this example.

10.4.3 The Percentage of Variation Explained: R^2

We now discuss another important measure of the goodness of fit of the least squares line: R^2 (pronounced "R-square"). Along with the standard error of estimate s_e, it is the most frequently quoted measure in applied regression analysis. With a value always between 0 and 1, R^2 always has exactly the same interpretations: It is the *fraction of variation of the dependent variable explained by the regression line*. (It is often expressed as a percentage, so you hear about the *percentage* of variation explained by the regression line.)

R^2 is the percentage of variation of the dependent variable explained by the regression.

To see more precisely what this means, we look briefly into the derivation of R^2. In the previous section we suggested that one way to measure the regression equation's ability to

[5]This requires that the residuals be at least approximately normally distributed, a requirement discussed in the next chapter.

predict is to compare the standard error of estimate, s_e, to the standard deviation of the dependent variable, s_Y. The idea is that s_e is (essentially) the standard deviation of the residuals, whereas s_Y is the standard deviation of the residuals from a horizontal regression line at height $\overline{Y}$, the sample mean of the dependent variable. Therefore, if s_e is small compared to s_Y (that is, if s_e/s_Y is small), the regression line is evidently doing a good job in explaining the variation of the dependent variable.

The R^2 measure is based on this idea. It is defined by Equation (10.8). (This value is obtained automatically with StatTools's regression procedure, or it can be calculated with Excel's RSQ function when there is a single X variable.) Equation (10.8) indicates that when the residuals are small, R^2 will be close to 1, but when they are large, R^2 will be close to 0.

Formula for R^2

$$R^2 = 1 - \frac{\Sigma e_i^2}{\Sigma(Y_i - \overline{Y})^2} \qquad \textbf{(10.8)}$$

R^2 measures the goodness of a linear fit. The better the linear fit is, the closer R^2 is to 1.

You can see from cell C9 of Figure 10.15 that the R^2 measure for the Pharmex drugstore data is 0.453. In words, the single explanatory variable Promote is able to explain only 45.3% of the variation in the Sales variable. This is not particularly good—the same conclusion we made when we based goodness of fit on s_e. There is still 54.7% of the variation left unexplained. Of course, we would like R^2 to be as close to 1 as possible. Usually, the only way to increase it is to use better and/or more explanatory variables.

Analysts often compare equations on the basis of their R^2 values. You can see from Figures 10.17 and 10.18 that the R^2 values using MachHrs and ProdRuns as single explanatory variables for the Bendrix overhead data are 39.9% and 27.1%, respectively. These provide one more piece of evidence that MachHrs is a slightly better predictor of Overhead than ProdRuns. Of course, they also suggest that the percentage of variation of Overhead explained could be increased by including *both* variables in a single equation. This is true, as you will see shortly.

In simple linear regression, R^2 is the square of the correlation between the dependent variable and the explanatory variable.

There is a good reason for the notation R^2. It turns out that R^2 is the square of the correlation between the observed Y values and the fitted $\hat{Y}$ values. This correlation appears in all regression outputs as the *multiple R*. For the Pharmex data it is 0.673, as seen in cell B9 of Figure 10.15. Aside from rounding, the square of 0.673 is 0.453, which is the R^2 value right next to it. In the case of simple linear regression, when there is only a single explanatory variable in the equation, the correlation between the Y variable and the fitted $\hat{Y}$ values is the same as the absolute value of the correlation between the Y variable and the explanatory X variable. For the Pharmex data you already saw that the correlation between Sales and Promote is indeed 0.673.

This interpretation of R^2 as the square of a correlation helps to clarify the issue of when a correlation is "large." For example, if the correlation between two variables Y and X is ± 0.8, the regression of Y on X will have an R^2 of 0.64; that is, the regression with X as the only explanatory variable will explain 64% of the variation in Y. If the correlation drops to ± 0.7, this percentage drops to 49%; if the correlation increases to ± 0.9, the percentage increases to 81%. The point is that before a single variable X can explain a large percentage of the variation in some other variable Y, the two variables must be highly correlated—in *either* a positive or negative direction.

Level A

1. Explore the relationship between the selling prices (Y) and the appraised values (X) of the 148 homes in the file P02_11.xlsx by estimating a simple linear regression model. Interpret the standard error of estimate s_e and R^2 and the least squares line for these data.
   a. Is there evidence of a *linear* relationship between the selling price and appraised value? If so, characterize the relationship. Is it positive or negative? Is it weak or strong?
   b. For which of the three remaining variables, the size of the home, the number of bedrooms, and the number of bathrooms, is the relationship with the home's selling price *stronger*? Justify your choice with additional simple linear regression models.

2. The file P02_10.xlsx contains midterm and final exam scores for 96 students in a corporate finance course. Each row contains the two exam scores for a given student, so you might expect them to be positively correlated.
   a. Create a scatterplot of the final exam score (Y) versus the midterm score (X). Based on the visual evidence, would you say that the scores for the two exams are strongly related? Is the relationship a linear one?
   b. Superimpose a trend line on the scatterplot, and use the option to display the equation and the R^2 value. What does this equation indicate in terms of predicting a student's final exam score from his or her midterm score? Be specific.
   c. Run a regression to confirm the trend-line equation from part **b**. What does the standard error of estimate say about the accuracy of the prediction requested in part **b**?

3. A company produces electric motors for use in home appliances. One of the company's production managers is interested in examining the relationship between inspection costs in a month (X) and the number of motors produced that month that were returned by dissatisfied customers (Y). He has collected the data in the file P10_03.xlsx for the past 36 months. Estimate a simple linear regression equation using the given data and interpret it for this production manager. Also, interpret s_e and R^2 for these data.

4. The owner of the Original Italian Pizza restaurant chain wants to understand which variable most strongly influences the sales of his specialty deep-dish pizza. He has gathered data on the monthly sales of deep-dish pizzas at his restaurants and observations on other potentially relevant variables for each of his 15 outlets in central Indiana. These data are provided in the file P10_04.xlsx. Estimate a simple linear regression equation between the quantity sold (Y) and each of the following candidates for the best explanatory variable: average price of deep-dish pizzas, monthly advertising expenditures, and disposable income per household in the areas surrounding the outlets. Which variable is *most* strongly associated with the number of pizzas sold? Explain your choice.

5. The human resources manager of DataCom, Inc., wants to examine the relationship between annual salaries (Y) and the number of years employees have worked at DataCom (X). These data have been collected for a sample of employees and are given in columns B and C of the file P10_05.xlsx.
   a. Estimate the relationship between Y and X. Interpret the least squares line.
   b. How well does the estimated simple linear regression equation fit the given data? Provide evidence for your answer.

6. The file P02_02.xlsx contains information on over 200 movies that came out during 2006 and 2007.
   a. Create two scatterplots and corresponding correlations, one of Total US Gross (Y) versus 7-day Gross (X) and one of Total US Gross (Y) versus 14-day Gross (X). Based on the visual evidence, is it possible to predict the total U.S. gross of a movie from its first week's gross or its first two weeks' gross?
   b. Run two simple regressions corresponding to the two scatterplots in part **a**. Explain exactly what they tell you about the movie business. How accurate would the two predictions requested in part **a** tend to be? Be as specific as possible.

7. Examine the relationship between the average utility bills for homes of a particular size (Y) and the average monthly temperature (X). The data in the file P10_07.xlsx include the average monthly bill and temperature for each month of the past year.
   a. Use the given data to estimate a simple linear regression equation. Interpret the least squares line.
   b. How well does the estimated regression equation fit the given data? How might you do a better job of explaining the variation of the average utility bills for homes of a certain size?

8. The file P10_08.xlsx contains data on the top 200 professional golfers in 2009. (The same data set, covering multiple years, was used in Example 3.4 in Chapter 3.)
   a. Create a new variable, Earnings per Round, and the ratio of Earnings to Rounds. Then create five

scatterplots and corresponding correlations, each with Earnings per Round on the *Y* axis. The *X*-axis variables are those that most golf enthusiasts probably think are related to Earnings per Round: Yards/Drive, Driving Accuracy, Greens in Regulation, Putting Average, and Sand Save Pct. Comment on the results. Are any of these highly related to Earnings per Round? Do the correlations have the signs you would expect (positive or negative)?

b. For the two most highly correlated variables with Earnings per Round (positive or negative), run the regressions corresponding to the scatterplots. Explain exactly what they tell you about predicting Earnings per Round. How accurate do you think these predictions would be?

9. Management of a home appliance store wants to understand the growth pattern of the monthly sales of Blu-ray disc players over the past two years. The managers have recorded the relevant data in the file P10_09.xlsx. Have the sales of this product been growing linearly over the past 24 months? Using simple linear regression, explain why or why not.

10. Do the selling prices of houses in a given community vary systematically with their sizes (as measured in square feet)? Answer this question by estimating a simple regression equation where the selling price of the house is the dependent variable and the size of the house is the explanatory variable. Use the sample data given in the file P10_10.xlsx. Interpret your estimated equation and the associated R^2.

11. The file P10_11.xlsx contains annual observations of the American minimum wage since 1955. Has the minimum wage been growing at roughly a *constant* rate over this period? Use simple linear regression analysis to address this question. Explain the results you obtain. (You can ignore the data in column C for now.)

12. Based on the data in the file P02_23.xlsx from the U.S. Department of Agriculture, explore the relationship between the number of farms (*X*) and the average size of a farm (*Y*) in the United States.

Specifically, estimate a simple linear regression equation and interpret it.

13. Estimate the relationship between monthly electrical power usage (*Y*) and home size (*X*) using the data in the file P10_13.xlsx. Interpret your results. How well does a simple linear regression equation explain the variation in monthly electrical power usage?

14. The file P02_12.xlsx includes data on the 50 top graduate programs in the United States, according to a recent *U.S. News & World Report* survey. Columns B, C, and D contain ratings: an overall rating, a rating by peer schools, and a rating by recruiters. The other columns contain data that might be related to these ratings.

a. Find a table of correlations between all of the numerical variables. From these correlations, which variables in columns E–L are most highly correlated with the various ratings?

b. For the Overall rating, run a regression using it as the dependent variable and the variable (from columns E–L) most highly correlated with it. Interpret this equation. Could you have guessed the value of R^2 before running the regression? Explain. What does the standard error of estimate indicate?

c. Repeat part **b** with the Peers rating as the dependent variable. Repeat again with the Recruiters rating as the dependent variable. Discuss any differences among the three regressions in parts **b** and **c**.

Level B

15. If you haven't already done Problem 6 on 2006–2007 movies, do it now. The scatterplots of Total US Gross versus 7-day Gross or 14-day Gross indicate some possible outliers at the right—the movies that did great during their first week or two. Identify these outliers (you can decide how many qualify) and move them out of the data set. Then redo Problem 6 without the outliers. Comment on whether you get very different results. Specifically, do these outliers affect the slope of either regression line? Do they affect the standard error of estimate or R^2?

10.5 MULTIPLE REGRESSION

In general, there are two possible approaches to obtaining improved fits. The first is to examine a scatterplot of residuals for nonlinear patterns and then make appropriate modifications to the regression equation. We will discuss this approach later in the chapter. The second approach is much more straightforward: Add more explanatory variables to the regression equation. In the Bendrix manufacturing example, we deliberately included only a single explanatory variable in the equation at a time to keep the equations simple. But because scatterplots indicate that both explanatory variables are also related to Overhead, it makes sense to try including both in the regression equation. With any luck, the linear fit should improve.

When you include several explanatory variables in the regression equation, you move into the realm of *multiple* regression. Some of the concepts from simple regression carry over naturally to multiple regression, but some change considerably. The following list provides a starting point that we expand on throughout this section.

Characteristics of Multiple Regression

- Graphically, you are no longer fitting a *line* to a set of points. If there are exactly two explanatory variables, you are fitting a *plane* to the data in three-dimensional space. There is one dimension for the dependent variable and one for each of the two explanatory variables. Although you can imagine a flat plane passing through a swarm of points, it is difficult to graph this on a two-dimensional screen. If there are more than two explanatory variables, then you can only imagine the regression plane; drawing in four or more dimensions is impossible.

- The regression equation is still estimated by the least squares method—that is, by minimizing the sum of squared residuals. However, it is definitely not practical to implement this method by hand. A statistical software package such as StatTools is required.

- Simple regression is actually a special case of multiple regression—that is, an equation with a single explanatory variable can be considered a "multiple" regression equation. This explains why it is possible to use StatTools's Multiple Regression procedure for simple regression.

- There is a slope term for each explanatory variable in the equation. The interpretation of these slope terms is somewhat different than in simple regression, as explained in the following subsection.

- The standard error of estimate and R^2 summary measures are almost exactly as in simple regression, as explained in section 10.5.2.

- Many *types* of explanatory variables can be included in the regression equation, as explained in section 10.6. To a large part, these are responsible for the wide applicability of multiple regression in the business world. However, the burden is on you to choose the best set of explanatory variables. This is generally not easy.

10.5.1 Interpretation of Regression Coefficients

A typical slope term measures the expected change in Y when the corresponding X increases by one unit.

If Y is the dependent variable and X_1 through X_k are the explanatory variables, then a typical multiple regression equation has the form shown in Equation (10.9), where a is again the Y-intercept, and b_1 through b_k are the slopes. Collectively, a and the bs in Equation (10.9) are called the **regression coefficients**. The intercept a is the expected value of Y when all of the Xs equal zero. (Of course, this makes sense only if it is practical for all of the Xs to equal zero, which is seldom the case.) Each slope coefficient is the expected change in Y when this particular X increases by one unit *and the other Xs in the equation remain constant*. For example, b_1 is the expected change in Y when X_1 increases by one unit and the other Xs in the equation, X_2 through X_k, remain constant.

General Multiple Regression Equation

$$\text{Predicted } Y = a + b_1X_1 + b_2X_2 + \cdots + b_kX_k \tag{10.9}$$

This extra proviso, "when the other Xs in the equation remain constant," is crucial for the interpretation of the regression coefficients. In particular, it means that the estimates of the bs depend on which other Xs are included in the regression equation. We illustrate these ideas in the following continuation of the Bendrix manufacturing example.

EXAMPLE | **10.2 EXPLAINING OVERHEAD COSTS AT BENDRIX (CONTINUED)**

Estimate and interpret the equation for Overhead when both explanatory variables, MachHrs and ProdRuns, are included in the regression equation.

Objective   To use StatTools's Regression procedure to estimate the equation for overhead costs at Bendrix as a function of machine hours and production runs.

Solution

To obtain the regression output, select Regression from the StatTools Regression and Classification dropdown list and fill out the resulting dialog box as shown in Figure 10.20. As before, choose the Multiple option, specify the single *D* variable and the two *I* variables, and check any optional graphs you want to see. (This time we have selected the first and third options.)

Figure 10.20

Multiple Regression Dialog Box

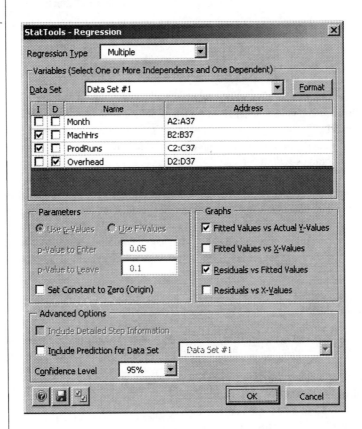

The main regression output appears in Figure 10.21. The coefficients in the range B18:B20 indicate that the estimated regression equation is

$$\text{Predicted Overhead} = 3997 + 43.54\text{MachHrs} + 883.62\text{ProdRuns} \qquad \textbf{(10.10)}$$

The interpretation of Equation (10.10) is that if the number of production runs is held constant, the overhead cost is expected to increase by \$43.54 for each extra machine hour, and if the number of machine hours is held constant, the overhead cost is expected to increase by \$883.62 for each extra production run. The Bendrix manager can interpret the intercept,

Figure 10.21

Multiple Regression Output for Bendrix Example

	A	B	C	D	E	F	G
7		Multiple R	R-Square	Adjusted R-Square	StErr of Estimate		
8	Summary						
9		0.9308	0.8664	0.8583	4108.993		
10							
11		Degrees of Freedom	Sum of Squares	Mean of Squares	F-Ratio	p-Value	
12	ANOVA Table						
13	Explained	2	3614020661	1807010330	107.0261	< 0.0001	
14	Unexplained	33	557166199.1	16883824.22			
15							
16		Coefficient	Standard Error	t-Value	p-Value	Confidence Interval 95%	
17	Regression Table					Lower	Upper
18	Constant	3996.678	6603.651	0.6052	0.5492	-9438.551	17431.907
19	MachHrs	43.536	3.589	12.1289	< 0.0001	36.234	50.839
20	ProdRuns	883.618	82.251	10.7429	< 0.0001	716.276	1050.960

$3997, as the fixed component of overhead. The slope terms involving MachHrs and ProdRuns are the variable components of overhead.

It is interesting to compare Equation (10.10) with the separate equations for Overhead involving only a single variable each. From the previous section these are

$$\text{Predicted Overhead} = 48621 + 34.7\text{MachHrs}$$

and

$$\text{Predicted Overhead} = 75606 + 655.1\text{ProdRuns}$$

Note that the coefficient of MachHrs has increased from 34.7 to 43.5 and the coefficient of ProdRuns has increased from 655.1 to 883.6. Also, the intercept is now lower than either intercept in the single-variable equations. In general, it is difficult to guess the changes that will occur when more explanatory variables are included in the equation, but it is likely that changes *will* occur.

The estimated coefficient of any explanatory variable typically depends on which other explanatory variables are included in the equation.

The reasoning is that when MachHrs is the only variable in the equation, ProdRuns constant is *not* being held constant—it is being ignored—so in effect the coefficient 34.7 of MachHrs indicates the effect of MachHrs *and* the omitted ProdRuns on Overhead. But when both variables are included, the coefficient 43.5 of MachHrs indicates the effect of MachHrs only, holding ProdRuns constant. Because the coefficients of MachHrs in the two equations have different *meanings*, it is not surprising that they result in different numerical estimates. ▪

FUNDAMENTAL INSIGHT

Multiple Regression, Correlations, and Scatterplots

When there are multiple potential Xs for a regression on Y, it is useful to calculate correlations and scatterplots of Y versus each X. But remember that correlations and scatterplots are for *two variables only*; they do not necessarily tell the whole story. Sometimes, as in this overhead example, a multiple regression can turn out quite differently than might be expected from correlations and scatterplots alone. Specifically, the R^2 value for the multiple regression can be considerably smaller or larger than might be expected.

10.5.2 Interpretation of Standard Error of Estimate and R^2

The multiple regression output in Figure 10.21 is very similar to simple regression output. In particular, cells C9 and E9 again show R^2 and the standard error of estimate s_e. Also, the square root of R^2 appears in cell B9. The interpretation of these quantities is almost exactly the same as in simple regression. The standard error of estimate is essentially the standard deviation of residuals, but it is now given by Equation (10.11), where n is the number of observations and k is the number of explanatory variables in the equation.

Formula for Standard Error of Estimate in Multiple Regression

$$s_e = \sqrt{\frac{\sum e_i^2}{n - k - 1}}$$

(10.11)

Fortunately, you can interpret s_e exactly as before. It is a measure of the typical prediction error when the multiple regression equation is used to predict the dependent variable. In this example, about two-thirds of the predictions should be within one standard error, or $4109, of the actual overhead cost. By comparing this with the standard errors from the single-variable equations for Overhead, $8585 and $9457, you can see that the multiple regression equation will tend to provide predictions that are more than twice as accurate as the single-variable equations—a big improvement.

The R^2 value is again the percentage of variation of the dependent variable explained by the combined set of explanatory variables. In fact, it even has the same formula as before [see Equation (10.8)]. For the Bendrix data you can see that MachHrs and ProdRuns combine to explain 86.6% of the variation in Overhead. This is a big improvement over the single-variable equations that were able to explain only 39.9% and 27.1% of the variation in Overhead. Remarkably, the combination of the two explanatory variables explains a larger percentage than the *sum* of their individual effects. This is not common, but this example shows that it is possible.

R^2 is always the square of the correlation between the actual and fitted Y values—in both simple and multiple regression.

The square root of R^2 shown in cell B9 of Figure 10.21 (the multiple R) is again the correlation between the fitted values and the observed values of the dependent variable. For the Bendrix data the correlation between them is 0.931, quite high. A graphical indication of this high correlation can be seen in one of the requested scatterplots, the plot of fitted versus observed values of Overhead. This scatterplot appears in Figure 10.22. If the regression equation gave *perfect* predictions, all of the points in this plot would lie on a 45° line—each fitted value would *equal* the corresponding observed value. Although a perfect fit virtually never occurs, the closer the points are to a 45° line, the better the fit is, as indicated by R^2 or its square root.

Although the R^2 value is one of the most frequently quoted values from a regression analysis, it does have one serious drawback: R^2 can only *increase* when extra explanatory

Figure 10.22

Scatterplot of Fitted Values Versus Observed Values of Overhead

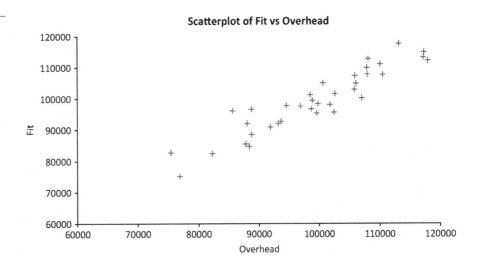

variables are added to an equation. This can lead to "fishing expeditions," where you keep adding variables to an equation, some of which have no conceptual relationship to the dependent variable, just to inflate the R^2 value. To avoid adding extra variables that do not really belong, an **adjusted R^2** value is typically listed in regression outputs. This adjusted value appears in cell D9 of Figure 10.21. Although it has no direct interpretation as "percentage of variation explained," it *can* decrease when unnecessary explanatory variables are added to an equation. Therefore, it serves as an index that you can monitor. If you add variables and the adjusted R^2 *decreases*, the extra variables are essentially not pulling their weight and should probably be omitted. We will say much more about this issue in the next chapter.

> The **adjusted R^2** is a measure that adjusts R^2 for the number of explanatory variables in the equation. It is used primarily to monitor whether extra explanatory variables really belong in the equation.

FUNDAMENTAL INSIGHT

R^2, Adjusted R^2, and Standard Error of Estimate

Sometimes a regression equation is "built" by successively adding explantory variables to an equation. As more variables are added, it is a mathematical fact that R^2 *must* increase; it cannot decrease. However, the standard error of estimate *can* increase, and the adjusted R^2 *can* decrease, each signaling that the extra variables are not useful and should probably be omitted from the equation. In fact, the only purpose of adjusted R^2 is to monitor whether the equation is getting better or worse as more variables are added.

PROBLEMS

Level A

16. A trucking company wants to predict the yearly maintenance expense (Y) for a truck using the number of miles driven during the year (X_1) and the age of the truck (X_2, in years) at the beginning of the year. The company has gathered the data given in the file P10_16.xlsx, where each observation corresponds to a particular truck.
   a. Estimate a multiple regression equation using the given data. Interpret each of the estimated regression coefficients. Why is the magnitude of the Miles Driven coefficient so much lower than the magnitude of the Age of Truck coefficient? Is it because Miles Driven is not as important in predicting Maintenance Expense?
   b. Interpret the standard error of estimate s_e and R^2 for these data.

17. DataPro is a small but rapidly growing firm that provides electronic data-processing services to commercial firms, hospitals, and other organizations. For each of the past 12 months, DataPro has tracked the number of contracts sold, the average contract price, advertising expenditures, and personal selling expenditures. These data are provided in P10_17.xlsx. Using the number of contracts sold as the dependent variable, estimate a multiple regression equation with three explanatory variables. Interpret each of the estimated regression coefficients, the standard error of estimate, and R^2.

18. An antique collector believes that the price received for a particular item increases with its age and with the number of bidders. The file P10_18.xlsx contains data on these three variables for 32 recently auctioned comparable items.
   a. Estimate a multiple regression equation using the given data. Interpret each of the estimated regression coefficients. Is the antique collector correct in believing that the price received for the item increases with its age and with the number of bidders?
   b. Interpret the standard error of estimate s_e and R^2. Does it appear that predictions of price from this equation will be very accurate?

19. Stock market analysts are continually looking for reliable predictors of stock prices. Consider the problem of modeling the price per share of electric utility stocks (Y). Two variables thought to influence this stock price are return on average equity (X_1) and annual dividend rate (X_2). The stock price, returns on equity, and dividend rates on a randomly selected day for 16 electric utility stocks are provided in the file P10_19.xlsx.

a. Estimate a multiple regression equation using the given data. Interpret each of the estimated regression coefficients.

b. Interpret the standard error of estimate s_e, R^2, and the adjusted R^2. Does it appear that predictions of price from this equation will be very accurate?

20. The manager of a commuter rail transportation system was recently asked by her governing board to determine which factors have a significant impact on the demand for rides in the large city served by the transportation network. The system manager collected data on variables thought to be possibly related to the number of weekly riders on the city's rail system. The file P10_20.xlsx contain these data.

a. What do you expect the signs of the coefficients of the explanatory variables in this multiple regression equation to be? Why? (Answer this *before* running the regression.)

b. Estimate a multiple regression equation using the given data. Interpret each of the estimated regression coefficients. Are the signs of the estimated coefficients consistent with your expectations in part **a**?

c. What proportion of the total variation in the number of weekly riders is *not* explained by this estimated multiple regression equation?

21. Consider the enrollment data for *Business Week*'s top U.S. graduate business programs in the file P10_21.xlsx. Use the data in the MBA Data sheet to estimate a multiple regression equation to assess whether there is a relationship between the total number of full-time students (Enrollment) and the following explanatory variables: (a) the proportion of female students, (b) the proportion of minority students, and (c) the proportion of international students enrolled at these business schools.

a. Interpret the coefficients of the estimated regression equation. Do any of these results surprise you? Explain.

b. How well does the estimated regression equation fit the given data?

22. A regional express delivery service company recently conducted a study to investigate the relationship between the cost of shipping a package (Y), the package weight (X_1), and the distance shipped (X_2). Twenty packages were randomly selected from among the large number received for shipment, and a detailed analysis of the shipping cost was conducted for each

package. These sample observations are given in the file P10_22.xlsx.

a. Estimate a simple linear regression equation involving shipping cost and package weight. Interpret the slope coefficient of the least squares line and the R^2 value.

b. Add another explanatory variable, distance shipped, to the regression model in part **a**. Estimate and interpret this expanded equation. How does the R^2 value for this multiple regression equation compare to that of the simple regression equation in part **a**? Explain any difference between the two R^2 values. Interpret the *adjusted* R^2 value for the revised equation.

Level B

23. The owner of a restaurant in Bloomington, Indiana, has recorded sales data for the past 19 years. He has also recorded data on potentially relevant variables. The entire data set appears in the file P10_23.xlsx.

a. Estimate a simple linear regression equation involving annual sales (the dependent variable) and the size of the population residing within 10 miles of the restaurant (the explanatory variable). Interpret the R^2 value.

b. Add another explanatory variable—annual advertising expenditures—to the regression equation in part **a**. Estimate and interpret this expanded equation. How does the R^2 value for this equation compare to the equation in part **a**? Explain any difference between the two R^2 values. What, if anything, does the *adjusted* R^2 value for the revised equation indicate?

c. Add one more explanatory variable to the multiple regression equation estimated in part **b**. In particular, estimate and interpret the coefficients of a multiple regression equation that includes the *previous* year's advertising expenditure. How does the inclusion of this third explanatory variable affect the R^2 and adjusted R^2 values, in comparison to the corresponding values for the equation of part **b**? Explain any changes in these values.

24. Continuing Problem 8 on the 2009 golfer data in the file P10_08.xlsx, the simple linear regressions for Earnings per Round were perhaps not as good as you expected. Explore several multiple regressions for Earnings per Round, using the variables in columns I–M and R. Proceed as follows.

a. Create a table of correlations for these variables.

b. Run a regression of Earnings per Round versus the most highly correlated variable (positive or negative) with Earnings per Round. Then run a second regression with the two most highly correlated variables with Earnings per Round. Then run a third with the three most highly correlated, and so on until all six explanatory variables are in the equation.

c. Comment on the changes you see from one equation to the next. Does the coefficient of a variable entered earlier change as you enter more variables? How much better do the equations get, in terms of standard error of estimate and R^2, as you enter more variables? Does adjusted R^2 ever indicate that an equation is *worse* than the one before it?

d. The bottom line is whether these variables, as a whole, do a very good job of predicting Earnings per Round. Would you say they do? Why or why not?

25. Using the sample data given in the file P10_10.xlsx, use multiple regression to predict the selling price of houses in a given community. Proceed as follows.

a. Add one explanatory variable at a time and estimate each regression equation along the way. Report and explain changes in the standard error of estimate s_e, R^2, and adjusted R^2 as each explanatory variable is added to the model. Does it matter which order you add the variables? Try at least two different orderings to answer this question.

b. Interpret each of the estimated regression coefficients in the full equation, that is, the equation with all explanatory variables included.

c. What proportion of the total variation in the selling price is explained by the multiple regression equation that includes all four explanatory variables?

10.6 MODELING POSSIBILITIES

Once you move from simple to multiple regression, the floodgates open. All types of explanatory variables are potential candidates for inclusion in the regression equation. In this section we examine several new types of explanatory variables. These include dummy variables, interaction variables, and nonlinear transformations. The techniques in this section provide you with many alternative approaches to modeling the relationship between a dependent variable and potential explanatory variables. In many applications these techniques produce much better fits than you could obtain without them.

FUNDAMENTAL INSIGHT

Modeling Possibilities

As the title of this section suggests, these techniques are modeling *possibilities*. They provide a wide variety of explanatory variables to choose from. However, this does not mean that it is wise to include all or even many of these new types of explanatory variables in any particular regression equation. The chances are that only a few, if any, will significantly improve the fit. Knowing which explanatory variables to include requires a great deal of practical experience with regression, as well as a thorough understanding of the data in its context. The material in this section should *not* be an excuse for a mindless fishing expedition.

10.6.1 Dummy Variables

Some potential explanatory variables are categorical and cannot be measured on a quantitative scale. However, these categorical variables are often related to the dependent variable, so you need a way to include them in a regression equation. The trick is to use **dummy** variables, also called **indicator** or **0–1** variables. Dummy variables are variables that indicate the category a given observation is in. If a dummy variable for a given category equals 1, the observation is in that category; if it equals 0, the observation is not in that category.

> A **dummy variable** is a variable with possible values 0 and 1. It equals 1 if the observation is in a particular category and 0 if it is not.

Categorical variables are used in two situations. The first and perhaps most common situation is when a categorical variable has only two categories. A good example of this is a gender variable that has the two categories "male" and "female." In this case only a *single* dummy variable is required, and you have the choice of assigning the 1s to either category. If the dummy variable is called Gender, you can code Gender as 1 for males and 0 for females, or you can code Gender as 1 for females and 0 for males. You just need to be consistent and specify explicitly which coding scheme you are using.

The other situation is when there are more than two categories. A good example of this is when you have quarterly time series data and you want to treat the quarter of the year as a categorical variable with four categories, 1 through 4. Then you can create four dummy variables, Q1 through Q4. For example, Q2 equals 1 for all second-quarter observations and 0 for all other observations. Although you can create four dummy variables, only three of them—*any* three—can be used in a regression equation, as will be explained shortly.

The following example illustrates how to create, use, and interpret dummy variables in regression analysis.

| EXAMPLE | 10.3 POSSIBLE GENDER DISCRIMINATION IN SALARY AT FIFTH NATIONAL BANK OF SPRINGFIELD |

The Fifth National Bank of Springfield is facing a gender discrimination suit.[6] The charge is that its female employees receive substantially smaller salaries than its male employees. The bank's employee data are listed in the file Bank Salaries.xlsx. For each of its 208 employees, the data set includes the following variables:

- EducLev: education level, a categorical variable with categories 1 (finished high school), 2 (finished some college courses), 3 (obtained a bachelor's degree), 4 (took some graduate courses), 5 (obtained a graduate degree)

- JobGrade: a categorical variable indicating the current job level, the possible levels being 1 through 6 (6 is highest)

- YrsExper: years of experience with this bank

- Age: employee's current age

- Gender: a categorical variable with values "Female" and "Male"

- YrsPrior: number of years of work experience at another bank prior to working at Fifth National

- PCJob: a categorical yes/no variable depending on whether the employee's current job is computer-related

- Salary: current annual salary

Figure 10.23 lists a few of the observations. Do these data provide evidence that there is discrimination against females in terms of salary?

Objective To use StatTools's Regression procedure to analyze whether the bank discriminates against females in terms of salary.

---

[6]This example and the accompanying data set are based on a real case from 1995. Only the bank's name has been changed.

Figure 10.23

Selected Data for
Bank Example

	A	B	C	D	E	F	G	H	I
1	Employee	EducLev	JobGrade	YrsExper	Age	Gender	YrsPrior	PCJob	Salary
2	1	3	1	3	26	Male	1	No	$32,000
3	2	1	1	14	38	Female	1	No	$39,100
4	3	1	1	12	35	Female	0	No	$33,200
5	4	2	1	8	40	Female	7	No	$30,600
6	5	3	1	3	28	Male	0	No	$29,000
7	6	3	1	3	24	Female	0	No	$30,500
8	7	3	1	4	27	Female	0	No	$30,000
9	8	3	1	8	33	Male	2	No	$27,000
10	9	1	1	4	62	Female	0	No	$34,000
11	10	3	1	9	31	Female	0	No	$29,500
12	11	3	1	9	34	Female	2	No	$26,800
13	12	2	1	8	37	Female	8	No	$31,300
14	13	2	1	9	37	Female	0	No	$31,200
15	14	2	1	10	58	Female	6	No	$34,700
16	15	3	1	4	33	Female	0	No	$30,000

Solution

A naive approach to this problem is to compare the average female salary to the average male salary. This can be done with a pivot table, as in Chapter 3, or with a more formal hypothesis test, as in Chapter 9. Using these methods, you can check that the average of all salaries is $39,922, the female average is $37,210, the male average is $45,505, and the difference between the male and female averages is statistically significant at any reasonable level of significance. In short, the females definitely earn less. But perhaps there is a reason for this. They might have lower education levels, they might have been hired more recently, and so on. The question is whether the difference between female and male salaries is still evident after taking these other attributes into account. This is a perfect task for regression.

The first task is to create dummy variables for the various categorical variables. You can do this manually with IF functions or you can use StatTools's Dummy procedure. To do it manually, create a dummy variable Female based on Gender in column J by entering the formula

=IF(F45= "Female",1,0)

in cell J4 and copying it down. Note that females are coded as 1s and males as 0s. (Remember that the quotes are necessary when a text value is used in an IF function.)

StatTools's Dummy procedure is somewhat easier, especially when there are multiple categories. For example, to create five dummies for the education levels, select Dummy from the StatTools Data Utilities dropdown menu, select the Create One Dummy Variable for Each Distinct Category option, and select the EducLev variable to base the dummies on. This creates five dummy columns with variable names EducLev=1 through EducLev=5. You could follow the same procedure to create six dummies, JobGrade=1 through JobGrade=6, for the job grade categories.

It is also possible to add dummies to effectively collapse categories.

Sometimes you might want to collapse several categories. For example, you might want to collapse the five education categories into three categories: 1, (2,3), and (4,5). The new second category includes employees who have taken undergraduate courses or have completed a bachelor's degree, and the new third category includes employees who have taken graduate courses or have completed a graduate degree. It is easy to do this. You can again use IF functions, or you can simply add the EducLev=2 and EducLev=3 columns to get the dummy for the new second category. Similarly, you add the EducLev=4 and EducLev=5 columns for the new third category. (Do you see why this works?)

Once the dummies have been created, you can run a regression analysis with Salary as the dependent variable, using any combination of numerical and dummy explanatory variables. However, there are two rules you must follow:

1. You shouldn't use any of the *original* categorical variables, such as EducLev, that the dummies are based on.

2. You should always use *one fewer dummy* than the number of categories for any categorical variable.

Always include one fewer dummy than the number of categories. The omitted dummy corresponds to the reference category.

This second rule is a technical one. If you violate it, the statistical software (StatTools or any other package) will display an error message. For example, if you want to use education level as an explanatory variable, you should enter only four of the five dummies EducLev=1 through EducLev=5. *Any* four of these can be used. The omitted dummy then corresponds to the *reference* category. The interpretation of any dummy variable coefficient is relative to this reference category. When there are only two categories, as with the gender variable, the common procedure is to name the variable with the category, such as Female, that corresponds to the 1s. If you create the dummy variables manually, you probably will not even bother to create a dummy for males. In this case "Male" automatically becomes the reference category.

To explain dummy variables in regression, it is useful to proceed in several steps in this example. (After you get used to the procedure, you can combine all of these steps into a single step. Alternatively, you can use a stepwise procedure, as explained in the next chapter.) The first step is to estimate a regression equation with only one explanatory variable, Female. The output appears in Figure 10.24, and the resulting equation is

$$\text{Predicted Salary} = 45505 - 8296\text{Female} \qquad \textbf{(10.12)}$$

Figure 10.24

Output for Bank Example with a Single Explanatory Variable

	A	B	C	D	E	F	G
7		Multiple R	R-Square	Adjusted R-Square	StErr of Estimate		
8	Summary						
9		0.3465	0.1201	0.1158	10584.3		
10							
11		Degrees of Freedom	Sum of Squares	Mean of Squares	F-Ratio	p-Value	
12	ANOVA Table						
13	Explained	1	3149633845	3149633845	28.1151	< 0.0001	
14	Unexplained	206	23077473386	112026569.8			
15							
16		Coefficient	Standard Error	t-Value	p-Value	Confidence Interval 95%	
17	Regression Table					Lower	Upper
18	Constant	45505.4	1283.5	35.4533	< 0.0001	42974.9	48036.0
19	Female	-8295.5	1564.5	-5.3024	< 0.0001	-11380.0	-5211.0

To interpret regression equations with dummy variables, it is useful to rewrite the equation for each category.

To interpret this equation, recall that Female has only two possible values, 0 and 1. If you substitute Female=1 into Equation (10.12), you obtain

$$\text{Predicted Salary} = 45505 - 8296(1) = 37209$$

Because Female=1 corresponds to females, this equation simply indicates the average female salary. Similarly, if you substitute Female=0 into Equation (10.12), you obtain

$$\text{Predicted Salary} = 45505 - 8296(0) = 45505$$

Because Female=0 corresponds to males, this equation indicates the average male salary. Therefore, the interpretation of the −8296 coefficient of the Female dummy variable is straightforward. It is the average female salary relative to the reference (male) category. In short, females get paid $8296 less on average than males.

However, Equation (10.12) tells only part of the story. It ignores all information except for gender. The next step is to expand this equation by adding the experience variables

YrsPrior and YrsExper. The output with the Female dummy variable and these two experience variables appears in Figure 10.25. The corresponding regression equation is

$$\text{Predicted Salary} = 35492 + 988\text{YrsExper} + 131\text{YrsPrior} - 8080\text{Female} \qquad \textbf{(10.13)}$$

Figure 10.25

Regression Output
with Two Numerical
Explanatory
Variables Included

	A	B	C	D	E	F	G
7		Multiple R	R-Square	Adjusted R-Square	StErr of Estimate		
8	Summary						
9		0.7016	0.4923	0.4848	8079.4		
10							
11		Degrees of Freedom	Sum of Squares	Mean of Squares	F-Ratio	p-Value	
12	ANOVA Table						
13	Explained	3	12910668018	4303556006	65.9279	< 0.0001	
14	Unexplained	204	13316439212	65276662.81			
15							
16		Coefficient	Standard Error	t-Value	p-Value	Confidence Interval 95%	
17	Regression Table					Lower	Upper
18	Constant	35491.7	1341.0	26.4661	< 0.0001	32847.6	38135.7
19	YrsExper	988.0	80.9	12.2083	< 0.0001	828.4	1147.6
20	YrsPrior	131.3	180.9	0.7259	0.4687	-225.4	488.1
21	Female	-8080.2	1198.2	-6.7438	< 0.0001	-10442.6	-5717.8

It is again useful to write Equation (10.13) in two forms: one for females (substituting Female=1) and one for males (substituting Female=0). After doing the arithmetic, they become

$$\text{Predicted Salary} = 27412 + 988\text{YrsExper} + 131\text{YrsPrior}$$

and

$$\text{Predicted Salary} = 35492 + 988\text{YrsExper} + 131\text{YrsPrior}$$

Except for the intercept term, these equations are identical. You can now interpret the coefficient −8080 of the Female dummy variable as the average salary disadvantage for females relative to males *after controlling for job experience*. Gender discrimination still appears to be a very plausible conclusion. However, note that the R^2 value is only 49.2%. Perhaps there is still more to the story.

The next step is to add education level to the equation by including four of the five education level dummies. Although *any* four could be used, we use EducLev=2 through EducLev=5, so that the lowest level becomes the reference category. (This should lead to *positive* coefficients for these dummies, which are easier to interpret.) The resulting output appears in Figure 10.26. The estimated regression equation is now

$$\text{Predicted Salary} = 26613 + 1033\text{YrsExper} + 362\text{YrsPrior} - 4501\text{Female}$$
$$+ 160\text{EducLev}=2 + 4765\text{EducLev}=3 + 7320\text{EducLev}=4 + 11770\text{EducLev}=5 \qquad \textbf{(10.14)}$$

Figure 10.26

Regression Output
with Education
Dummies Included

	A	B	C	D	E	F	G
7		Multiple R	R-Square	Adjusted R-Square	StErr of Estimate		
8	Summary						
9		0.8030	0.6449	0.6324	6824.4		
10							
11		Degrees of Freedom	Sum of Squares	Mean of Squares	F-Ratio	p-Value	
12	ANOVA Table						
13	Explained	7	16912692100	2416098871	51.8787	< 0.0001	
14	Unexplained	200	9314415131	46572075.65			
15							
16		Coefficient	Standard Error	t-Value	p-Value	Confidence Interval 95%	
17	Regression Table					Lower	Upper
18	Constant	26613.4	1794.1	14.8335	< 0.0001	23075.5	30151.2
19	YrsExper	1032.9	69.6	14.8404	< 0.0001	895.7	1170.2
20	YrsPrior	362.2	158.1	2.2908	0.0230	50.4	674.0
21	Female	-4501.3	1085.8	-4.1458	< 0.0001	-6642.3	-2360.3
22	EducLev = 2	160.2	1656.0	0.0968	0.9230	-3105.2	3425.7
23	EducLev = 3	4764.6	1473.4	3.2336	0.0014	1859.1	7670.0
24	EducLev = 4	7319.8	2694.2	2.7169	0.0072	2007.2	12632.5
25	EducLev = 5	11770.2	1510.2	7.7937	< 0.0001	8792.2	14748.2

Now there are two categorical variables involved, gender and education level. However, you can still write a separate equation *for each combination* of categories by setting the dummies to appropriate values. For example, the equation for females at education level 5 is found by setting Female and EducLev=5 equal to 1, and setting the other education dummies equal to 0. After combining terms, this equation is

$$\text{Predicted Salary} = 33882 + 1033\text{YrsExper} + 362\text{YrsPrior}$$

The intercept 33882 is the intercept from Equation (10.14), 26613, plus the coefficients of Female and EducLev=5.

Equation (10.14) can be interpreted as follows. For either gender and any education level, the expected increase in salary for one extra year of experience with Fifth National is $1033; the expected increase in salary for one extra year of prior experience with another bank is $362. The coefficients of the education dummies indicate the average increase in salary an employee can expect relative to the reference (lowest) education level. For example, an employee with education level 4 can expect to earn $7320 more than an employee with education level 1, all else being equal. Finally, the key coefficient, −$4501 for females, indicates the average salary disadvantage for females relative to males, given that they have the same experience levels *and* the same education levels. Note that the R^2 value is now 64.5%, quite a bit larger than when the education dummies were not included. We appear to be getting closer to the truth. In particular, you can see that there appears to be gender discrimination in salaries, even after accounting for job experience and education level.

One further explanation for gender differences in salary might be job grade. Perhaps females tend to be in lower job grades, which would help explain why they get lower salaries on average. One way to check this is with a pivot table, as in Figure 10.27, with job grade in the row area, gender in the column area, and counts, displayed as percentages of columns in the values area. Clearly, females tend to be concentrated at the lower job grades. For example, 28.85% of all employees are at the lowest job grade, but 34.29% of all females are at this grade and only 17.65% of males are at this grade. The opposite is true at the higher job grades. This certainly helps to explain why females get lower salaries on average.

Figure 10.27

Pivot Table of Job Grade Counts for Bank Data

	A	B	C	D
1				
2				
3	Count of Employee	Gender		
4	JobGrade	Female	Male	Grand Total
5	1	34.29%	17.65%	28.85%
6	2	20.71%	19.12%	20.19%
7	3	25.71%	10.29%	20.67%
8	4	12.14%	16.18%	13.46%
9	5	6.43%	17.65%	10.10%
10	6	0.71%	19.12%	6.73%
11	Grand Total	100.00%	100.00%	100.00%

It is possible to go one step further to see the effect of job grade on salary. As with the education dummies, the lowest job grade is used as the reference category and only the five dummies for the other categories are included. Two other potential explanatory variables can be added to the equation: Age and HasPCJob, a dummy based on the PCJob categorical variable. The regression output for this equation with all variables appears in Figure 10.28.

Figure 10.28

Regression Output with Other Variables Added

	A	B	C	D	E	F	G
7		Multiple	R-Square	Adjusted	StErr of		
8	Summary	R		R-Square	Estimate		
9		0.8748	0.7652	0.7482	5648.1		
10							
11		Degrees of	Sum of	Mean of	F-Ratio	p-Value	
12	ANOVA Table	Freedom	Squares	Squares			
13	Explained	14	20070250768	1433589341	44.9390	< 0.0001	
14	Unexplained	193	6156856463	31900810.69			
15							
16		Coefficient	Standard	t-Value	p-Value	Confidence Interval 95%	
17	Regression Table		Error			Lower	Upper
18	Constant	29689.9	2490.0	11.9236	< 0.0001	24778.8	34601.1
19	YrsExper	515.6	98.0	5.2621	< 0.0001	322.3	708.8
20	Age	-9.0	57.7	-0.1553	0.8767	-122.8	104.8
21	YrsPrior	167.7	140.4	1.1943	0.2338	-109.3	444.7
22	Female	-2554.5	1012.0	-2.5242	0.0124	-4550.4	-558.5
23	EducLev = 2	-485.6	1398.7	-0.3472	0.7289	-3244.2	2273.1
24	EducLev = 3	527.9	1357.5	0.3889	0.6978	-2149.6	3205.4
25	EducLev = 4	285.2	2404.7	0.1186	0.9057	-4457.7	5028.1
26	EducLev = 5	2690.8	1620.9	1.6601	0.0985	-506.1	5887.7
27	JobGrade = 2	1564.5	1185.8	1.3194	0.1886	-774.2	3903.2
28	JobGrade = 3	5219.4	1262.4	4.1345	< 0.0001	2729.5	7709.2
29	JobGrade = 4	8594.8	1496.0	5.7451	< 0.0001	5644.2	11545.5
30	JobGrade = 5	13659.4	1874.3	7.2879	< 0.0001	9962.7	17356.1
31	JobGrade = 6	23832.4	2799.9	8.5119	< 0.0001	18310.1	29354.7
32	HasPCJob	4922.8	1473.8	3.3402	0.0010	2016.0	7829.7

As expected, the coefficients of the job grade dummies are all positive, and they increase as the job grade increases—it pays to be in the higher job grades. The effect of age appears to be minimal, and there appears to be a "bonus" of close to $5000 for having a PC-related job. The R^2 value has now increased to 76.5%, and the penalty for being a female has decreased to $2555—still large but not as large as before.

The regression indicates that being in lower job grades implies lower salaries, but it doesn't explain why females are in the lower job grades in the first place.

However, even if this penalty, the coefficient of Female in this last equation, is considered "small," is it convincing evidence against the argument for gender discrimination? We believe the answer is no. We have used variations in job grades to reduce the penalty for being female. But the question is why females are predominantly in the low job grades. Perhaps this is the real source of gender discrimination. Perhaps management is not advancing the females as quickly as it should, which naturally results in lower salaries for females. In a sense, JobGrade is not really an explanatory variable; it is a dependent variable.

We conclude this example for now, but we will say more about it in the next two subsections. ∎

10.6.2 Interaction Variables

Consider the following regression equation for a dependent variable Y versus a numerical variable X and a dummy variable D. If the estimated equation is of the form

$$\hat{Y} = a + b_1 X + b_2 D \tag{10.15}$$

then, as in the previous section, this equation can be written as two separate equations:

$$\hat{Y} = (a + b_2) + b_1 X$$

and

$$\hat{Y} = a + b_1 X$$

The first corresponds to $D = 1$, and the second corresponds to $D = 0$. The only difference between these two equations is the intercept term; the slope for each is b_1. Geometrically, they correspond to two *parallel* lines that are a vertical distance b_2 apart. For example, if D corresponds to gender, there is a female line and a parallel male line. The effect of X on Y is the same for females and males. When X increases by one unit, Y is expected to change by b_1 units for males or females.

In effect, when you include *only* a dummy variable in a regression equation, as in Equation (10.15), you are allowing the intercepts of the two lines to differ (by an amount b_2), but you are *forcing* the lines to be parallel. To be more realistic, you might want to allow them to have different slopes, in addition to possibly different intercepts. You can do this by including an **interaction variable**. Algebraically, an interaction variable is the *product* of two variables. Its inclusion allows the effect of one of the variables on Y to depend on the value of the other variable.

> An **interaction variable** is the product of two explanatory variables. You can include such a variable in a regression equation if you believe the effect of one explanatory variable on Y depends on the value of another explanatory variable.

Suppose you create the interaction variable XD (the product of X and D) and then estimate the equation

$$\hat{Y} = a + b_1X + b_2D + b_3XD$$

As usual, this equation can be rewritten as two separate equations, depending on whether $D = 0$ or $D = 1$. If $D = 1$, terms can be combined to write

$$\hat{Y} = (a + b_2) + (b_1 + b_3)X$$

If $D = 0$, the dummy and interaction variables drop out and the equation becomes

$$\hat{Y} = a + b_1X$$

The notation is not important. The important part is that the interaction term, b_3XD, allows the slope of the regression line to differ between the two categories.

The following continuation of the bank discrimination example illustrates one possible use of interaction variables.

EXAMPLE | **10.3 POSSIBLE GENDER DISCRIMINATION IN SALARY AT FIFTH NATIONAL BANK OF SPRINGFIELD (CONTINUED)**

Earlier you estimated an equation for Salary using the numerical explanatory variables YrsExper and YrsPrior and the dummy variable Female. If you drop the YrsPrior variable from this equation (for simplicity) and rerun the regression, you obtain the equation

$$\text{Predicted Salary} = 35824 + 981\text{YrsExper} - 8012\text{Female} \qquad (10.16)$$

The R^2 value for this equation is 49.1%. If an interaction variable between YrsExper and Female is added to this equation, what is its effect?

Objective To use multiple regression with an interaction variable to see whether the effect of years of experience on salary is different across the two genders.

Solution

You first need to form an interaction variable that is the product of YrsExper and Female. This can be done in two ways in Excel. You can do it manually with an Excel formula that multiplies the two variables involved, or you can use the Interaction option from the StatTools Data Utilities dropdown menu. For the latter, select the Two Numeric Variables option in the Interaction Between dropdown list, and select Female and YrsExper as the variables to be used to create the interaction variable.[7]

Once the interaction variable has been created, you can include it in the regression equation in addition to the other variables in Equation (10.16). The multiple regression output appears in Figure 10.29. The estimated regression equation is

$$\text{Predicted Salary} = 30430 + 1528\text{YrsExper} + 4098\text{Female}$$
$$- 1248\text{Interaction(YrsExper,Female)}$$

where Interaction(YrsExper,Female) is StatTools's default name for the interaction variable. As before, it is useful to write this as two separate equations, one for females and one for males. The female equation (Female=1, so that Interaction(YrsExper,Female) = YrsExper) is

$$\text{Predicted Salary} = (30430 + 4098) + (1528 - 1248)\text{YrsExper}$$
$$= 34528 + 280\text{YrsExper}$$

and the male equation (Female=0, so that Interaction(YrsExper,Female) = 0) is

$$\text{Predicted Salary} = 30430 + 1528\text{YrsExper}$$

Figure 10.29
Regression Output with an Interaction Variable

	A	B	C	D	E	F	G
7		Multiple R	R-Square	Adjusted R-Square	StErr of Estimate		
8	Summary						
9		0.7991	0.6386	0.6333	6816.3		
10							
11		Degrees of Freedom	Sum of Squares	Mean of Squares	F-Ratio	p-Value	
12	ANOVA Table						
13	Explained	3	16748875071	5582958357	120.1620	< 0.0001	
14	Unexplained	204	9478232160	46461922.35			
15							
16		Coefficient	Standard Error	t-Value	p-Value	Confidence Interval 95%	
17	Regression Table					Lower	Upper
18	Constant	30430.0	1216.6	25.0129	< 0.0001	28031.4	32828.7
19	YrsExper	1527.8	90.5	16.8887	< 0.0001	1349.4	1706.1
20	Female	4098.3	1665.8	2.4602	0.0147	813.8	7382.7
21	Interaction(YrsExper,Female)	-1247.8	136.7	-9.1296	< 0.0001	-1517.3	-978.3

Graphically, these equations appear as in Figure 10.30. The Y-intercept for the female line is slightly higher—females with no experience with Fifth National tend to start out slightly higher than males—but the slope of the female line is much smaller. That is, males tend to move up the salary ladder much more quickly than females. Again, this provides another argument, although a somewhat different one, for gender discrimination against females. Notice that the R^2 value with the interaction variable has increased from 49.1% to 63.9%. The interaction variable has definitely added to the explanatory power of the equation.

[7]See the StatTools online help for this data utility. It explains the various options for creating interaction variables.

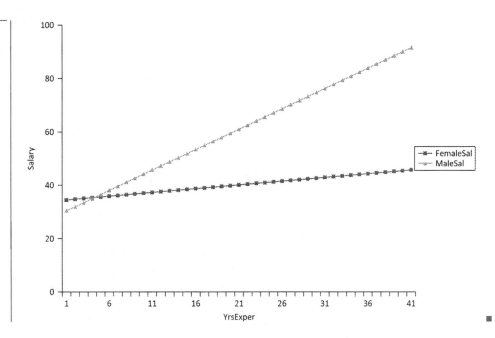

Figure 10.30

Nonparallel Female and Male Salary Lines

This example illustrates just one possible use of interaction variables. The product of *any* two variables, a numerical and a dummy variable, two dummy variables, or even two numerical variables, can be used. The trick is to interpret the results correctly, and the easiest way to do this is the way we have been doing it—by writing several separate equations and seeing how they differ. To illustrate one further possibility (among many), suppose you include the variables YrsExper, Female, and HighJob in the equation for Salary, along with interactions between Female and YrsExper and between Female and HighJob. Here, HighJob is a new dummy variable that is 1 for job grades 4 to 6 and is 0 for job grades 1 to 3. (It can be calculated as the sum of the dummies JobGrade=4 through JobGrade=6.) The resulting equation is

$$\text{Predicted Salary} = 28168 + 1261\text{YrsExper} + 9242\text{HighJob} + 6601\text{Female}$$
$$- 1224\text{Interaction(YrsExper,Female)} + 1564\text{Interaction(Female,HighJob)} \quad \textbf{(10.17)}$$

and the R^2 value is now 76.6%.

The interpretation of Equation (10.17) is quite a challenge because it is really composed of four separate equations, one for each combination of Female and HighJob. For females in the high job category, the equation becomes

$$\text{Predicted Salary} = (28168 + 9242 + 6601 + 1564) + (1261 - 1224)\text{YrsExper}$$
$$= 45575 + 37\text{YrsExper}$$

and for females in the low job category it is

$$\text{Predicted Salary} = (28168 + 6601) + (1261 - 1224)\text{YrsExper}$$
$$= 34769 + 37\text{YrsExper}$$

Similarly, for males in the high job category, the equation becomes

$$\text{Predicted Salary} = (28168 + 9242) + 1261\text{YrsExper}$$
$$= 37410 + 1261\text{YrsExper}$$

and for males in the low job category it is

$$\text{Predicted Salary} = 28168 + 1261\text{YrsExper}$$

Putting this into words, the various coefficients can be interpreted as follows.

Interpretation of Regression Coefficients

■ The intercept 28168 is the average *starting* salary (that is, with no experience at Fifth National) for males in the low job category.

■ The coefficient 1261 of YrsExper is the expected increase in salary per extra year of experience for males (in either job category).

■ The coefficient 9242 of HighJob is the expected salary premium for males starting in the high job category instead of the low job category.

■ The coefficient 6601 of Female is the expected starting salary premium for females relative to males, given that they start in the low job category.

■ The coefficient −1224 of Interaction(YrsExper,Female) is the penalty per extra year of experience for females relative to males—that is, male salaries increase this much more than female salaries each year.

■ The coefficient 1564 of Interaction(Female,HighJob) is the extra premium (in addition to the male premium) for females starting in the high job category instead of the low job category.

FUNDAMENTAL INSIGHT

Interaction Variables

As this example indicates, interaction variables can make a regression quite difficult to interpret, and they are certainly not always necessary. However, without them, the effect of each X on Y is *independent* of the values of the other Xs. If you believe, for example, that the effect of years of experience on salary is different for males than it is for females, the *only* way to capture this behavior is to include an interaction variable between years of experience and gender.

There are clearly pros and cons to adding interaction variables. On the plus side, they allow for more complex and interesting models, and they can lead to significantly better fits. On the minus side, they can become extremely difficult to interpret correctly. Therefore, we recommend that you add them only when there is good economic and statistical justification for doing so.

Postscript to Example 10.3

When regression analysis is used in a legal case, as it was in the bank gender discrimination example, it can uncover multiple versions of the "truth." That is, by including or omitting various variables, the resulting equations can imply quite different things about the issue in question, in this case, gender discrimination. If one side claims, for example, that the equation

$$\text{Predicted Salary} = 35492 + 988\text{YrsExper} + 131\text{YrsPrior} - 8080\text{Female}$$

is the true equation for explaining how salaries are determined at the bank, it is ludicrous for them to claim that the bank literally does it this way. No one believes that bank executives sit down and say: "We will start everyone at $35,492. Then we will add $988 for every year of experience with our bank and $131 for every year of prior work experience at another bank. Finally, we will subtract $8080 from this total if the person is female." All the analysts can claim is that the given regression equation is consistent, to a greater or lesser extent, with the observed data. If a number of regression equations, such as the ones estimated in this example, all point to lower salaries for females after controlling for other factors, then it doesn't matter whether management is deliberately discriminating against females according to some preconceived formula; the regression analysis indicates that females *are* compensated less than males with the same qualifications. Without a smoking gun, it is very difficult for either side to *prove* anything, but regression analysis permits either side to present evidence that is most consistent with the data.

10.6.3 Nonlinear Transformations

The general linear regression equation has the form

$$\text{Predicted } Y = a + b_1 X_1 + b_2 X_2 + \cdots + b_k X_k$$

You typically include nonlinear transformations in a regression equation because of economic considerations or curvature detected in scatterplots.

It is *linear* in the sense that the right side of the equation is a constant plus a sum of products of constants and variables. However, there is no requirement that the dependent variable Y or the explanatory variables X_1 through X_k be the *original* variables in the data set. Most often they are, but they can also be transformations of original variables. You already saw one example of this in the previous section with interaction variables. They are not original variables but are instead products of original (or even transformed) variables. The software treats them in the same way as original variables; only the interpretation differs. In this section we look at several possible **nonlinear transformations** of variables. These are often used because of curvature detected in scatterplots. They can also arise because of economic considerations. That is, economic theory often leads to particular nonlinear transformations.

You can transform the dependent variable Y or any of the explanatory variables, the Xs. You can also do both. In either case there are a few nonlinear transformations that are typically used. These include the natural logarithm, the square root, the reciprocal, and the square. The purpose of each of these is usually to "straighten out" the points in a scatterplot. If several different transformations straighten out the data equally well, the one that is easiest to interpret is preferred.

We begin with a small example where only the X variable needs to be transformed.

EXAMPLE | 10.4 DEMAND AND COST FOR ELECTRICITY

The Public Service Electric Company produces different quantities of electricity each month, depending on the demand. The file Cost of Power.xlsx lists the number of units of electricity produced (Units) and the total cost of producing these (Cost) for a 36-month period. The data appear in Figure 10.31. How can regression be used to analyze the relationship between Cost and Units?

Figure 10.31

Data for Electric Power Example

	A	B	C
1	Month	Cost	Units
2	1	45623	601
3	2	46507	738
4	3	43343	686
5	4	46495	736
6	5	47317	756
7	6	41172	498
8	7	43974	828
9	8	44290	671
10	9	29297	305
11	10	47244	637
12	11	43185	499
13	12	42658	578

Objective To see whether the cost of supplying electricity is a nonlinear function of demand, and, if it is, what form the nonlinearity takes.

Solution

A good place to start is with a scatterplot of Cost versus Units. This appears in Figure 10.32. It indicates a definite positive relationship and one that is nearly linear. However, there is also some evidence of curvature in the plot. The points increase slightly less rapidly as Units increases from left to right. In economic terms, there might be economies of scale, so that the marginal cost of electricity decreases as more units of electricity are produced.

Figure 10.32

Scatterplot of Cost Versus Units for Electricity Example

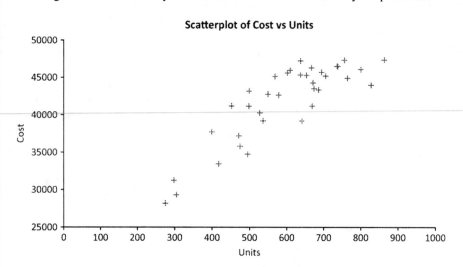

Nevertheless, you can first use regression to estimate a *linear* relationship between Cost and Units. The resulting regression equation is

$$\text{Predicted Cost} = 23651 + 30.53\text{Units}$$

The corresponding R^2 and s_e are 73.6% and $2734. It is always a good idea to request a scatterplot of the residuals versus the fitted values. This scatterplot is shown in Figure 10.33. Note that the residuals to the far left and the far right are all negative, whereas the majority of the residuals in the middle are positive. Admittedly, the pattern is far from perfect—there are several negative residuals in the middle—but this plot certainly suggests nonlinear behavior.

Figure 10.33

Residuals from a Straight-Line Fit

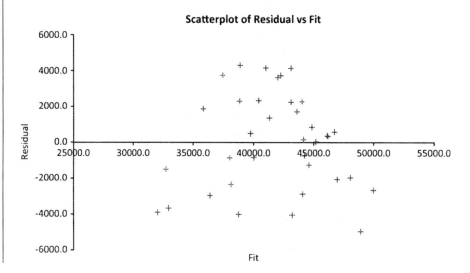

A scatterplot of residuals versus fitted values often indicates the need for a nonlinear transformation.

This negative–positive–negative behavior of residuals suggests a *parabola*—that is, a **quadratic** relationship with the *square* of Units included in the equation. The next step is to create a new variable (Units)^2 in the data set. You can do this manually (with the formula =C4^2 in cell D4, copied down) or with the Transform item in the StatTools Data Utilities dropdown menu.[8] This latter method has the advantage that it allows you to transform several variables simultaneously. Then you can use multiple regression to estimate the equation for Cost with *both* explanatory variables, Units and (Units)^2, included. The resulting equation, as shown in Figure 10.34, is

$$\text{Predicted Cost} = 5793 + 98.35\text{Units} - 0.0600(\text{Units})^2 \qquad \textbf{(10.18)}$$

Note that R^2 has increased to 82.2% and s_e has decreased to $2281.

Figure 10.34

Regression Output with Squared Term Included

	A	B	C	D	E	F	G
7		Multiple	R-Square	Adjusted	StErr of		
8	Summary	R		R-Square	Estimate		
9		0.9064	0.8216	0.8108	2280.800		
10							
11		Degrees of	Sum of	Mean of	F-Ratio	p-Value	
12	ANOVA Table	Freedom	Squares	Squares			
13	Explained	2	790511518.3	395255759.1	75.9808	< 0.0001	
14	Unexplained	33	171667570.7	5202047.597			
15							
16			Standard			Confidence Interval 95%	
17	Regression Table	Coefficient	Error	t-Value	p-Value	Lower	Upper
18	Constant	5792.80	4763.06	1.2162	0.2325	-3897.72	15483.31
19	Units	98.350	17.237	5.7058	< 0.0001	63.282	133.419
20	(Units)^2	-0.0600	0.0151	-3.9806	0.0004	-0.0906	-0.0293

One way to see how this regression equation fits the scatterplot of Cost versus Units (in Figure 10.32) is to use Excel's Trendline option. To do so, activate the scatterplot, right-click on any point, select Add Trendline, and select the Polynomial type or order 2, that is, a quadratic. A graph of Equation (10.18) is superimposed on the scatterplot, as shown in Figure 10.35. It shows a reasonably good fit, plus an obvious curvature.

The main downside to a quadratic regression equation, as in Equation (10.18), is that there is no easy way to interpret the coefficients of Units and (Units)^2. For example, you can't conclude from the 98.35 coefficient of Units that Cost increases by 98.35 dollars when Units increases by one. The reason is that when Units increases by one, (Units)^2 doesn't

Figure 10.35

Quadratic Fit in Electricity Example

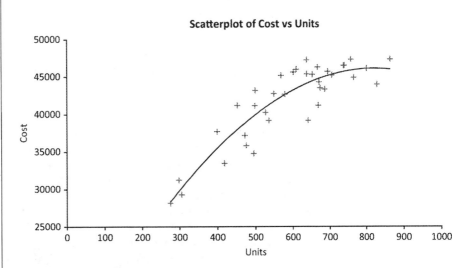

Scatterplot of Cost vs Units

[8]StatTools provides four nonlinear transformations: natural logarithm, square, square root, and reciprocal.

Excel's Trendline option allows you to superimpose a number of different curves on a scatterplot.

stay constant; it *also* increases. All you can say is that the terms in Equation (10.18) combine to explain the nonlinear relationship between units produced and total cost.

Note that the coefficient of (Units)^2, −0.0600 is a small negative value. First, the fact that it is negative makes the parabola bend downward. This produces the decreasing marginal cost behavior, where every extra unit of electricity incurs a smaller cost. Actually, the curve described by Equation (10.18) eventually goes *downhill* for large values of Units, but this part of the curve is irrelevant because the company evidently never produces such large quantities. Second, you should not be fooled by the small magnitude of this coefficient. Remember that it is the coefficient of Units *squared*, which is a large quantity. Therefore, the effect of the product −0.0600(Units)^2 is sizable.

There is at least one other possibility you can examine. Rather than a quadratic fit, you can try a logarithmic fit. In this case you need to create a new variable, Log(Units), the natural logarithm of Units, and then regress Cost against the *single* variable Log(Units). To create the new variable, you can use a formula with Excel's LN function or you can use the Transform option from StatTools Data Utilities. Also, you can superimpose a logarithmic curve on the scatterplot of Cost versus Units by using Excel's Trendline feature with the logarithm option. This curve appears in Figure 10.36. To the naked eye, it appears to be similar, and about as good a fit, as the quadratic curve in Figure 10.35.

Figure 10.36
Logarithmic Fit to Electricity Data

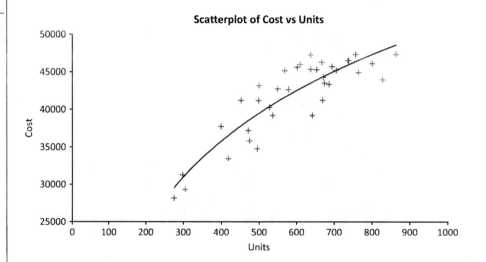

The resulting regression equation is

$$\text{Predicted Cost} = -63993 + 16654\text{Log(Units)} \qquad \textbf{(10.19)}$$

and the R^2 and s_e values are 79.8% and 2393. These latter values indicate that the logarithmic fit is not quite as good as the quadratic fit. However, the advantage of the logarithmic equation is that it is easier to interpret. In fact, one reason logarithmic transformations of variables are used so widely in regression analysis is that they are fairly easy to interpret.

In the present case, where the log of an *explanatory* variable is used, you can interpret its coefficient as follows. Suppose that Units increases by 1%, for example, from 600 to 606. Then Equation (10.19) implies that the expected Cost will increase by approximately 0.01(16654) = 166.54 dollars. In words, every 1% increase in Units is accompanied by an expected $166.54 increase in Cost. Note that for larger values of Units, a 1% increase represents a larger absolute increase (from 700 to 707 instead of from 600 to 606, say). But each such 1% increase entails the *same* increase in Cost. This is another way of describing the decreasing marginal cost property. ∎

In general, if b is the coefficient of the log of X, then the expected change in Y when X increases by 1% is approximately 0.01 times b.

The electricity example has shown two possible nonlinear transformations of the *explanatory* variable (or variables) that you can use. All you need to do is create the transformed Xs and run the regression. The interpretation of statistics such as R^2 and s_e is exactly the same as before; only the interpretation of the coefficients of the transformed Xs changes. It is also possible to transform the dependent variable Y. Now, however, you must be careful when interpreting summary statistics such as R^2 and s_e, as explained in the following examples.

A logarithmic transformation of Y is often useful when the distribution of Y values is skewed to the right.

Each of these examples transforms the dependent variable Y by taking its natural logarithm and then using the log of Y as the new dependent variable. This approach has been used in a wide variety of business applications. Essentially, it is often a good option when the distribution of Y is skewed to the right, with a few very large values and many small to medium values. The effect of the logarithm transformation is to spread the small values out and squeeze the large values together, making the distribution more symmetric. This is illustrated in Figures 10.37 and 10.38 for a hypothetical distribution of household incomes. The histogram of incomes in Figure 10.37 is clearly skewed to the right. However, the histogram of the natural log of income in Figure 10.38 is much more nearly symmetric—and, for technical reasons, more suitable for use as the dependent variable in regression.

Figure 10.37

Skewed Distribution of Income

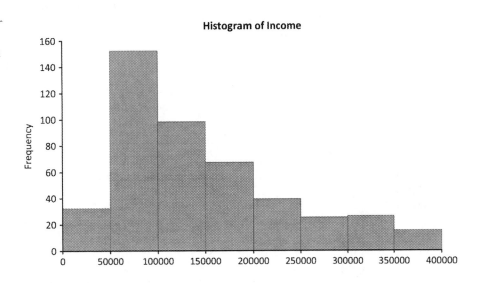

Figure 10.38

Symmetric Distribution of Log(Income)

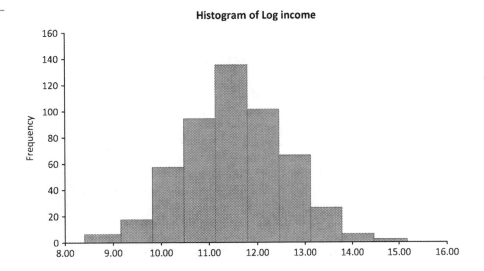

EXAMPLE

10.3 Possible Gender Discrimination in Salary at Fifth National Bank of Springfield (continued)

Returning to the bank discrimination example, a glance at the distribution of salaries of the 208 employees shows some skewness to the right—a few employees make substantially more than the majority of employees. Therefore, it might make more sense to use the natural logarithm of Salary as the dependent variable, not Salary. If you do this, how can you interpret the results?

Objective To reanalyze the bank salary data, now using the logarithm of salary as the dependent variable.

Solution

All of the previous analyses with this data set could be repeated with Log(Salary) as the dependent variable. For the sake of discussion, we look only at the regression equation with Female and YrsExper as explanatory variables. After creating the Log(Salary) variable and running the regression, the output in Figure 10.39 results. The estimated regression equation is

$$\text{Predicted Log(Salary)} = 10.4907 + 0.0188\text{YrsExper} - 0.1616\text{Female} \qquad \textbf{(10.20)}$$

The R^2 and s_e values are 42.4% and 0.1794. For comparison, when this same equation was estimated with Salary as the dependent variable, R^2 and s_e were 49.1% and 8.070.

Figure 10.39
Regression Output with Log of Salary as Dependent Variable

	A	B	C	D	E	F	G
7		Multiple		Adjusted	StErr of		
8	*Summary*	R	R-Square	R-Square	Estimate		
9		0.6514	0.4243	0.4187	0.1794		
10							
11		Degrees of	Sum of	Mean of			
12	*ANOVA Table*	Freedom	Squares	Squares	F-Ratio	p-Value	
13	Explained	2	4.861326452	2.430663226	75.5556	< 0.0001	
14	Unexplained	205	6.59495595	0.032170517			
15							
16			Standard			Confidence Interval 95%	
17	*Regression Table*	Coefficient	Error	t-Value	p-Value	Lower	Upper
18	Constant	10.4907	0.0280	374.8768	< 0.0001	10.4355	10.5458
19	YrsExper	0.0188	0.0018	10.5556	< 0.0001	0.0153	0.0224
20	Female	-0.1616	0.0265	-6.0936	< 0.0001	-0.2139	-0.1093

When the logarithm of Y is used in the regression equation, the interpretations of s_e and R^2 are different because the units of the dependent variable are completely different.

You must be careful when interpreting R^2 and s_e. Neither is directly comparable to the R^2 or s_e value with Salary as the dependent variable. Recall that R^2 in general is the percentage of the dependent variable explained by the regression equation. The problem here is that the two R^2 values are percentages explained of *different* dependent variables, Log(Salary) and Salary. The fact that one is smaller than the other (42.4% versus 49.1%) does not necessarily mean that it corresponds to a worse fit. They simply are not comparable.

The situation is even worse with s_e. Each s_e is a measure of a typical residual, but the residuals in the Log(Salary) equation are in log dollars, whereas the residuals in the Salary equation are in dollars. These units are completely different. For example, the log of \$1000 is only 6.91. Therefore, it is no surprise that s_e for the Log(Salary) equation is *much* smaller than s_e for the Salary equation. If you want comparable standard error measures for the two equations, you should take antilogs of fitted values from the Log(Salary) equation to convert them back to dollars, subtract these from the original Salary values, and take the standard deviation of these "residuals." (The EXP function in Excel can be used to take antilogs.) You can check that the resulting standard deviation is 7774.[9] This is somewhat smaller than s_e from the Salary equation, an indication of a slightly better fit.

Finally, it is fairly easy to interpret Equation (10.20) itself. When the dependent variable is Log(Y) and a term on the right-hand side of the equation is of the form bX, then whenever X increases by one unit, the predicted value of Y changes by a constant *percentage*, and this percentage is approximately equal to b (written as a percentage). For example, if $b = 0.035$, then when X increases by one unit, the predicted value of Y increases by approximately 3.5%. Applied to Equation (10.20), this means that for each extra year of experience with Fifth National, an employee's salary can be expected to increase by about 1.88%. To interpret the Female coefficient, note that the only possible increase in Female is one unit (from 0 for male to 1 for female). When this occurs, the expected percentage *decrease* in salary is approximately 16.16%. In other words, Equation (10.20) implies that females can expect to make about 16% less than men for comparable years of experience. ■

Any coefficient b can now be interpreted as the approximate percentage change in Y when the corresponding X increases by one unit.

We are not necessarily claiming that the bank data are fit better with Log(Salary) as the dependent variable than with Salary—it appears to be a virtual toss-up. However, the lessons from this example are important in general. They are as follows.

1. The R^2 values with Y and Log(Y) as dependent variables are not directly comparable. They are percentages explained of *different* variables.

2. The s_e values with Y and Log(Y) as dependent variables are usually of totally different magnitudes. To make the s_e from the log equation comparable, you need to go through the procedure described in the example so that the residuals are in *original* units.

3. To interpret any term of the form bX in the log equation, you should first express b as a percentage. For example, $b = 0.035$ becomes 3.5%. Then when X increases by one unit, the expected *percentage* change in Y is approximately this percentage b.

Remember these points, especially the third, when using the logarithm of Y as the dependent variable.

The log transformation of a dependent variable Y is used frequently. This is partly because it induces nice statistical properties (such as making the distribution of Y more symmetric). But an important advantage of this transformation is its ease of interpretation in terms of percentage changes.

Constant Elasticity Relationships

A particular type of nonlinear relationship that has firm grounding in economic theory is called a **constant elasticity relationship**. It is also called a **multiplicative relationship**. It has the form shown in Equation (10.21).

Formula for Multiplicative Relationship
$$\text{Predicted } Y = aX_1^{b_1} X_2^{b_2} \cdots X_k^{b_k} \tag{10.21}$$

One property of this type of relationship is that the effect of a one-unit change in any X on Y depends on the levels of the other Xs in the equation. This is not true for the *additive* relationships of the form

$$\text{Predicted } Y = a + b_1X_1 + b_2X_2 + \cdots + b_kX_k$$

[9]To make the two "standard deviations" comparable, we use the denominator $n - 3$ in each.

that we have been discussing. For additive relationships, when any X increases by one unit, the predicted value of Y changes by the corresponding b units, regardless of the levels of the other Xs. However, multiplicative relationships have the following nice property.

> In a **multiplicative** (or **constant elasticity**) **relationship**, the dependent variable is expressed as a *product* of explanatory variables raised to powers. When any explanatory variable X changes by 1%, the predicted value of the dependent variable changes by a constant *percentage*, regardless of the value of this X or the values of the other Xs.

The term *constant elasticity* comes from economics. Economists define the elasticity of Y with respect to X as the percentage change in Y that accompanies a 1% increase in X. Often this is in reference to a demand–price relationship. Then the *price elasticity* is the percentage decrease in demand when price increases by 1%. Usually, the elasticity depends on the current value of X. For example, the price elasticity when the price is $35 might be different than when the price is $50. However, if the relationship is of the form

$$\text{Predicted } Y = aX^b$$

then the elasticity is *constant*, the same for any value of X. In fact, it is approximately equal to the exponent b. For example, if Predicted $Y = 2X^{-1.5}$, the constant elasticity is approximately -1.5, so that when X increases by 1%, the predicted value of Y decreases by approximately 1.5%.

The constant elasticity for any X is approximately equal to the exponent of that X.

The constant elasticity property carries over to the multiple-X relationship in Equation (10.21). Then each exponent is the approximate elasticity for its X. For example, if Predicted $Y = 2X_1^{-1.5}X_2^{0.7}$, you can make the following statements:

- When X_1 increases by 1%, the predicted value of Y decreases by approximately 1.5%, regardless of the current values of X_1 and X_2.

- When X_2 increases by 1%, the predicted value of Y increases by approximately 0.7%, regardless of the current values of X_1 and X_2.

You can use linear regression to estimate the nonlinear relationship in Equation (10.21) by taking natural logarithms of *all* variables. Here two properties of logarithms are used: (1) the log of a product is the sum of the logs, and (2) the log of X^b is b times the log of X. Therefore, taking logs of both sides of Equation (10.21) gives

$$\text{Predicted } \text{Log}(Y) = \text{Log}(a) + b_1\text{Log}(X_1) + \cdots + b_k\text{Log}(X_k)$$

This equation is *linear* in the log variables $\text{Log}(X_1)$ through $\text{Log}(X_k)$, so you can estimate it in the usual way with multiple regression. You can then interpret the coefficients of the explanatory variables directly as elasticities. The following example illustrates the method.

FUNDAMENTAL INSIGHT

Using Logarithmic Transformations in Regression

If scatterplots suggest nonlinear relationships, there are an unlimited number of nonlinear transformations of Y and/or the Xs that could be tried in a regression analysis. The reason that logarithmic transformations are arguably the most frequently used nonlinear transformations, besides the fact that they often produce good fits, is that they can be interpreted naturally in terms of percentage changes. In real studies, this interpretability is an important advantage over other potential nonlinear transformations.

EXAMPLE | 10.5 FACTORS RELATED TO SALES OF DOMESTIC AUTOMOBILES

The file Car Sales.xlsx contains annual data (1970–1999) on domestic auto sales in the United States. The data are listed in Figure 10.40. The variables are defined as

- Sales: annual domestic auto sales (in number of units)
- PriceIndex: consumer price index of transportation
- Income: real disposable income
- Interest: prime rate of interest

Our goal is to estimate and interpret a multiplicative (constant elasticity) relationship between Sales and PriceIndex, Income, and Interest.

Objective   To use logarithms of variables in a multiple regression to estimate a multiplicative relationship for automobile sales as a function of price, income, and interest rate.

Figure 10.40   Data for Automobile Demand Example

	A	B	C	D	E	F	G	H	I
1	Year	Sales	PriceIndex	Income	Interest				
2	1970	7,115,270	37.5	2630	7.91%				
3	1971	8,676,410	39.5	2745.3	5.72%	Sources: Automotive News, Market			
4	1972	9,321,310	39.9	2874.3	5.25%	Data Book (various issues) for column			
5	1973	9,618,510	41.2	3072.3	8.03%	B, from Economic Report of the			
6	1974	7,448,340	45.8	3051.9	10.81%	President, 2000, for columns C, D, E			
7	1975	7,049,840	50.1	3108.5	7.86%				
8	1976	8,606,860	55.1	3243.5	6.84%				
9	1977	9,104,930	59	3360.7	6.83%				
10	1978	9,304,250	61.7	3527.5	9.06%				
11	1979	8,316,020	70.5	3628.6	12.67%				
12	1980	6,578,360	83.1	3658	15.27%				
13	1981	6,206,690	93.2	3741.1	18.87%				
14	1982	5,756,610	97	3791.7	14.86%				
15	1983	6,795,230	99.3	3906.9	10.79%				
16	1984	7,951,790	103.7	4207.6	12.04%				
17	1985	8,204,690	106.4	4347.8	9.93%				
18	1986	8,222,480	102.3	4486.6	8.33%				
19	1987	7,080,890	105.4	4582.5	8.21%				
20	1988	7,526,334	108.7	4784.1	9.32%				
21	1989	7,014,850	114.1	4906.5	10.87%				
22	1990	6,842,733	120.5	5041.2	10.01%				
23	1991	6,072,255	123.8	5033	8.46%				
24	1992	6,216,488	126.5	5189.3	6.25%				
25	1993	6,674,458	130.4	5261.3	6.00%				
26	1994	7,181,975	134.3	5397.2	7.15%				
27	1995	7,023,843	139.1	5539.1	8.83%				
28	1996	7,139,884	143	5677.7	8.27%				
29	1997	6,907,992	144.3	5854.5	8.44%				
30	1998	6,756,804	141.6	6168.6	8.35%				
31	1999	6,987,208	144.4	6320	8.00%				

Solution

The first step is to take natural logs of all four variables. (You can do this in one step with the StatTools Transform utility or you can use Excel's LN function.) Then you can run a multiple regression, with Log(Quantity) as the dependent variable and Log(PriceIndex), Log(Income), and Log(Interest) as the explanatory variables. The resulting output is shown in Figure 10.41. The corresponding equation for Log(Quantity) is

$$\text{Predicted Log(Sales)} = 14.126 - 0.384\text{Log(PriceIndex)} + 0.388\text{Log(Income)} - 0.070\text{Log(Interest)}$$

Figure 10.41 Regression Output for Multiplicative Relationship

	A	B	C	D	E	F	G
7		Multiple	R-Square	Adjusted	StErr of		
8	Summary	R		R-Square	Estimate		
9		0.6813	0.4642	0.4023	0.1053		
10							
11		Degrees of	Sum of	Mean of	F-Ratio	p-Value	
12	ANOVA Table	Freedom	Squares	Squares			
13	Explained	3	0.249567775	0.083189258	7.5073	0.0009	
14	Unexplained	26	0.288107728	0.011081066			
15							
16		Coefficient	Standard	t-Value	p-Value	Confidence Interval 95%	
17	Regression Table		Error			Lower	Upper
18	Constant	14.1260	1.9838	7.1206	< 0.0001	10.0482	18.2037
19	Log(PriceIndex)	-0.3837	0.2091	-1.8351	0.0780	-0.8135	0.0461
20	Log(Income)	0.3881	0.3621	1.0720	0.2936	-0.3561	1.1324
21	Log(Interest)	-0.0698	0.0893	-0.7821	0.4412	-0.2534	0.1137

If you like, you can convert this back to original variables, that is, back to multiplicative form, by taking antilogs. The result is

$$\text{Predicted Sales} = 1364048\text{PriceIndex}^{-0.384}\text{Income}^{0.388}\text{Interest}^{-0.070}$$

The constant 1364048 is the antilog of 14.126 (and be calculated in Excel with the EXP function).

In either form the equation implies that the elasticities are approximately equal to -0.384, 0.388, and -0.070. When PriceIndex increases by 1%, the predicted value of Sales tends to decrease by about 0.384%; when Income increases by 1%, the predicted value of Sales tends to increase by about 0.388%; and when Interest increases by 1%, the predicted value of Sales tends to decrease by about 0.070%.

Does this multiplicative equation provide a better fit to the automobile data than an additive relationship? Without doing considerably more work, it is difficult to answer this question with any certainty. As discussed in the previous example, it is *not* sufficient to compare R^2 and s_e values for the two fits. Again, the reason is that one has Log(Sales) as the dependent variable, whereas the other has Sales, so the R^2 and s_e measures aren't comparable. We simply state that the multiplicative relationship provides a reasonably good fit (for example, a scatterplot of its fitted values versus residuals shows no unusual patterns), and it makes sense economically. But the additive equation is arguably just about as good.

Before leaving this example, we note that the results for this data set are not quite as clear as they might appear. (This is often the case with real data.) First, the correlation between Sales and Income, or between Log(Sales) and Log(Income), is negative, not positive. However, because of multicollinearity, a topic discussed in the next chapter, the regression coefficient of Log(Income) is positive. Second, most of the behavior appears to be driven by the early years. If you rerun the analysis from 1980 on, you will discover almost no relationship between Sales and the other variables. ▪

One final example of a multiplicative relationship is the *learning curve* model. A **learning curve** relates the unit production time (or cost) to the cumulative volume of output since that production process first began. Empirical studies indicate that production times tend to decrease by a relatively constant *percentage* every time cumulative output doubles. To model this phenomenon, let Y be the time required to produce a unit of output, and let X be the *cumulative* amount of output that has been produced so far. If we assume that the relationship between Y and X is of the constant elasticity form

$$\text{Predicted } Y = aX^b$$

then it can be shown that whenever X doubles, the predicted value of Y decreases to a *constant* percentage of its previous value. This constant is often called the *learning rate*. For example, if the learning rate is 80%, then each doubling of cumulative production yields a 20% reduction in unit production time. It can be shown that the learning rate satisfies the equation

$$b = \text{LN(learning rate)/LN(2)} \qquad \textbf{(10.22)}$$

(where LN refers to the natural logarithm). So once you estimate b, you can use Equation (10.22) to estimate the learning rate.

The following example illustrates a typical application of the learning curve model.

EXAMPLE | **10.6 THE LEARNING CURVE FOR PRODUCTION OF A NEW PRODUCT AT PRESARIO**

The Presario Company produces a variety of small industrial products. It has just finished producing 22 batches of a new product (new to Presario) for a customer. The file Learning Curve.xlsx contains the times (in hours) to produce each batch. These data are listed in Figure 10.42. Clearly, the times have tended to decrease as Presario has gained more experience in making the product. Does the multiplicative learning model apply to these data, and what does it imply about the learning rate?

Objective   To use a multiplicative regression equation to estimate the learning rate for production time.

Solution

One way to check whether the multiplicative learning model is reasonable is to create the log variables Log(Time) and Log(Batch) in the usual way and then see whether a scatterplot of Log(Time) versus Log(Batch) is approximately *linear*. The multiplicative model implies that it should be. Such a scatterplot appears in Figure 10.43, along with a superimposed linear trend line. The fit appears to be quite good.

The relationship can be estimated by regressing Log(Time) on Log(Batch). The resulting equation is

$$\text{Predicted Log(Time)} = 4.834 - 0.155\text{Log(Batch)} \qquad \textbf{(10.23)}$$

Figure 10.42

Data for Learning Curve Example

	A	B
1	Batch	Time
2	1	125.00
3	2	110.87
4	3	105.35
5	4	103.34
6	5	98.98
7	6	99.90
8	7	91.49
9	8	93.10
10	9	92.23
11	10	86.19
12	11	82.09
13	12	82.32
14	13	87.67
15	14	81.72
16	15	83.72
17	16	81.53
18	17	80.46
19	18	76.53
20	19	82.06
21	20	82.81
22	21	76.52
23	22	78.45

Figure 10.43

Scatterplot of Log Variables with Linear Trend Superimposed

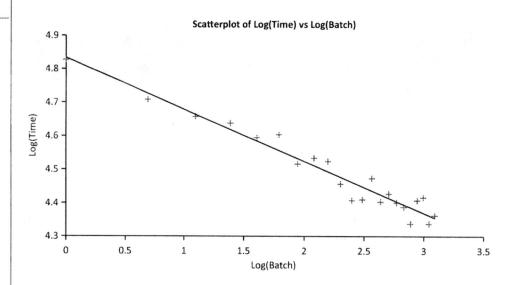

There are a couple of ways to interpret this equation. First, because it is a constant elasticity relationship, the coefficient −0.155 can be interpreted as an elasticity. That is, when Batch increases by 1%, Time tends to decrease by approximately 0.155%.

Although this interpretation is correct, it is not as useful as the "doubling" interpretation discussed previously. Equation (10.22) states that the estimated learning rate satisfies

$$-0.155 = \text{LN(learning rate)}/\text{LN}(2)$$

Solving for the learning rate (multiply through by LN(2) and then take antilogs), you can see that it is 0.898, or approximately 90%. In words, whenever cumulative production doubles, the time to produce a batch decreases by about 10%.

Presario could use this regression equation to predict future production times. For example, suppose the customer places an order for 15 more batches of the same product. Note that Presario is already partway up the learning curve, that is, these batches are numbers 23 through 37, and the company already has experience producing the product. You can use Equation (10.23) to predict the log of production time for each batch. Then you can take their antilogs and sum them to obtain the total production time. The calculations are shown in rows 24 through 39 of Figure 10.44. You enter the batch numbers and calculate their logs in columns A and C. Then you substitute the values of Log(Batch) in column C into equation (10.23) to obtain the predicted values of Log(Time) in column E. Finally, you use Excel's EXP function to calculate the antilogs of these predictions in column B, and you calculate their sum in cell B39. The total predicted time to finish the order is about 1115 hours.

Figure 10.44

Using the Learning Curve Model for Predictions

	A	B	C	D	E	F
21	20	82.81	2.995732274	4.416548827		
22	21	76.52	3.044522438	4.337552145		
23	22	78.45	3.091042453	4.362461479		
24	23	77.324	3.135494216	4.348009995		
25	24	76.816	3.17805383	4.341413654		
26	25	76.332	3.218875825	4.335086627		
27	26	75.869	3.258096538	4.329007785		
28	27	75.426	3.295836866	4.323158388		
29	28	75.003	3.33220451	4.317521744		
30	29	74.596	3.36729583	4.312082919		
31	30	74.205	3.401197382	4.306828497		
32	31	73.829	3.433987204	4.301746382		
33	32	73.466	3.465735903	4.296825631		
34	33	73.117	3.496507561	4.292056313		
35	34	72.779	3.526360525	4.287429384		
36	35	72.453	3.555348061	4.282936587		
37	36	72.137	3.583518938	4.278570366		
38	37	71.832	3.610917913	4.274323782		
39		1115.183	←———	Predicted time for next 15 batches		

PROBLEMS

Level A

26. In a study of housing demand, a county assessor is interested in developing a regression model to estimate the selling price of residential properties within her jurisdiction. She randomly selects 15 houses and records the selling price in addition to the following values: the size of the house (in square feet), the total number of rooms in the house, the age of the house, and an indication of whether the house has an attached garage. These data are stored in the file P10_26.xlsx.

   a. Estimate and interpret a multiple regression equation that includes the four potential explanatory variables. How do you interpret the coefficient of the Attached Garage variable?

   b. Evaluate the estimated regression equation's goodness of fit.

   c. Use the estimated equation to predict the sales price of a 3000-square-foot, 20-year-old home that has seven rooms but no attached garage. How accurate is your prediction?

27. A manager of boiler drums wants to use regression analysis to predict the number of worker-hours needed to erect the drums in future projects. Data for 36 randomly selected boilers have been collected. In addition to worker-hours (Y), the variables measured include boiler capacity, boiler design pressure, boiler type, and drum type. All of these measurements are listed in the file P10_27.xlsx.
   a. Estimate an appropriate multiple regression equation to predict the number of worker-hours needed to erect boiler drums.
   b. Interpret the estimated regression coefficients.
   c. According to the estimated regression equation, what is the difference between the mean number of worker-hours required for erecting industrial and utility field boilers?
   d. According to the estimated regression equation, what is the difference between the mean number of worker-hours required for erecting boilers with steam drums and those with mud drums?
   e. Given the estimated regression equation, predict the number of worker-hours needed to erect a utility-field, steam-drum boiler with a capacity of 550,000 pounds per hour and a design pressure of 1400 pounds per square inch. How accurate is your prediction?
   f. Given the estimated regression equation, predict the number of worker-hours needed to erect an industrial-field, mud-drum boiler with a capacity of 100,000 pounds per hour and a design pressure of 1000 pounds per square inch. How accurate is your prediction?

28. Suppose that a regional express delivery service company wants to estimate the cost of shipping a package (Y) as a function of cargo type, where cargo type includes the following possibilities: fragile, semifragile, and durable. Costs for 15 randomly chosen packages of approximately the same weight and same distance shipped, but of different cargo types, are provided in the file P10_28.xlsx.
   a. Estimate an appropriate multiple regression equation to predict the cost of shipping a given package.
   b. Interpret the estimated regression coefficients. You should find that the estimated intercept and slope of the equation are sample means. Which sample means are they?
   c. According to the estimated regression equation, which cargo type is the *most* costly to ship? Which cargo type is the *least* costly to ship?
   d. How well does the estimated equation fit the given sample data? How do you think the model's goodness of fit could be improved?
   e. Given the estimated regression equation, predict the cost of shipping a package with semifragile cargo.

29. The file P10_11.xlsx contains annual observations (in column B) of the American minimum wage. The basic question here is whether the minimum wage has been growing at roughly a *constant* rate over this period.
   a. Create a time series graph for these data. Comment on the observed behavior of the minimum wage over time.
   b. Estimate a linear regression equation of the minimum wage versus time (the Year variable). What does the estimated slope indicate?
   c. Analyze the residuals from the equation in part **b**. Are they essentially random? If not, return to part **b** and revise your equation appropriately. Then interpret the revised equation.

30. Estimate a regression equation that *adequately* estimates the relationship between monthly electrical power usage (Y) and home size (X) using the data in the file P10_13.xlsx. Interpret your results. How well does your model explain the variation in monthly electrical power usage?

31. An insurance company wants to determine how its annual operating costs depend on the number of home insurance (X_1) and automobile insurance (X_2) policies that have been written. The file P10_31.xlsx contains relevant information for 10 branches of the insurance company. The company believes that a multiplicative model might be appropriate because operating costs typically increase by a constant percentage as the number of either type of policy increases by a given percentage. Use the given data to estimate a multiplicative model for this insurance company. Interpret your results. Does a multiplicative model provide a good fit with these data? Answer by calculating the appropriate standard error of estimate and R^2 value, based on *original* units of the dependent variable.

32. Suppose that an operations manager is trying to determine the number of labor hours required to produce the ith unit of a certain product. Consider the data provided in the file P10_32.xlsx. For example, the second unit produced required 517 labor hours, and the 600th unit required 34 labor hours.
   a. Use the given data to estimate a relationship between the total number of units produced and the labor hours required to produce the last unit in the total set. Interpret your findings.
   b. Use your estimated relationship to predict the number of labor hours that will be needed to produce the 800th unit.

Level B

33. The human resources manager of DataCom, Inc., wants to predict the annual salaries of given employees using the potential explanatory variables in the file P10_05.xlsx.

a. Estimate an appropriate multiple regression equation to predict the annual salary of a given DataCom employee using all of the data in columns C–H.

b. Interpret the estimated regression coefficients.

c. According to the estimated regression model, is there a difference between the mean salaries earned by male and female employees at DataCom? If so, how large is the difference? According to your equation, does this difference depend on the values of the other explanatory variables? Explain.

d. According to the estimated regression model, is there a difference between the mean salaries earned by employees in the sales department and those in the advertising department at DataCom? If so, how large is the difference? According to your equation, does this difference depend on the values of the other explanatory variables? Explain.

e. According to the estimated regression model, in which department are DataCom employees paid the *highest* mean salary (after controlling for other explanatory variables)? In which department are DataCom employees paid the *lowest* mean salary?

f. Given the estimated regression model, predict the annual salary of a female employee who served in a similar department at another company for 10 years prior to coming to work at DataCom. This woman, a graduate of a four-year collegiate business program, has been supervising 12 subordinates in the purchasing department since joining the organization five years ago.

34. Does the rate of violent crime acts vary across different regions of the United States? Answer this with the (somewhat old), 1999 data in the file P10_34.xlsx as requested below.

a. Estimate an appropriate regression model to explain the variation in violent crime rate across the four given regions of the United States. Interpret the estimated equation. Rank the four regions from highest to lowest according to their mean violent crime rate. Could you have done this without regression? Explain.

b. How would you modify the regression model in part **a** to account for possible differences in the violent crime rate across the various subdivisions of the given regions? Estimate your revised regression equation and interpret your findings. Rank the nine subdivisions from highest to lowest according to their mean violent crime rate.

35. Continuing Problems 6 and 15 on the 2006–2007 movie data in the file P02_02.xlsx, create a new variable Total Revenue that is the sum of Total US Gross, International Gross, and US DVD Sales. How well can this new variable be predicted from the data in columns C–F? For Distributor, relabel the categories so that there are only two: Large Distributor and Small Distributor. The former is any distributor that had at least 12 movies in this period, and the latter is all the rest. For Genre, relabel the categories to be Comedy, Drama, Adventure, Action, Thriller/Suspense, and Other. (Other includes Black Comedy, Documentary, Horror, Musical, and Romantic Comedy.) Interpret the coefficients of the estimated regression equation. How would you explain the results to someone in the movie business? Do you think that predictions of total revenue from this regression equation will be very accurate? Why?

36. Continuing Problem 18, suppose that the antique collector believes that the *rate of increase* of the auction price with the age of the item will be driven upward by a large number of bidders. How would you revise the multiple regression equation developed previously to model this feature of the problem?

a. Estimate your revised equation using the data in the file P10_18.xlsx.

b. Interpret each of the estimated coefficients in your revised model.

c. Does this revised model fit the given data better than the original multiple regression model? Explain why or why not.

37. Continuing Problem 19, revise the previous multiple regression equation to include an interaction term between the return on average equity (X_1) and annual dividend rate (X_2).

a. Estimate your revised equation using the data provided in the file P10_19.xlsx.

b. Interpret each of the estimated coefficients in your revised equation. In particular, how do you interpret the coefficient for the interaction term in the revised equation?

c. Does this revised equation fit the given data better than the original multiple regression equation? Explain why or why not.

38. Continuing Problem 22, suppose that one of the managers of this regional express delivery service company is trying to decide whether to add an interaction term involving the package weight (X_1) and the distance shipped (X_2) in the previous multiple regression equation.

a. Why would the manager want to add such a term to the regression equation?

b. Estimate the revised equation using the data given in the file P10_22.xlsx.

c. Interpret each of the estimated coefficients in your revised equation. In particular, how do you interpret the coefficient for the interaction term in the revised equation?

d. Does this revised equation fit the data better than the original multiple regression equation? Explain why or why not.

10.7 VALIDATION OF THE FIT

The fit from a regression analysis is often overly optimistic. When you use the least squares procedure on a given set of data, all of the idiosyncrasies of the particular data set are exploited to obtain the best possible fit. However, there is no guarantee that the fit will be as good when the estimated regression equation is applied to *new* data. In fact, it usually isn't. This is particularly important when the goal is to use the regression equation to predict new values of the dependent variable. The usual situation is that you use a given data set to estimate a regression equation. Then you gather new data on the *explanatory* variables and use these, along with the already-estimated regression equation, to predict the new (but unknown) values of the dependent variable.

One way to see whether this procedure will be successful is to split the original data set into two subsets: one subset for estimation and one subset for validation. A regression equation is estimated from the first subset. Then the values of explanatory variables from the second subset are substituted into this equation to obtain predicted values for the dependent variable. Finally, these predicted values are compared to the *known* values of the dependent variable in the second subset. If the agreement is good, there is reason to believe that the regression equation will predict well for new data. This procedure is called **validating the fit**.

This validation procedure is fairly simple to perform in Excel. We illustrate it for the Bendrix manufacturing data in Example 10.2. (See the file Overhead Costs Validation.xlsx.) There we used 36 monthly observations to regress Overhead on

---

FUNDAMENTAL INSIGHT

Training and Validation Sets

This practice of *partitioning* a data set into a set for estimation and a set for validation is becoming much more common as larger data sets become available. It allows you to see how a given procedure such as regression works on a data set where you *know* the Ys. If it works well, you have more confidence that it will work well on a new data set where you do *not* know the Ys. This partitioning is a routine part of data mining, the exploration of large data sets. In data mining, the first data set is usually called the *training* set, and the second data set is called the *validation* or *testing* set.

MachHrs and ProdRuns. For convenience, the regression output is repeated in Figure 10.45. In particular, it shows an R^2 value of 86.6% and an s_e value of $4109.

Now suppose that this data set is from one of Bendrix's two plants. The company would like to predict overhead costs for the other plant by using data on machine hours and production runs at the other plant. The first step is to see how well the regression from

Figure 10.45   Multiple Regression Output for Bendrix Example

	A	B	C	D	E	F	G
7		Multiple	R-Square	Adjusted	StErr of		
8	Summary	R		R-Square	Estimate		
9		0.9308	0.8664	0.8583	4108.993		
10							
11		Degrees of	Sum of	Mean of	F-Ratio	p-Value	
12	ANOVA Table	Freedom	Squares	Squares			
13	Explained	2	3614020661	1807010330	107.0261	< 0.0001	
14	Unexplained	33	557166199.1	16883824.22			
15							
16		Coefficient	Standard	t-Value	p-Value	Confidence Interval 95%	
17	Regression Table		Error			Lower	Upper
18	Constant	3996.678	6603.651	0.6052	0.5492	-9438.551	17431.907
19	MachHrs	43.536	3.589	12.1289	< 0.0001	36.234	50.839
20	ProdRuns	883.618	82.251	10.7429	< 0.0001	716.276	1050.960

Figure 10.45 fits data from the other plant. This validation on the 36 months of data is shown in Figure 10.46.

Figure 10.46

Validation of Bendrix Regression Results

	A	B	C	D	E	F
1	Validation data					
2						
3	Coefficients from regression equation (based on original data)					
4		Constant	MachHrs	ProdRuns		
5		3996.6782	43.5364	883.6179		
6						
7	Comparison of summary measures					
8		Original	Validation			
9	R-square	0.8664	0.7733			
10	StErr of Est	4108.99	5256.50			
11						
12	Month	MachHrs	ProdRuns	Overhead	Fitted	Residual
13	1	1374	24	92414	85023	7391
14	2	1510	35	92433	100663	-8230
15	3	1213	21	81907	75362	6545
16	4	1629	27	93451	98775	-5324
17	5	1858	28	112203	109629	2574
18	6	1763	40	112673	116096	-3423
19	7	1449	44	104091	105960	-1869
20	8	1422	46	104354	106552	-2198
45	33	1534	38	104946	104359	587
46	34	1529	29	94325	96189	-1864
47	35	1389	47	98474	105999	-7525
48	36	1350	34	90857	92814	-1957

To obtain the results in this figure, proceed as follows.

PROCEDURE FOR VALIDATING REGRESSION RESULTS

1 Copy old results. Copy the results from the original regression to the ranges B5:D5 and B9:B10.

2 Calculate fitted values and residuals. The fitted values are now the predicted values of overhead for the other plant, based on the original regression equation. Find these by substituting the new values of MachHrs and ProdRuns into the original equation. Specifically, enter the formula

=$B$5+SUMPRODUCT($C$5:$D$5,B13:C13)

in cell E13 and copy it down. Then calculate the residuals (prediction errors for the other plant) by entering the formula

=D13-E13

in cell F13 and copying it down.

3 Calculate summary measures. You can see how well the original equation fits the new data by calculating R^2 and s_e values. Recall that R^2 in general is the square of the correlation between observed and fitted values. Therefore, enter the formula

=CORREL(E13:E48,D13:D48)^2

in cell C9. The *se* value is essentially the average of the squared residuals, but it uses the denominator $n - 3$ (when there are two explanatory variables) rather than $n - 1$. Therefore, enter the formula

=SQRT(SUMSQ((F13:F48)/33)

in cell C10.

Excel's SUMSQ function is often handy. It sums the squares of values in a range.

The results in Figure 10.46 are typical. The validation results are usually not as good as the original results. The value of R^2 has decreased from 86.6% to 77.3%, and the value of s_e has increased from \$4109 to \$5257. Nevertheless, Bendrix might conclude that the original regression equation is adequate for making future predictions at either plant.

10.8 CONCLUSION

In this chapter we have illustrated how to fit an equation to a set of points and how to interpret the resulting equation. We have also discussed two measures, R^2 and s_e, that indicate the goodness of fit of the regression equation. Although the general technique is called *linear* regression, it can be used to estimate nonlinear relationships through suitable transformations of variables. We are not finished with our study of regression, however. In the next chapter we make some statistical assumptions about the regression model and then discuss the types of inferences that can be made from regression output. In particular, we discuss the accuracy of the estimated regression coefficients, the accuracy of predictions made from the regression equation, and the choice of explanatory variables to include in the regression equation.

Summary of Key Terms

Term	Symbol	Explanation	Excel	Page	Equation
Regression analysis		A general method for estimating the relationship between a dependent variable and one or more explanatory variables		531	
Dependent (or response) variable	Y	The variable being estimated or predicted in a regression analysis		532	
Explanatory (or independent) variables	$X_1, X_2,$ and so on	The variables used to explain or predict the dependent variable		532	
Simple regression		A regression model with a single explanatory variable	StatTools/ Regression & Classification/ Regression	532	
Multiple regression		A regression model with any number of explanatory variables	StatTools/ Regression & Classification/ Regression	532	
Correlation	r_{XY}	A measure of the strength of the linear relationship between two variables X and Y	=CORREL (range1, range2), or StatTools/ Summary Statistics/ Correlation and Covariance	540	10.1

(continued)

Term	Symbol	Explanation	Excel	Page	Equation
Fitted value		The predicted value of the dependent variable, found by substituting explanatory values into the regression equation		543	10.2
Residual		The difference between the actual and fitted values of the dependent variable		543	10.2
Least squares line		The regression equation that minimizes the sum of squared residuals	StatTools/ Regression & Classification/ Regression	544	10.3, 10.4
Standard error of estimate	s_e	Essentially, the standard deviation of the residuals; indicates the magnitude of the prediction errors	StatTools/ Regression & Classification/ Regression	549	10.7, 10.11
R-square	R^2	The percentage of variation in the response variable explained by the regression model	StatTools/ Regression & Classification/ Regression	558	10.8
Adjusted R^2		A measure similar to R^2, but adjusted for the number of explanatory variables in the equation		558	
Regression coefficients	b_1, b_2, and so on	The coefficients of the explanatory variables in a regression equation	StatTools/ Regression & Classification/ Regression	554	10.9
Dummy (or indicator) variables		Variables coded as 0 or 1, used to capture categorical variables in a regression analysis	StatTools/ Data Utilities/ Dummy	560	
Interaction variables		Products of explanatory variables, used when the effect of one on the dependent variable depends on the value of the other	StatTools/ Data Utilities/ Interaction	567	
Nonlinear transformations		Variables created to capture nonlinear relationships in a regression model	StatTools/ Data Utilities/ Transform	571	
Quadratic model		A regression model with linear and squared explanatory variables	StatTools/ Regression & Classification/ Regression	573	
Model with logarithmic transformations		A regression model using logarithms of Y and/or Xs	StatTools/ Regression & Classification/ Regression	574	
Constant elasticity (or multiplicative relationship)		A relationship where predicted Y changes by a constant percentage when any X changes by 1%; requires logarithmic transformations	StatTools/ Regression & Classification/ Regression	577	10.21
Learning curve		A particular multiplicative relationship used to indicate how cost or time in production decreases over time	StatTools/ Regression & Classification/ Regression	581	10.22
Validation of fit		Checks how well a regression model based on one sample predicts a related sample	StatTools/ Regression & Classification/ Regression	586	

PROBLEMS

Conceptual Questions

C.1. Consider the relationship between yearly wine consumption (liters of alcohol from drinking wine, per person) and yearly deaths from heart disease (deaths per 100,000 people) in 19 developed countries. Suppose that you read a newspaper article in which the reporter states the following:

Researchers find that the correlation between yearly wine consumption and yearly deaths from heart disease is −0.84. Thus, it is reasonable to conclude that increased consumption of alcohol from wine causes fewer deaths from heart disease in industrialized societies.

Comment on the reporter's interpretation of the correlation in this situation.

C.2. "It is generally appropriate to delete all outliers in a data set that are apparent in a scatterplot." Do you agree with this statement? Explain.

C.3. How would you interpret the relationship between two numeric variables when the estimated least squares regression line for them is essentially *horizontal* (i.e., flat)?

C.4. Suppose that you generate a scatterplot of residuals versus fitted values of the dependent variable for an estimated regression equation. Furthermore, you find the correlation between the residuals and fitted values to be 0.829. Does this provide a good indication that the estimated regression equation is satisfactory? Explain why or why not.

C.5. Suppose that you have generated three alternative multiple regression equations to explain the variation in a particular dependent variable. The regression output for each equation can be summarized as follows:

	Equation 1	Equation 2	Equation 3
No. of Xs	4	6	9
R^2	0.76	0.77	0.79
Adjusted R^2	0.75	0.74	0.73

Which of these equation would you select as "best"? Explain your choice.

C.6. Suppose you want to investigate the relationship between a dependent variable Y and two potential explanatory variables X_1 and X_2. Is the R^2 value for the equation with both X variables included necessarily at least as large as the R^2 value from each equation with only a single X? Explain why or why not. Could the R^2 value for the equation with

both X variables included be *larger* than the sum of the R^2 values from the separate equations, each with only a single X included? Is there any intuitive explanation for this?

C.7. Suppose you believe that two variables X and Y are related, but you have no idea which way the causality goes. Does X cause Y or vice versa (or maybe even neither)? Can you tell by regressing Y on X and then regressing X on Y? Explain. Also, provide at least one real example where the direction of causality would be ambiguous.

C.8. Suppose you have two columns of monthly data, one on advertising expenditures and one on sales. If you use this data set, as is, to regress sales on advertising, will it adequately capture the behavior that advertising in one month doesn't really affect sales in *that* month but only in *future* months? What should you do, in terms of regression, to capture this timing effect?

C.9. Suppose you want to predict reading speed using, among other variables, the device the person is reading from. This device could be a regular book, an iPhone, a Kindle, or others. Therefore, you create dummy variables for device. How, exactly, would you do it? If you use regular book as the reference category and another analyst uses, say, Kindle as the reference category, will you get the same regression results? Explain.

C.10. Explain the benefits of using natural logarithms of variables, either of Y or of the Xs, as opposed to other possible nonlinear functions, when scatterplots (or possibly economic considerations) indicate that nonlinearities should be taken into account. Explain exactly how you interpret regression coefficients if logs are taken only of Y, only of the Xs, or of both Y and the Xs.

C.11. The number of cars per 1000 people is known for virtually every country in the world. For many countries, however, per capita income is not known. How might you estimate per capita income for countries where it is unknown?

Level A

39. Many companies manufacture products that are at least partially produced using chemicals (e.g., paint, gasoline, and steel). In many cases, the quality of the finished product is a function of the temperature and pressure at which the chemical reactions take place. Suppose that a particular manufacturer wants to model the quality (Y) of a product as a function of the temperature (X_1) and the pressure (X_2) at which it is produced. The file P10_39.xlsx contains data obtained from a carefully designed experiment involving these variables. Note that the assigned quality score can range from a minimum of 0 to a maximum of 100 for each manufactured product.

    a. Estimate a multiple regression equation that includes the two given explanatory variables. Does the estimated equation fit the data well?

    b. Add an interaction term between temperature and pressure and run the regression again. Does the inclusion of the interaction term improve the model's goodness of fit?

    c. Interpret each of the estimated coefficients in the two equations. How are they different? How do you interpret the coefficient for the interaction term in the second equation?

40. A power company located in southern Alabama wants to predict the peak power load (i.e., the maximum amount of power that must be generated each day to meet demand) as a function of the daily high temperature (X). A random sample of 25 summer days is chosen, and the peak power load and the high temperature are recorded each day. The file P10_40.xlsx contains these observations.

    a. Create a scatterplot for these data. Comment on the observed relationship between Y and X.

    b. Estimate an appropriate regression equation to predict the peak power load for this power company. Interpret the estimated regression coefficients.

    c. Analyze the estimated equation's residuals. Do they suggest that the regression equation is adequate? If not, return to part **b** and revise your equation. Continue to revise the equation until the results are satisfactory.

    d. Use your final equation to predict the peak power load on a summer day with a high temperature of 100 degrees.

41. Management of a home appliance store would like to understand the growth pattern of the monthly sales of Blu-ray disc players over the past two years. Managers have recorded the relevant data in the file P10_09.xlsx.

    a. Create a scatterplot for these data. Comment on the observed behavior of monthly sales at this store over time.

    b. Estimate an appropriate regression equation to explain the variation of monthly sales over the given time period. Interpret the estimated regression coefficients.

    c. Analyze the estimated equation's residuals. Do they suggest that the regression equation is adequate? If not, return to part **b** and revise your equation. Continue to revise the equation until the results are satisfactory.

42. A small computer chip manufacturer wants to forecast monthly operating costs as a function of the number of units produced during a month. The company has collected the 16 months of data in the file P10_42.xlsx.

    a. Determine an equation that can be used to predict monthly production costs from units produced. Are there any outliers?

    b. How could the regression line obtained in part **a** be used to determine whether the company was efficient or inefficient during any particular month?

43. The file P02_07.xlsx includes data on 204 employees at the (fictional) company Beta Technologies.

    a. Create a recoded version of Education, where 0 or 2 is recoded as 1, 4 is recoded as 2, and 6 or 8 is recoded as 3. Then create dummy variables for these three categories.

    b. Use pivot tables to explore whether average salary depends on gender, and whether it depends on the recoded Education. Then use scatterplots to explore whether salary is related to age, prior experience, and Beta experience. Briefly state your results.

    c. Run a regression of salary versus gender, prior experience, Beta experience, and any two of the education dummies, and interpret the results.

    d. If any of the potential explanatory variables seems to be unrelated to salary, based on the results from part **b**, run one or more regressions without such a variable. Comment on whether it makes much of a difference in the regression outputs.

44. The file P10_44.xlsx contains data that relate the unit cost of producing a fuel pressure regulator to the cumulative number of fuel pressure regulators produced at an automobile production plant. For example, the 4000th unit cost $13.70 to produce.

    a. Fit a learning curve to these data.

    b. You would predict that doubling cumulative production reduces the cost of producing a regulator by what amount?

45. The *beta* of a stock is found by running a regression with the monthly return on a market index as the explanatory variable and the monthly return on the stock as the dependent variable. The beta of the stock is then the slope of this regression line.

    a. Explain why most stocks have a positive beta.

    b. Explain why a stock with a beta with absolute value greater than one is more volatile than the market index and a stock with a beta less than one (in absolute value) is less volatile than the market index.

    c. Use the data in the file P10_45.xlsx to estimate the beta for each of the four companies listed: Caterpillar, Goodyear, McDonalds, and Ford. Use the S&P 500 as the market index.

    d. For each of these companies, what percentage of the variation in its returns is explained by the variation in the market index? What percentage is unexplained by variation in the market index?

e. Verify (using Excel's COVAR and VARP functions) that the beta for each company is given by

$$\frac{\text{Covariance between Company and Market}}{\text{Variance of Market}}$$

Also, verify that the correlation between each company's returns and the market's returns is the square root of R^2.

46. Continuing the previous problem, explore whether the beta for these companies changes through time. For example, are the betas based on 1990s data different from those based on 2000s data? Or are data based on only five years of data different from those based on longer time periods?

47. The file Catalog Marketing.xlsx contains recent data on 1000 HyTex customers. (This is the same data set used in Example 2.7 in Chapter 2.)

a. Create a pivot table of average amount spent versus the number of catalogs sent. Is there any evidence that these two variables are related? Would it make sense to enter Catalogs, as is, in a regression equation for AmountSpent, or should dummies be used? Explain.

b. Create a pivot table of average amount spent versus History. Is there any evidence that these two variables are related? Would it make sense to enter History, as is, in a regression equation for AmountSpent, or should dummies be used? Explain.

c. Answer part b with History replaced by Age.

d. Base on your results from parts a through c, estimate an appropriate regression equation for AmountSpent, using the appropriate forms for Catalogs, History, and Age, plus the variables Gender, OwnHome, Married, and Close. Interpret this equation and comment on its usefulness in predicting AmountSpent.

48. The file P10_48.xlsx contains monthly sales and price of a popular candy bar.

a. Describe the type of relationship between price and sales (linear/nonlinear, strong/weak).

b. What percentage of variation in monthly sales is explained by variation in price? What percentage is unexplained?

c. If the price of the candy bar is $1.05, predict monthly candy bar sales.

d. Use the regression output to determine the correlation between price and candy bar sales.

e. Are there any outliers?

49. The file P10_49.xlsx contains the amount of money spent advertising a product and the number of units sold for eight months.

a. Assume that the only factor influencing monthly sales is advertising. Fit the following three curves to these data: linear ($Y = a + bX$), exponential ($Y = ab^X$), and multiplicative ($Y = aX^b$). Which equation fits the data best?

b. Interpret the best-fitting equation.

c. Using the best-fitting equation, predict sales during a month in which $60,000 is spent on advertising.

50. A golf club manufacturer is trying to determine how the price of a set of clubs affects the demand for clubs. The file P10_50.xlsx contains the price of a set of clubs and the monthly sales.

a. Assume the only factor influencing monthly sales is price. Fit the following three curves to these data: linear ($Y = a + bX$), exponential ($Y = ab^X$), and multiplicative ($Y = aX^b$). Which equation fits the data best?

b. Interpret your best-fitting equation.

c. Using the best-fitting equation, predict sales during a month in which the price is $470.

51. The file P03_55.xlsx lists the average salary for each Major League Baseball (MLB) team from 2004 to 2009, along with the number of team wins in each of these years.

a. Rearrange the data so that there are four long columns: Team, Year, Salary, and Wins. There should be 6*30 values for each.

b. Create a scatterplot of Wins (Y) versus Salary (X). Is there any indication of a relationship between these two variables? Is it a linear relationship?

c. Run a regression of Wins versus Salary. What does it say, if anything, about teams buying their way to success?

52. Repeat the previous problem with the basketball data in the file P03_56.xlsx. (Now there will be 5*30 rows in the rearranged data set.)

53. Repeat Problem 51 with the football data in the file P03_57.xlsx. (Now there will be 8*32 rows in the rearranged data set.)

54. The Baker Company wants to develop a budget to predict how overhead costs vary with activity levels. Management is trying to decide whether direct labor hours (DLH) or units produced is the better measure of activity for the firm. Monthly data for the preceding 24 months appear in the file P10_54.xlsx. Use regression analysis to determine which measure, DLH or Units (or both), should be used for the budget. How would the regression equation be used to obtain the budget for the firm's overhead costs?

55. The auditor of Kiely Manufacturing is concerned about the number and magnitude of year-end adjustments that are made annually when the financial statements of Kiely Manufacturing are prepared. Specifically, the auditor suspects that the management of Kiely

Manufacturing is using discretionary write-offs to manipulate the reported net income. To check this, the auditor has collected data from 25 companies that are similar to Kiely Manufacturing in terms of manufacturing facilities and product lines. The cumulative reported third-quarter income and the final net income reported are listed in the file P10_55.xlsx for each of these 25 companies. If Kiely Manufacturing reports a cumulative third-quarter income of $2,500,000 and a preliminary net income of $4,900,000, should the auditor conclude that the relationship between cumulative third-quarter income and the annual income for Kiely Manufacturing differs from that of the 25 companies in this sample? Explain why or why not.

56. The file P10_56.xlsx contains some interesting data on the U.S. presidential elections from 1880 through 2008. The variable definitions are on the Source sheet. The question is whether the Vote variable can be predicted very well from the other variables.
    a. Create pivot tables and/or scatterplots to check whether Vote appears to be related to the other variables. Comment on the results.
    b. Run a regression of Vote versus the other variables (not including Year). Do the coefficients go in the direction (positive or negative) you would expect? If you were going to use the regression equation to predict Vote for the 2012 election and you had the relevant data for the explanatory variables for 2012, how accurate do you think your prediction would be?

Level B

57. We stated in the beginning of the chapter that regression can be used to understand the way the world works. That is, you can look at the regression coefficients (their signs and magnitudes) to see the effects of the explanatory variables on the dependent variable. However, is it possible that apparently small changes in the data can lead to very different-looking equations? The file P10_57.xlsx lets you explore this question. Columns K–R contain data on over 100 (fictional) homes that were recently sold. The regression equation for this original data set is given in the range T15:U21. (It was found with StatTools in the usual way.) Columns C–I contain slight changes to the original data, with the amount of change determined by the adjustable parameters in row 2. (Look at the formulas in columns C–I to see how the original data have been changed randomly.) The regression equation for the changed data appears in the range T6:U12. It has been calculated through special matrix functions (not StatTools), so that it changes automatically when the random data change. (These require the 1s in column B.) Experiment by pressing the F9 key or changing the adjustable parameters to see how much the two regression equations can differ.

After experimenting, briefly explain how you think housing pricing works—or can you tell?

58. The file P02_35.xlsx contains data from a survey of 500 randomly selected households. For this problem, use Monthly Payment as the dependent variable in several regressions, as explained below.
    a. Beginning with Family Size, iteratively add one explanatory variable and estimate the resulting regression equation to explain the variation in Monthly Payment. If adding any explanatory variable causes the *adjusted* R^2 measure to fall, do not include that variable in subsequent versions of the regression model. Otherwise, include the variable and consider adding the next variable in the set. Which variables are included in the final version of your regression model? (Add dummies for Location in a single step, and use Total Income rather than First Income and Second Income separately.)
    b. Interpret the final estimated regression equation you obtained through the process outlined in part **a**. Also, interpret the standard error of estimate s_e, R^2, and the adjusted R^2 for the final estimated model.

59. (This problem is based on an actual court case in Philadelphia.) In the 1994 congressional election, the Republican candidate outpolled the Democratic candidate by 400 votes (excluding absentee ballots). The Democratic candidate outpolled the Republican candidate by 500 absentee votes. The Republican candidate sued (and won), claiming that vote fraud must have played a role in the absentee ballot count. The Republican's lawyer ran a regression to predict (based on past elections) how the absentee ballot margin could be predicted from the votes tabulated on voting machines. Selected results are given in the file P10_59.xlsx. Show how this regression could be used by the Republican to "prove" his claim of vote fraud.

60. In the world of computer science, Moore's law is famous. Although there are various versions of this law, they all say something to the effect that computing power *doubles* every two years. Several researchers estimated this law with regression using real data in 2006. Their paper can be found online at http://download.intel.com/pressroom/pdf/computer trendsrelease.pdf. For example, one interesting chart appears on page S1, backed up with regression results on another page. What exactly do these results say about doubling every two years (or do they contradict Moore's law)?

61. (The data for this problem are fictitious, but they are not far off.) For each of the top 25 business schools, the file P10_61.xlsx contains the average salary of a professor. Thus, for Indiana University (number 15 in the rankings), the average salary is $46,000. Use this information and regression to show that IU is doing a great job with its available resources.

62. Suppose the correlation between the average height of parents and the height of their firstborn male child is 0.5. You are also told that:
   - The average height of all parents is 66 inches.
   - The standard deviation of the average height of parents is 4 inches.
   - The average height of all male children is 70 inches.
   - The standard deviation of the height of all male children is 4 inches.

   If a mother and father are 73 and 80 inches tall, respectively, how tall do you predict their son to be? Explain why this is called "regression toward the mean."

63. Do increased taxes increase or decrease economic growth? The file P10_63.xlsx lists tax revenues as a percentage of gross domestic product (GDP) and the average annual percentage growth in GDP per capita for nine countries during the years 1970 through 1994. Do these data support or contradict the dictum of supply-side economics?

64. For each of the four data sets in the file P10_64.xlsx, calculate the least squares line. For which of these data sets would you feel comfortable in using the least squares line to predict Y?

65. Suppose you run a regression on a data set of Xs and Ys and obtain a least squares line of $Y = 12 - 3X$.
   a. If you double each value of X, what is the new least squares line?
   b. If you triple each value of Y, what is the new least squares line?
   c. If you add 6 to each value of X, what is the new least squares line?
   d. If you subtract 4 from each value of Y, what is the new least squares line?

66. The file P10_66.xlsx contains monthly cost accounting data on overhead costs, machine hours, and direct material costs. This problem will help you explore the meaning of R^2 and the relationship between R^2 and correlations.
   a. Create a table of correlations between the individual variables.
   b. If you ignore the two explanatory variables Machine Hours and Direct Material Cost and predict each Overhead Cost as the *mean* of Overhead Cost, then a typical "error" is Overhead Cost minus the mean of Overhead Cost. Find the sum of squared errors using this form of prediction, where the sum is over all observations.
   c. Now run three regressions: (1) Overhead Cost (OHCost) versus Machine Hours, (2) OHCost versus Direct Material Cost, and (3) OHCost versus both Machine Hours and Direct Material Cost. (The first two are simple regressions, the third is a multiple regression.) For each, find the sum of squared residuals, and divide this by

the sum of squared errors from part **b**. What is the relationship between this ratio and the associated R^2 for that equation? (Now do you see why R^2 is referred to as the percentage of variation explained?)
   d. For the first two regressions in part **c**, what is the relationship between R^2 and the corresponding correlation between the dependent and explanatory variable? For the third regression it turns out that the R^2 can be expressed as a complicated function of all three correlations in part **a**. That is, the function involves not just the correlations between the dependent variable and each explanatory variable, but also the correlation between the explanatory variables. Note that this R^2 is not just the sum of the R^2 values from the first two regressions in part **c**. Why do you think this is true, intuitively? However, R^2 for the multiple regression is still the square of a correlation—namely, the correlation between the observed and predicted values of OHCost. Verify that this is the case for these data.

67. The file P10_67.xlsx contains hypothetical starting salaries for MBA students directly after graduation. The file also lists their years of experience prior to the MBA program and their class rank in the MBA program (on a 0–100 scale).
   a. Estimate the regression equation with Salary as the dependent variable and Experience and Class Rank as the explanatory variables. What does this equation imply? What does the standard error of estimate s_e tell you? What about R^2?
   b. Repeat part **a**, but now include the interaction term Experience*Class Rank (the product) in the equation as well as Experience and Class Rank individually. Answer the same questions as in part **a**. What evidence is there that this extra variable (the interaction variable) is worth including? How do you interpret this regression equation? Why might you expect the interaction to be present in real data of this type?

68. In a study published in 1985 in *Business Horizons*, Platt and McCarthy employed multiple regression analysis to explain variations in compensation among the CEOs of large companies. (Although the data set is old, we suspect the results would be similar with more current data.) Their primary objective was to discover whether levels of compensations are affected more by short-run considerations—"I'll earn more now if my company does well in the short run"—or long-run considerations—"My best method for obtaining high compensation is to stay with my company for a long time." The study used as its dependent variable the total compensation for each of the 100 highest paid CEOs in 1981. This variable was defined as the sum of salary, bonuses, and other benefits (measured in

$1000s). The following potential explanatory variables were considered. To capture short-run effects, the average of the company's previous five years' percentage changes in earnings per share (EPS) and the projected percentage change in next year's EPS were used. To capture the long-run effect, age and years as CEO, two admittedly correlated variables, were used. Dummy variables for the CEO's background (finance, marketing, and so on) were also considered. Finally, the researchers considered several nonlinear and interaction terms based on these variables. The best-fitting equation was the following:

$$\text{Total Compensation} = -3493 + 898.7*\text{Years as CEO}$$
$$+ 9.28*(\text{Years as CEO})^2 - 17.19*\text{Years as CEO}*\text{Age}$$
$$+ 88.27*\text{Age} + 867.4*\text{Finance}$$

(The last variable is a dummy variable, equal to 1 if the CEO had a finance background, 0 otherwise.) The corresponding R^2 was 19.4%.

a. Explain what this equation implies about CEO compensations.

b. The researchers drew the following conclusions. First, it appears that CEOs should indeed concentrate on long-run considerations—namely, those that keep them on their jobs the longest. Second, the absence of the short-run company-related variables from the equations helps to confirm the conjecture that CEOs who concentrate on earning the quick buck for their companies may not be acting in their best self-interest. Finally, the positive coefficient of the dummy variable may imply that financial people possess skills that are vitally important, and firms therefore outbid one another for the best financial talent. Based on the data given, do you agree with these conclusions?

c. Consider a CEO (other than those in the study) who has been in his position for 10 years and has a financial background. Predict his total yearly compensation (in $1000s) if he is 50 years old and then if he is 55 years old. Explain why the difference between these two predictions is not 5(88.27), where 88.27 is the coefficient of the Age variable.

69. The Wilhoit Company has observed that there is a linear relationship between indirect labor expense

and direct labor hours. Data for direct labor hours and indirect labor expense for 18 months are given in the file P10_69.xlsx. At the start of month 7, all cost categories in the Wilhoit Company increased by 10%, and they stayed at this level for months 7 through 12. Then at the start of month 13, another 10% across-the-board increase in all costs occurred, and the company operated at this price level for months 13 through 18.

a. Plot the data. Verify that the relationship between indirect labor expense and direct labor hours is approximately linear within each six-month period. Use regression (three times) to estimate the slope and intercept during months 1 through 6, during months 7 through 12, and during months 13 through 18.

b. Use regression to fit a straight line to all 18 data points simultaneously. What values of the slope and intercept do you obtain?

c. Perform a price level adjustment to the data and re-estimate the slope and intercept using all 18 data points. Assuming no cost increases for month 19, what is your prediction for indirect labor expense if there are 35,000 direct labor hours in month 19?

d. Interpret your results. What causes the difference in the linear relationship estimated in parts **b** and **c**?

70. The Bohring Company manufactures a sophisticated radar unit that is used in a fighter aircraft built by Seaways Aircraft. The first 50 units of the radar unit have been completed, and Bohring is preparing to submit a proposal to Seaways Aircraft to manufacture the next 50 units. Bohring wants to submit a competitive bid, but at the same time, it wants to ensure that all the costs of manufacturing the radar unit are fully covered. As part of this process, Bohring is attempting to develop a standard for the number of labor hours required to manufacture each radar unit. Developing a labor standard has been a continuing problem in the past. The file P10_70.xlsx lists the number of labor hours required for each of the first 50 units of production. Bohring accountants want to see whether regression analysis, together with the concept of learning curves, can help solve the company's problem.

CASE 10.1 QUANTITY DISCOUNTS AT THE FIRM CHAIR COMPANY

The Firm Chair Company manufactures customized wood furniture and sells the furniture in large quantities to major furniture retailers. Jim Bolling has recently been assigned to analyze the company's pricing policy. He has been told that quantity discounts were usually given. For example, for one type of chair, the pricing changed at quantities of 200 and 400—that is, these were the price breaks, where the marginal cost of the next chair changed. For this type of chair, the file Firm Chair.xlsx contains the quantity and total price to the customer for 81 orders. Use regression to help Jim discover the pricing structure that Firm Chair evidently used. (*Note:* A linear regression of TotPrice versus Quantity will give you a "decent" fit, but you can do much better by introducing appropriate variables into the regression.) ■

Sales of single-family houses have been brisk in Mid City this year. This has especially been true in older, more established neighborhoods, where housing is relatively inexpensive compared to the new homes being built in the newer neighborhoods. Nevertheless, there are also many families who are willing to pay a higher price for the prestige of living in one of the newer neighborhoods. The file Mid City.xlsx contains data on 128 recent sales in Mid City. For each sale, the file shows the neighborhood (1, 2, or 3) in which the house is located, the number of offers made on the house, the square footage, whether the house is made primarily of brick, the number of bathrooms, the number of bedrooms, and the selling price. Neighborhoods 1 and 2 are more traditional neighborhoods, whereas neighborhood 3 is a newer, more prestigious neighborhood.

Use regression to estimate and interpret the pricing structure of houses in Mid City. Here are some considerations.

1. Do buyers pay a premium for a brick house, all else being equal?

2. Is there a premium for a house in neighborhood 3, all else being equal?

3. Is there an *extra* premium for a brick house in neighborhood 3, in addition to the usual premium for a brick house?

4. For purposes of estimation and prediction, could neighborhoods 1 and 2 be collapsed into a single "older" neighborhood? ■

Howie's Bakery is one of the most popular bakeries in town, and the favorite at Howie's is French bread. Each day of the week, Howie's bakes a number of loaves of French bread, more or less according to a daily schedule. To maintain its fine reputation, Howie's gives away to charity any loaves not sold on the day they are baked. Although this occurs frequently, it is also common for Howie's to run out of French bread on any given day—more demand than supply. In this case, no extra loaves are baked that day; the customers have to go elsewhere (or come back to Howie's the next day) for their French bread. Although French bread at Howie's is always popular, Howie's stimulates demand by running occasional 10% off sales.

Howie's has collected data for 20 consecutive weeks, 140 days in all. These data are listed in the file **Howies Bakery.xlsx**. The variables are Day (Monday–Sunday), Supply (number of loaves baked that day), OnSale (whether French bread is on sale that day), and Demand (loaves actually sold that day). Howie's would like you to see whether regression can be used successfully to estimate Demand from the other data in the file. Howie reasons that if these other variables can be used to predict Demand, then he might be able to determine his daily supply (number of loaves to bake) in a more cost-effective way.

How successful is regression with these data? Is Howie correct that regression can help him determine his daily supply? Is any information missing that would be useful? How would you obtain it? How would you use it? Is this extra information *really* necessary? ■

Financial advisors offer many types of advice to customers, but they generally agree that one of the best things people can do is invest as much as possible in tax-deferred retirement plans. Not only are the earnings from these investments exempt from income tax (until retirement), but the investment itself is tax-exempt. This means that if a person invests, say, $10,000 of his $100,000 income in a tax-deferred retirement plan, he pays income tax that year on only $90,000 of his income. This is probably the best method available to most people for avoiding tax payments. However, which group takes advantage of this attractive investment opportunity: everyone, people with low salaries, people with high salaries, or who?

The file Retirement Plan.xlsx lets you investigate this question. It contains data on 194 (hypothetical) couples: number of dependent children, combined annual salary of husband and wife, current mortgage on home, average amount of other (non-mortgage) debt, and percentage of combined income invested in tax-deferred retirement plans (assumed to be limited to 15%, which is realistic). Using correlations, scatterplots, and regression analysis, what can you conclude about the tendency of this group of people to invest in tax-deferred retirement plans? ■

Regression Analysis: Statistical Inference

PREDICTING MOVIE REVENUES

In the opener for Chapter 3, we discussed the article by Simonoff and Sparrow (2000) that examined movie revenues for 311 movies released in 1998 and late 1997. We saw that movie revenues were related to several variables, including genre, Motion Picture Association of America (MPAA) rating, country of origin, number of stars in the cast, whether the movie was a sequel, and whether the movie was released during a few choice times. In Chapter 3, we were limited to looking at summary measures and charts of the data. Now that we are studying regression, we can look further into the analysis performed by Simonoff and Sparrow. Specifically, they examined whether these variables, plus others, are effective in predicting movie revenues.

The authors report the results from three multiple regression models. All of these used the logarithm of the total U.S. gross revenue from the film as the dependent variable. (They used the *logarithm* because the distribution of gross revenues is very positively skewed.) The first model used only the *prerelease* variables listed in the previous paragraph. The values of these variables were all known prior to the movie's release. Therefore, the purpose of this model was to see how well revenues could be predicted *before* the movie was released.

The second model used the variables from model 1, along with two variables that could be observed after the first week of the movie's release: the first weekend gross and the number of screens the movie opened on. (Actually, the logarithms of these latter two variables were used, again because of positive skewness. Also, the authors found it necessary to run two separate regressions at this stage—one for movies that opened on 10 or fewer screens, and another for movies that opened on more than 10 screens.) The idea here was that the success or failure of many movies depends to a large extent on how they do right after they are released. Therefore, it was expected that this information would add significantly to the predictive power of the regression model.

The third model built on the second by adding an additional explanatory variable: the number of Oscar nominations the movie received for key awards (Best Picture, Best Director, Best Actor, Best Actress, Best Supporting Actor, and Best Supporting Actress). This information is often not known until well after a movie's release, but it was hypothesized that Oscar nominations would lead to a significant increase in a movie's revenues, and that a regression model with this information could lead to very different predictions of revenue.

Simonoff and Sparrow found that the coefficients of the first regression model were in line with the box plots shown earlier in Figure 3.1 of Chapter 3. For example, the variables that measured the number of star actors and actresses were both positive and significant, indicating that star power tends to lead to larger revenues. However, the predictive power of this model was poor. Given its standard error of prediction (and taking into account that the *logarithm* of revenue was the dependent variable), the authors stated that "the predictions of total grosses for an individual movie can be expected to be off by as much as a multiplicative factor of 100 high or low." It appears that there is no way to predict which movies will succeed and which will fail based on prerelease data only.

The second model added considerable predictive power. The regression equations indicated that gross revenue is positively related to first weekend gross and negatively related to the number of opening screens, both of these variables being significant. As for prediction, the factor of 100 mentioned in the previous paragraph decreased to a factor of 10 (for movies with 10 or fewer opening screens) or 2 (for movies with more than 10 opening screens). This is still not perfect—predictions of total revenue made after the movie's first weekend can still be pretty far off—but this additional information about initial success certainly helps.

The third model added only slightly to the predictive power, primarily because so few of the movies (10 out of 311) received Oscar nominations for key awards. However, the predictions for those that did receive nominations increased considerably. For example, the prediction for the multiple Oscar nominee *Saving Private Ryan,* based on the second model, was 194.622 (millions of dollars). Its prediction based on the third model increased to a whopping 358.237. (Interestingly, the prediction for this movie from the first model was only 14.791, and its actual gross revenue was 216.119. Perhaps the reason *Saving Private Ryan* did not make as much as the third model predicted was that the Oscar nominations were announced about nine months after its release—too long after release to do much good.)

Simonoff and Sparrow then used their third model to predict gross revenues for 24 movies released in 1999—movies that were not in the data set used to estimate the regression model. They found that 21 out of 24 of the resulting 95% prediction intervals captured the actual gross revenues, which is about what would be expected. However, many of these prediction intervals were extremely wide, and several of the predictions were well above or below the actual revenues. The authors conclude by quoting Tim Noonan, a former movie executive: "Since predicting gross is extremely difficult, you have to serve up a [yearly] slate of movies and know that over time you'll have 3 or 4 to the left and 2 or 3 to the right. You must make sure you are doing things that mitigate your downside risk." ■

11.1 INTRODUCTION

In the previous chapter you learned how to fit a regression equation to a set of points by using the least squares method. The purpose of this regression equation is to provide a good fit to the points in the sample so that you can understand the relationship between a dependent variable and one or more explanatory variables. The entire emphasis of the discussion in the previous chapter was on finding a regression model that fits the observations in the sample. In this chapter we take a slightly different point of view: We assume that the observations in the sample are taken from some larger population. For example, the sample of 50 regions from the Pharmex drugstore example could represent a sample of all the regions where Pharmex does business. In this case, we might be interested in the relationship between variables in the entire population, not just in the sample.

There are two basic problems we discuss in this chapter. The first has to do with a *population regression model*. We want to infer its characteristics—that is, its intercept and slope term(s)—from the corresponding terms estimated by least squares. We also want to know which explanatory variables belong in the equation. There are typically a large number of *potential* explanatory variables, and it is often not clear which of these do the best job of explaining variation in the dependent variable. In addition, we would like to infer whether there is any population regression equation worth pursuing. It is possible that the potential explanatory variables provide very little explanation of the dependent variable.

The second problem we discuss in this chapter is *prediction*. We touched on the prediction problem in the previous chapter, primarily in the context of predicting the dependent variable for part of the sample held out for validation purposes. In reality, we had the values of the dependent variable for that part of the sample, so prediction was not really necessary. Now we go beyond the sample and predict values of the dependent variable for *new* observations. There is no way to check the accuracy of these predictions, at least not right away, because the true values of the dependent variable are not yet known. However, it is possible to calculate prediction intervals to measure the accuracy of the predictions.

11.2 THE STATISTICAL MODEL

To perform statistical inference in a regression context, you must first make several assumptions about the population. Throughout the analysis these assumptions remain exactly that—they are only assumptions, not facts. These assumptions represent an idealization of reality, and as such, they are never likely to be entirely satisfied for the population in any real study. From a practical point of view, all you can ask is that they represent a close approximation to reality. If this is the case, then the analysis in this chapter is valid. But if the assumptions are grossly violated, statistical inferences that are based on these assumptions should be viewed with suspicion. Although you can never be entirely certain of the validity of the assumptions, there are ways to check for gross violations, and we discuss some of these.

Regression Assumptions

1. There is a population regression line. It joins the *means* of the dependent variable for all values of the explanatory variables. For any fixed values of the explanatory variables, the mean of the errors is zero.

2. For any values of the explanatory variables, the variance (or standard deviation) of the dependent variable is a constant, the same for all such values.

3. For any values of the explanatory variables, the dependent variable is normally distributed.

4. The errors are probabilistically independent.

Because these assumptions are so crucial to the regression analysis that follows, it is important to understand exactly what they mean. Assumption 1 is probably the most important. It implies that for some set of explanatory variables, there is an exact linear relationship in the population between the *means* of the dependent variable and the values of the explanatory variables.

These explanatory variables could be original variables or variables you create, such as dummies, interactions, or nonlinear transformations.

To be more specific, let Y be the dependent variable, and assume that there are k explanatory variables, X_1 through X_k. Let $\mu_{Y|X_1,...,X_k}$ be the mean of all Ys for any fixed values of the Xs. Then assumption 1 implies that there is an exact linear relationship between the mean $\mu_{Y|X_1,...,X_k}$ and the Xs. That is, it implies that there are coefficients α and β_1 through β_k such that the following equation holds for all values of the Xs:

Population Regression Line Joining Means

$$\mu_{Y|X_1,...,X_k} = \alpha + \beta_1 X_1 + \cdots + \beta_k X_k \tag{11.1}$$

We commonly use Greek letters to denote population parameters and regular letters for their sample estimates.

In the terminology of the previous chapter, α is the intercept term, and β_1 through β_k are the slope terms. We use Greek letters for these coefficients to denote that they are *unobservable* population parameters. Assumption 1 implies the existence of a population regression equation and the corresponding α and βs. However, it tells us nothing about the *values* of these parameters. They still need to be estimated from sample data, using the least squares method to do so.

Equation (11.1) says that the *means* of the Ys lie on the population regression line. However, it is clear from a scatterplot that most *individual Y*s do not lie on this line. The vertical distance from any point to the line is called an **error**. The error for any point, labeled ε, is the difference between Y and $\mu_{Y|X_1,...,X_k}$, that is,

$$Y = \mu_{Y|X_1,...,X_k} + \varepsilon$$

By substituting the assumed linear form for $\mu_{Y|X_1,...,X_k}$, we obtain Equation (11.2). This equation states that each value of Y is equal to a fitted part plus an error. The fitted part is the linear expression $\alpha + \beta_1 X_1 + \cdots + \beta_k X_k$. The error ε is sometimes positive, in which case the point is above the regression line, and sometimes negative, in which case the point is below the regression line. The last part of assumption 1 states that these errors average to zero in the population, so that the positive errors cancel the negative errors.

Population Regression Line with Error

$$Y = \alpha + \beta_1 X_1 + \cdots + \beta_k X_k + \varepsilon \tag{11.2}$$

Note that an error ε is not quite the same as a residual e. An error is the vertical distance from a point to the (unobservable) population regression line. A residual is the vertical distance from a point to the *estimated* regression line. Residuals can be calculated from observed data; errors cannot.

Assumption 2 concerns variation around the population regression line. Specifically, it states that the variation of the Ys about the regression line is the *same,* regardless of the values of the Xs. A technical term for this property is **homoscedasticity**. A simpler term is **constant error variance**. In the Pharmex example (Example 11.1), constant error variance implies that the variation in Sales values is the same regardless of the value of Promote. As another example, recall the Bendrix manufacturing example (Example 11.2). There we related overhead costs (Overhead) to the number of machine hours (MachHrs) and the number of production runs (ProdRuns). Constant error variance implies that overhead costs vary just as much for small values of MachHrs and ProdRuns as for large values—or any values in between.

There are many situations where assumption 2 is questionable. The variation in Y often increases as X increases—a violation of assumption 2. We presented an example of this in Figure 10.10 (repeated here in Figure 11.1), which is based on customer spending at a mail-order company. This scatterplot shows the amount spent versus salary for a sample of the company's customers. Clearly, the variation in the amount spent increases as salary increases, which makes intuitive sense. Customers with small salaries have little disposable income, so they all tend to spend small amounts for mail-order items. Customers with large salaries have more disposable income. Some of them spend a lot of it on mail-order items and some spend only a little of it—hence, a larger variation. Scatterplots with this "fan" shape are not at all uncommon in real studies, and they exhibit a clear violation of assumption 2.[1] We say that the data in this graph exhibit **heteroscedasticity**, or more simply, **nonconstant error variance**. These terms are summarized in the following box.

Homoscedasticity means that the variability of Y values is the same for all X values.

Heteroscedasticity means that the variability of Y values is larger for some X values than for others.

Figure 11.1

Illustration of Nonconstant Error Variance

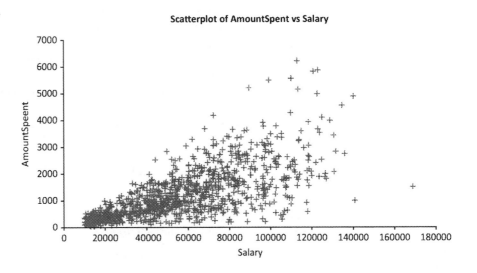

Scatterplot of AmountSpent vs Salary

[1]The fan shape in Figure 11.1 is probably the most common form of nonconstant error variance, but it is not the only possible form.

The easiest way to detect nonconstant error variance is through a visual inspection of a scatterplot. You create a scatterplot of the dependent variable versus an explanatory variable X and see whether the points vary more for some values of X than for others. You can also examine the residuals with a residual plot, where residual values are on the vertical axis and some other variable (Y or one of the Xs) is on the horizontal axis. If the residual plot exhibits a fan shape or other evidence of nonconstant error variance, this also indicates a violation of assumption 2.

Assumption 3 is equivalent to stating that the errors are normally distributed. You can check this by forming a histogram (or a Q-Q plot) of the residuals. If assumption 3 holds, the histogram should be approximately symmetric and bell-shaped, and the points in the Q-Q plot should be close to a 45° line.[2] But if there is an obvious skewness, too many residuals more than, say, two standard deviations from the mean, or some other nonnormal property, this indicates a violation of assumption 3.

Finally, assumption 4 requires probabilistic independence of the errors. Intuitively, this assumption means that information on some of the errors provides no information on the values of other errors. For example, if you are told that the overhead costs for months 1 through 4 are all above the regression line (positive residuals), you cannot infer anything about the residual for month 5 if assumption 4 holds.

Assumption 4 (independence of residuals) is usually in doubt only for time series data.

For cross-sectional data there is generally little reason to doubt the validity of assumption 4 unless the observations are ordered in some particular way. For cross-sectional data assumption 4 is usually taken for granted. However, for time series data, assumption 4 is often violated. This is because of a property called *autocorrelation*. For now, we simply mention that one output given automatically in many regression packages is the *Durbin–Watson statistic*. The Durbin–Watson statistic is one measure of autocorrelation and thus it measures the extent to which assumption 4 is violated. We briefly discuss this Durbin–Watson statistic toward the end of this chapter and in the next chapter.

One other assumption is important for numerical calculations. No explanatory variable can be an *exact* linear combination of any other explanatory variables. Another way of stating this is that there should be no exact linear relationship between any set of explanatory variables. This would be violated, for example, if one variable were an exact multiple of another, or if one variable were equal to the sum of several other variables. More generally, the violation occurs if one of the explanatory variables can be written as a weighted sum of several of the others. This is called *exact multicollinearity*.

Exact multicollinearity means that at least one of the explanatory variables is redundant and is not needed in the regression equation.

If exact multicollinearity exists, it means that there is *redundancy* in the data. One of the Xs could be eliminated without any loss of information. Here is a simple example. Suppose that MachHrs1 is machine hours measured in hours, and MachHrs2 is machine hours measured in *hundreds* of hours. Then it is clear that these two variables contain exactly the same information, and either of them could (and should) be eliminated.

As another example, suppose that Ad1, Ad2, and Ad3 are the amounts spent on radio ads, television ads, and newspaper ads. Also, suppose that TotalAd is the amount spent on radio, television, and newspaper ads combined. Then there is an exact linear relationship among these variables:

$$\text{TotalAd} = \text{Ad1} + \text{Ad2} + \text{Ad3}$$

In this case there is no need to include TotalAd in the analysis because it contains no information that is not already contained in the variables Ad1, Ad2, and Ad3. Therefore, TotalAd should be eliminated from the analysis.

---

[2]A Q-Q (quantile-quantile) plot is used to detect nonnormality. It is available in StatTools from the Normality Tests dropdown list. Nonnormal data often produce a Q-Q plot that is close to a 45° line in the middle of the plot but deviates from this line in one or both of the tails.

StatTools Tip StatTools issues a warning if it detects an exact linear relationship between explanatory variables in a regression model.

Generally, it is fairly simple to spot an exact linear relationship such as these, and then to eliminate it by excluding the redundant variable from the analysis. However, if you do *not* spot the relationship and try to run the regression analysis with the redundant variable included, regression packages will typically respond with an error message. If the package interrupts the analysis with an error message containing the words "exact multicollinearity" or "linear dependence," you should look for a redundant explanatory variable. The message from StatTools in this case is shown in Figure 11.2. We got it by deliberately entering dummy variables from *each* category of a categorical variable—something we have warned you *not* to do.

Figure 11.2

Error Message from StatTools Indicating Exact Multicollinearity

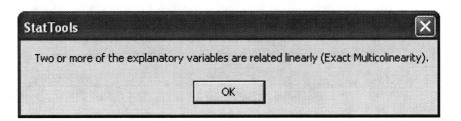

Although this problem can be a nuisance, it is usually caused by an oversight and can be fixed easily by eliminating a redundant variable. A more common and serious problem is *multicollinearity*, where explanatory variables are highly, but not exactly, correlated. A typical example is an employee's years of experience and age. Although these two variables are not equal for all employees, they are likely to be highly correlated. If they are both included as explanatory variables in a regression analysis, the software will not issue any error messages, but the estimates it produces can be unreliable and difficult to interpret. We will discuss multicollinearity in more detail later in this chapter.

11.3 INFERENCES ABOUT THE REGRESSION COEFFICIENTS

In this section we explain how to make inferences about the population regression coefficients from sample data. We begin by making the assumptions discussed in the previous section. In particular, the first assumption states that there is a population regression line. Equation (11.2) for this line is repeated here:

$$Y = \alpha + \beta_1 X_1 + \cdots + \beta_k X_k + \varepsilon$$

We refer to α and the βs collectively as the *regression coefficients*. Again, Greek letters are used to indicate that these quantities are unknown and unobservable. There is one other unknown constant in the model: the variance of the errors. Regression assumption 2 states that these errors have a constant variance, the same for all values of the Xs. We label this constant variance σ^2. Equivalently, the common standard deviation of the errors is σ.

This is how it looks in theory. There is a fixed set of explanatory variables, and given these variables, the problem is to estimate α, the βs, and σ. In practice, however, it is not usually this straightforward. In real regression applications the choice of relevant explanatory variables is almost never obvious. There are at least two guiding principles: relevance and data availability. You certainly want variables that are related to the dependent variable. The best situation is when there is an established economic or physical theory to guide you. For example, economic theory suggests that the demand for a product (dependent variable) is related to its price (possible explanatory variable). But there are not enough established theories to cover every situation. You often have to use the available data, plus some trial and error, to determine a *useful* set of explanatory variables. In this sense, it is usually pointless to search for one single "true" population regression equation. Instead, you typically estimate several competing models, each with a different set of explanatory variables, and ultimately select one of them as being the most useful.

Typically, the most challenging part of a regression analysis is deciding which explanatory variables to include in the regression equation.

Deciding which explanatory variables to include in a regression equation is probably the most difficult part of any applied regression analysis. Available data sets frequently offer an overabundance of potential explanatory variables. In addition, it is possible and often useful to create new variables from original variables, such as their logarithms. So where do you stop? Is it best to include every conceivable explanatory variable that might be related to the dependent variable? One overriding principle is **parsimony**—explaining the most with the least. For example, if a dependent variable can be explained just as well (or nearly as well) with two explanatory variables as with 10 explanatory variables, the principle of parsimony says to use only two. Models with fewer explanatory variables are generally easier to interpret, so they are preferred whenever possible.

> The principle of **parsimony** is to explain the most with the least. It favors a model with fewer explanatory variables, assuming that this model explains the dependent variable almost as well as a model with additional explanatory variables.

Before you can determine which equation has the best set of explanatory variables, however, you must be able to estimate the unknown parameters for a given equation. That is, for a given set of explanatory variables X_1 through X_k, you must be able to estimate α, the βs, and σ. You learned how to find point estimates of these parameters in the previous chapter. The estimates of α and the βs are the least squares estimates of the intercept and slope terms. For example, the 36 months of overhead data in the Bendrix example were used to estimate the equation

$$\text{Predicted Overhead} = 3997 + 43.54\text{MachHrs} + 883.62\text{ProdRuns}$$

This implies that the least squares estimates of α, β_1, and β_2 are 3997, 43.54, and 883.62. Furthermore, because the residuals are really estimates of the errors, the standard error of estimate s_e is an estimate of σ. For the same overhead equation this estimate is $s_e = \$4109$.

You learned in Chapter 8 that there is more to statistical estimation than finding point estimates of population parameters. Each potential sample from the population typically leads to *different* point estimates. For example, if Bendrix estimates the equation for overhead from a different 36-month period (or possibly from another of its plants), the results will almost certainly be different. Therefore, we now discuss how these point estimates vary from sample to sample.

11.3.1 Sampling Distribution of the Regression Coefficients

The key idea is again sampling distributions. Recall that the sampling distribution of any estimate derived from sample data is the distribution of this estimate over all possible samples. This idea can be applied to the least squares estimate of a regression coefficient. For example, the sampling distribution of b_1, the least squares estimate of β_1, is the distribution of b_1s you would see if you observed many samples and ran a least squares regression on each of them.

Mathematicians have used theoretical arguments to find the required sampling distributions. We state the main result as follows. Let β be any of the βs, and let b be the least squares estimate of β. If the regression assumptions hold, the standardized value $(b - \beta)/s_b$ has a t distribution with $n - k - 1$ degrees of freedom. Here, k is the number of explanatory variables included in the equation, and s_b is the estimated standard deviation of the sampling distribution of b.

Sampling Distribution of a Regression Coefficient

If the regression assumptions are valid, the standardized value

$$t = \frac{b - \beta}{s_b}$$

has a t distribution with $n - k - 1$ degrees of freedom.

This result has three important implications. First, the estimate b is *unbiased* in the sense that its mean is β, the true but unknown value of the slope. If bs were estimated from repeated samples, some would underestimate β and others would overestimate β, but on average they would be on target.

Second, the estimated standard deviation of b is labeled s_b. It is usually called the **standard error of b**. This standard error is related to the standard error of estimate s_e, but it is not the same. Generally, the formula for s_b is quite complicated, and it is not shown here, but its value is printed in all standard regression outputs. It measures how much the bs would vary from sample to sample. A small value of s_b is preferred—it means that b is a more accurate estimate of the true coefficient β.

Finally, the shape of the distribution of b is symmetric and bell-shaped. The relevant distribution is the t distribution with $n - k - 1$ degrees of freedom.

We have stated this result for a typical coefficient of one of the Xs. These are usually the coefficients of most interest. However, exactly the same result holds for the intercept term α. Now we illustrate how to use this result.

FUNDAMENTAL INSIGHT

Standard Errors in Regression

There are two quite different standard errors in regression outputs. The standard error of estimate, usually shown at the top of the output, is a measure of the error you are likely to make when you use the regression equation to predict a value of Y. In contrast, the standard errors of the coefficients measure the accuracy of the individual coefficients.

EXAMPLE 11.1 EXPLAINING OVERHEAD COSTS AT BENDRIX

This example is a continuation of the Bendrix manufacturing example from the previous chapter. As before, the dependent variable is Overhead and the explanatory variables are MachHrs and ProdRuns. What inferences can be made about the regression coefficients?

Objective To use standard regression output to make inferences about the regression coefficients of machine hours and production runs in the equation for overhead costs.

Solution

The output from StatTools's Regression procedure is shown in Figure 11.3. (See the file Overhead Costs.xlsx.) This output is practically identical to regression outputs from all

Figure 11.3   Regression Output for Bendrix Example

	A	B	C	D	E	F	G
7		Multiple	R-Square	Adjusted	StErr of		
8	Summary	R		R-Square	Estimate		
9		0.9308	0.8664	0.8583	4108.993		
10							
11		Degrees of	Sum of	Mean of	F-Ratio	p-Value	
12	ANOVA Table	Freedom	Squares	Squares			
13	Explained	2	3614020661	1807010330	107.0261	< 0.0001	
14	Unexplained	33	557166199.1	16883824.22			
15							
16		Coefficient	Standard	t-Value	p-Value	Confidence Interval 95%	
17	Regression Table		Error			Lower	Upper
18	Constant	3996.678	6603.651	0.6052	0.5492	-9438.551	17431.907
19	MachHrs	43.536	3.589	12.1289	< 0.0001	36.234	50.839
20	ProdRuns	883.618	82.251	10.7429	< 0.0001	716.276	1050.960

other statistical software packages. The estimates of the regression coefficients appear under the label Coefficient in the range B18:B20. These values estimate the true, but unobservable, population coefficients. The next column, labeled Standard Error, shows the s_b values. Specifically, 3.589 is the standard error of the coefficient of MachHrs, and 82.251 is the standard error of the coefficient of ProdRuns.

Each b represents a point estimate of the corresponding β, based on this particular sample. The corresponding s_b indicates the accuracy of this point estimate. For example, the point estimate of β_1, the effect on Overhead of a one-unit increase in MachHrs (when ProdRuns is held constant), is 43.536. You can be about 95% confident that the true β_1 is within two standard errors of this point estimate, that is, from approximately 36.357 to 50.715. Similar statements can be made for the coefficient of ProdRuns and the intercept (Constant) term. ▪

As with any population parameters, the sample data can be used to obtain confidence intervals for the regression coefficients. For example, the preceding paragraph implies that an approximate 95% confidence interval for the coefficient of MachHrs extends from approximately 36.357 to 50.715. More precisely, a confidence interval for any β is of the form

$$b \pm t\text{-multiple} \times s_b$$

where the t-multiple depends on the confidence level and the degrees of freedom (here $n - k - 1$). StatTools always provides these 95% confidence intervals for the regression coefficients automatically, as shown in the bottom right of Figure 11.3.

11.3.2 Hypothesis Tests for the Regression Coefficients and p-Values

There is another important piece of information in regression outputs: the t-values for the individual regression coefficients. These are shown in the "t-Value" column of the regression output in Figure 11.3. Each t-value is the ratio of the estimated coefficient to its standard error, as shown in Equation (11.3). Therefore, it indicates how many standard errors the regression coefficient is from zero. For example, the t-value for MachHrs is about 11.13, so the regression coefficient of MachHrs, 43.536, is more than 12 of its standard errors to the right of zero. Similarly, the coefficient of ProdRuns is more than 10 of its standard errors to the right of zero.

> **t-value for Test of Regression Coefficient**
>
> $$t\text{-value} = b/s_b \qquad\qquad\qquad\qquad \textbf{(11.3)}$$

A t-value can be used in an important hypothesis test for the corresponding regression coefficient. To motivate this test, suppose that you want to decide whether a particular explanatory variable belongs in the regression equation. A sensible criterion for making this decision is to check whether the corresponding regression coefficient is zero. If a variable's coefficient is zero, there is no point in including this variable in the equation; the zero coefficient will cancel its effect on the dependent variable.

Therefore, it is reasonable to test whether a variable's coefficient is zero. This is usually tested versus a *two-tailed* alternative. The null and alternative hypotheses are of the form $H_0:\beta = 0$ versus $H_a:\beta \neq 0$. If you can reject the null hypothesis and conclude that this coefficient is *not* zero, you then have an argument for including the variable in the regression equation. Conversely, if you cannot reject the null hypothesis, you might decide to eliminate this variable from the equation.

The t-value for a variable allows you to run this test easily. You simply compare the t-value in the regression output with a tabulated t-value and reject the null hypothesis only if the t-value from the computer output is greater in magnitude than the tabulated t-value.

The test for whether a regression coefficient is zero can be run by looking at the corresponding p-value: Reject the "equals zero" hypothesis if the p-value is small, say, less than 0.05.

Most statistical packages, including StatTools, make this test even easier to run by reporting the corresponding p-value for the test. This eliminates the need for finding the tabulated t-value. The p-value is interpreted exactly as in Chapter 9. It is the probability (in both tails) of the relevant t distribution beyond the listed t-value. For example, referring again to Figure 11.3, the t-value for MachHrs is 12.13, and the associated p-value is less than 0.0001. This means that there is virtually no probability beyond the observed t-value. In words, you are still not exactly sure of the true coefficient of MachHrs, but you are virtually sure it is not zero. The same can be said for the coefficient of ProdRuns.

In practice, you typically run a multiple regression with several explanatory variables and scan their p-values. If the p-value of a variable is low, then this variable should be kept in the equation; if the p-value is high, you might consider eliminating this variable from the equation. In section 11.5, we will discuss this *include/exclude decision* in greater depth and provide rules of thumb for the meaning of "low" and "high" p-values.

11.3.3 A Test for the Overall Fit: The ANOVA Table

The t-values for the regression coefficients allow you to see which of the potential explanatory variables are useful in explaining the dependent variable. But it is conceivable that *none* of these variables does a very good job. That is, it is conceivable that the entire group of explanatory variables explains only an insignificant portion of the variability of the dependent variable. Although this is the exception rather than the rule in most real applications, it can certainly happen. An indication of this is that you obtain a very small R^2 value. Because R^2 is the square of the correlation between the observed values of the dependent variable and the fitted values from the regression equation, another indication of a lack of fit is that this correlation (the "multiple R") is small. In this section we state a formal procedure for testing the overall fit, or explanatory power, of a regression equation.

Suppose that the dependent variable is Y and the explanatory variables are X_1 through X_k. Then the proposed population regression equation is

$$Y = \alpha + \beta_1 X_1 + \cdots + \beta_k X_k + \varepsilon$$

To say that this equation has absolutely no explanatory power means that the same value of Y will be predicted regardless of the values of the Xs. In this case it makes no difference which values of the Xs are used, because they all lead to the same predicted value of Y. But the only way this can occur is if all of the βs are 0. So the formal hypothesis test in this section is $H_0: \beta_1 = \cdots = \beta_k = 0$ versus the alternative that at least one of the βs is not zero. If the null hypothesis can be rejected, as it can in the majority of applications, this means that the explanatory variables *as a group* provide at least some explanatory power. These hypotheses are summarized as follows.

Hypotheses for ANOVA Test

The null hypothesis is that all coefficients of the explanatory variables are zero. The alternative is that at least one of these coefficients is not zero.

At first glance it might appear that this null hypothesis can be tested by looking at the individual *t*-values. If they are all small (statistically insignificant), then the null hypothesis of no fit cannot be rejected; otherwise, it can be rejected. However, as you will see in the next section, it is possible, because of multicollinearity, to have small *t*-values even though the variables as a whole have *significant* explanatory power.

The alternative is to use an *F* test. This is sometimes referred to as the ANOVA (analysis of variance) test because the elements for calculating the required *F*-value are shown in an ANOVA table.[3] In general, an ANOVA table analyzes different sources of variation. In the case of regression, the variation in question is the variation of the dependent variable Y. The *total variation* of this variable is the sum of squared deviations about the mean and is labeled *SST* (sum of squares total).

$$SST = \sum (Y_i - \overline{Y})^2$$

The ANOVA table splits this total variation into two parts, the part *explained* by the regression equation, and the part left *unexplained*. The unexplained part is the sum of squared residuals, usually labeled *SSE* (sum of squared errors):

$$SSE = \sum e_i^2 = \sum (Y_i - \hat{Y}_i)^2$$

The explained part is then the difference between the total and unexplained variation. It is usually labeled *SSR* (sum of squares due to regression):

$$SSR = SST - SSE$$

The *F* test is a formal procedure for testing whether the explained variation is large compared to the unexplained variation. Specifically, each of these sources of variation has an associated degrees of freedom (*df*). For the explained variation, $df = k$, which is the number of explanatory variables. For the unexplained variation, $df = n - k - 1$, the sample size minus the total number of coefficients (including the intercept term). The ratio of either sum of squares to its degrees of freedom is called a mean square, or *MS*. The two mean squares in this case are *MSR* and *MSE*, given by

$$MSR = \frac{SSR}{k}$$

and

$$MSE = \frac{SSE}{n - k - 1}$$

---

[3]This ANOVA table is similar to the ANOVA table discussed in Chapter 9. However, we repeat the necessary material here for those who didn't cover that section.

Note that *MSE* is the square of the standard error of estimate, that is,

$$MSE = s_e^2$$

Finally, the ratio of these mean squares is the required *F*-ratio for the test:

$$F\text{-ratio} = \frac{MSR}{MSE}$$

When the null hypothesis of no explanatory power is true, this *F*-ratio has an *F* distribution with k and $n - k - 1$ degrees of freedom. If the *F*-ratio is small, the explained variation is small relative to the unexplained variation, and there is evidence that the regression equation provides little explanatory power. But if the *F*-ratio is large, the explained variation is large relative to the unexplained variation, and you can conclude that the equation does have some explanatory power.

As usual, the *F*-ratio has an associated *p*-value that allows you to run the test easily. In this case the *p*-value is the probability to the *right* of the observed *F*-ratio in the appropriate *F* distribution. This *p*-value is reported in most regression outputs, along with the elements that lead up to it. If it is sufficiently small, less than 0.05, say, then you can conclude that the explanatory variables as a whole have at least some explanatory power.

Although this test is run routinely in most applications, there is often little doubt that the equation has some explanatory power; the only questions are how much, and which explanatory variables provide the best combination. In such cases the *F*-ratio from the ANOVA table is typically "off the charts" and the corresponding *p*-value is practically zero. On the other hand, *F*-ratios, particularly large ones, should not necessarily be used to choose between equations with different explanatory variables included.

For example, suppose that one equation with three explanatory variables has an *F*-ratio of 54 with an extremely small *p*-value—very significant. Also, suppose that another equation that includes these three variables plus a few more has an *F*-ratio of 37 and also has a very small *p*-value. (When we say small, we mean *small*. These *p*-values are probably listed as <0.001.) Is the first equation better because its *F*-ratio is higher? Not necessarily. The two *F*-ratios imply only that both of these equations have a good deal of explanatory power. It is better to look at their s_e values (or adjusted R^2 values) and their *t*-values to choose between them.

The ANOVA table is part of the StatTools output for any regression run. It appeared for the Bendrix example in Figure 11.3, which is repeated for convenience in Figure 11.4. The ANOVA table is in rows 12 through 14. The degrees of freedom are in column B, the

Reject the null hypothesis—and conclude that these X variables have at least some explanatory power—if the F-value in the ANOVA table is large and the corresponding p-value is small.

Figure 11.4   Regression Output for Bendrix Example

	A	B	C	D	E	F	G
7		Multiple		Adjusted	StErr of		
8	Summary	R	R-Square	R-Square	Estimate		
9		0.9308	0.8664	0.8583	4108.993		
10							
11		Degrees of	Sum of	Mean of	F-Ratio	p-Value	
12	ANOVA Table	Freedom	Squares	Squares			
13	Explained	2	3614020661	1807010330	107.0261	< 0.0001	
14	Unexplained	33	557166199.1	16883824.22			
15							
16		Coefficient	Standard	t-Value	p-Value	Confidence Interval 95%	
17	Regression Table		Error			Lower	Upper
18	Constant	3996.678	6603.651	0.6052	0.5492	-9438.551	17431.907
19	MachHrs	43.536	3.589	12.1289	< 0.0001	36.234	50.839
20	ProdRuns	883.618	82.251	10.7429	< 0.0001	716.276	1050.960

sums of squares are in column C, the mean squares are in column D, the F-ratio is in cell E13, and its associated p-value is in cell F13. As predicted, this F-ratio is "off the charts," and the p-value is practically zero.

This information wouldn't be much comfort for the Bendrix manager who is trying to understand the causes of variation in overhead costs. This manager already *knows* that machine hours and production runs are related positively to overhead costs—everyone in the company knows that. What he really wants is a set of explanatory variables that yields a high R^2 and a low s_e. The low p-value in the ANOVA tables does not guarantee these. All it guarantees is that MachHrs and ProdRuns are of *some* help in explaining variations in Overhead.

As this example indicates, the ANOVA table can be used as a screening device. If the explanatory variables do not explain a significant percentage of the variation in the dependent variable, then you can either discontinue the analysis or search for an entirely new set of explanatory variables. But even if the F-ratio in the ANOVA table is extremely significant (as it usually is), there is no guarantee that the regression equation provides a good enough fit for practical uses. This depends on other measures such as s_e and R^2.

PROBLEMS

Note: Student solutions for problems whose numbers appear within a colored box are available for purchase at www.cengagebrain.com.

Level A

1. Explore the relationship between the selling prices (Y) and the appraised values (X) of the 148 homes in the file P02_11.xlsx by estimating a simple linear regression equation. Find a 95% confidence interval for the model's slope parameter (β_1). What does this confidence interval tell you about the relationship between Y and X for these data?

2. The owner of the Original Italian Pizza restaurant chain would like to predict the sales of his specialty, deep-dish pizza. He has gathered data on the monthly sales of deep-dish pizzas at his restaurants and observations on other potentially relevant variables for each of his 15 outlets in central Indiana. These data are provided in the file P10_04.xlsx.
   a. Estimate a multiple regression model between the quantity sold (Y) and the explanatory variables in columns C–E.
   b. Is there evidence of any violations of the key assumptions of regression analysis?
   c. Which of the variables in this equation have regression coefficients that are statistically different from zero at the 5% significance level?
   d. Given your findings in part **c**, which variables, if any, would you choose to remove from the equation estimated in part **a**? Why?

3. The file P02_10.xlsx contains midterm and final exam scores for 96 students in a corporate finance course.

Based on a regression equation for the final exam score as a function of the midterm exam score, find a 95% confidence interval for the slope of the population regression line. State exactly what this confidence interval indicates.

4. A trucking company wants to predict the yearly maintenance expense (Y) for a truck using the number of miles driven during the year (X_1) and the age of the truck (X_2, in years) at the beginning of the year. The company has gathered the information given in the file P10_16.xlsx. Each observation corresponds to a particular truck.
   a. Estimate a multiple regression equation using the given data.
   b. Does autocorrelation appear to be a problem? What about multicollinearity? What about heteroscedasticity?
   c. Find 95% confidence intervals for the regression coefficients of X_1 and X_2. Based on these interval estimates, which variable, if any, would you choose to remove from the equation estimated in part **a**? Why?

5. Based on the data in the file P02_23.xlsx from the U.S. Department of Agriculture, explore the relationship between the number of farms (X) and the average size of a farm (Y) in the United States.
   a. Use the given data to estimate a simple linear regression model.
   b. Test whether there is sufficient evidence to conclude that the slope parameter (β_1) is *less than* zero. Use a 5% significance level.

c. Based on your finding in part **b**, is it possible to conclude that a linear relationship exists between the number of farms and the average farm size during the given time period? Explain.

6. An antique collector believes that the price received for a particular item increases with its age and the number of bidders. The file P10_18.xlsx contains data on these three variables for 32 recently auctioned comparable items.
  a. Estimate an appropriate multiple regression model using the given data.
  b. Interpret the ANOVA table for this model. In particular, does this set of explanatory variables provide at least *some* power in explaining the variation in price? Report a *p*-value for this hypothesis test.

7. The file P02_02.xlsx contains information on over 200 movies that came out during 2006 and 2007. Run a regression of Total US Gross versus 7-day Gross, and then run a multiple regression of Total US Gross versus 7-day Gross and 14-day Gross. Report the 95% confidence interval for the coefficient of 7-day Gross in each equation. What exactly do these confidence intervals tell you about the effect of 7-day Gross on Total US Gross? Why are they not at all the same? What is the relevant population that this data set is a sample from?

8. The file P10_10.xlsx contains data on 150 homes that were sold recently in a particular community.
  a. Find a table of correlations between all of the variables. Do the correlations between Price and each of the other variables have the sign (positive or negative) you would expect? Explain briefly.
  b. Run a regression of Price versus Rooms. What does the 95% confidence interval for the coefficient of Rooms tell you about the effect of Rooms on Price for the entire population of such homes?
  c. Run a multiple regression of Price versus Home Size, Lot Size, Rooms, and Bathrooms. What is the 95% confidence interval for the coefficient of Rooms now? Why do you think it can be so different from the one in part **b**? Based on this regression, can you reject the null hypothesis that the population regression coefficient of Rooms is zero versus a two-tailed alternative? What does this mean?

9. Suppose that a regional express delivery service company wants to estimate the cost of shipping a package (Y) as a function of cargo type, where cargo type includes the following possibilities: fragile, semifragile, and durable. Costs for 15 randomly chosen packages of approximately the same weight and same distance shipped, but of different cargo types, are provided in the file P10_28.xlsx.

  a. Estimate an appropriate multiple regression equation to predict the cost of shipping a given package.
  b. Interpret the ANOVA table for this model. In particular, do the explanatory variables included in your equation in part **a** provide at least *some* power in explaining the variation in shipping costs? Report a *p*-value for this hypothesis test.

10. The file P10_05.xlsx contains salaries for a sample of DataCom employees, along with several variables that might be related to salary. Run a multiple regression of Salary versus Years Employed, Years Education, Gender, and Number Supervised. For each of these variables, explain exactly what the results in the Coefficient, Standard Error, t-Value, and p-Value columns mean. Based on the results, can you reject the null hypothesis that the population coefficient of any of these variables is zero versus a two-tailed alternative at the 5% significance level? If you can, what would you probably do next in the analysis?

Level B

11. A multiple regression with 36 observations and three explanatory variables yields the ANOVA table in Table 11.1.
  a. Complete this ANOVA table.
  b. Can you conclude at the 1% significance level that these three explanatory variables have *some* power in explaining variation in the dependent variable?

Table 11.1 ANOVA Table

	Degrees of Freedom	Sum of Squares
Explained		1211
Unexplained		
Total		2567

12. Suppose you find the ANOVA table shown in Table 11.2 for a simple linear regression.

Table 11.2 ANOVA Table

	Degrees of Freedom	Sum of Squares
Explained		52
Unexplained	87	
Total		1598

  a. Find the correlation between X and Y, assuming that the slope of the least squares line is negative.
  b. Find the *p*-value for the test of the hypothesis of no explanatory power at all. What does it tell you in this particular case?

11.4 MULTICOLLINEARITY

Recall that the coefficient of any variable in a regression equation indicates the effect of this variable on the dependent variable, provided that the other variables in the equation remain constant. Another way of stating this is that the coefficient represents the effect of this variable on the dependent variable *in addition to* the effects of the other variables in the equation. In the Bendrix example, if MachHrs and ProdRuns are included in the equation for Overhead, the coefficient of MachHrs indicates the *extra* amount MachHrs explains about variation in Overhead, in addition to the amount already explained by ProdRuns. Similarly, the coefficient of ProdRuns indicates the extra amount ProdRuns explains about variation in Overhead, in addition to the amount already explained by MachHrs. Therefore, the relationship between an explanatory variable X and the dependent variable Y is not always accurately reflected in the coefficient of X; it depends on which *other X*s are included or not included in the equation.

This is especially true when *multicollinearity* exists. By definition, **multicollinearity** is the presence of a fairly strong linear relationship between two or more explanatory variables, and it can make regression output difficult to interpret.

> **Multicollinearity** occurs when there is a fairly strong linear relationship among a set of explanatory variables.

Consider the following example. It is a rather contrived example, but it is useful for illustrating the potential effects of multicollinearity.

EXAMPLE | **11.2 HEIGHT AS A FUNCTION OF FOOT LENGTH**

We want to explain a person's height by means of foot length. The dependent variable is Height, and the explanatory variables are Right and Left, the length of the right foot and the length of the left foot, respectively. What can occur when Height is regressed on *both* Right and Left?

Objective   To illustrate the problem of multicollinearity when both foot length variables are used in a regression for height.

Solution

Clearly, there is no need to include both Right and Left in an equation for Height—either one of them suffices—but we include them both to make a point. It is likely that there is a large correlation between height and foot size, so you would expect this regression equation to do a good job. For example, the R^2 value will probably be large. But what about the coefficients of Right and Left? Here there is a problem. The coefficient of Right indicates the right foot's effect on Height in addition to the effect of the left foot. This additional effect is probably minimal. That is, after the effect of Left on Height has been taken into account, the extra information provided by Right is probably minimal. But it goes the other way also. The extra effect of Left, in addition to that provided by Right, is probably also minimal.

To show what can happen numerically, we used simulation to generate a hypothetical data set of heights and left and right foot lengths. We did this so that, except for random error, height is approximately 31.8 plus 3.2 times foot length (all expressed in inches). (See Figure 11.5 and the file Heights Simulation.xlsx. You can check the formulas in

Figure 11.5 One Example of Height versus Foot Length

	A	B	C	D	E	F	G	H	I	J
1	Parameters of foot size distribution				Parameters of regression, given generic foot size					
2	Mean	12.95			Intercept	31.8				
3	Stdev1	3.1			Slope	3.2				
4	Stdev2	0.2			StErr of Est	3.0				
5										
6	Generic foot size	Left	Right	Height			Correlations	Squares		
7	15.381	15.063	15.111	83.631	Left vs Right		0.996			
8	9.614	9.467	9.707	65.59	Left vs Height		0.960	0.922		
9	10.067	9.827	9.878	63.918	Right vs Height		0.954	0.911		
10	12.071	11.688	11.962	70.89						
11	18.015	18.061	17.971	93.567	Regression equation					
12	13.567	13.676	13.164	77.095	Variable		Coeff	StErr	t-value	p-value
13	17.099	17.446	17.132	87.843	Constant		30.583	1.279	23.908	0.0000
14	18.784	18.49	18.878	90.079	Left		4.385	1.131	3.876	0.0002
15	11.035	11.003	10.922	67.118	Right		-1.046	1.122	-0.932	0.3535
16	10.271	10.055	10.196	63.502	Sum of coeffs		3.339			
17	10.884	10.715	11.295	66.552						
18	12.481	12.685	12.588	74.764	SSE		1017.020			
19	13.861	13.744	13.883	80.754	MSE		10.485			
20	4.008	4.031	4.441	38.922	StErr of est		3.238			
21	14.227	13.958	14.113	75.058						
22	13.537	13.211	13.888	78.243	R-square		0.923			
23	13.028	12.608	12.957	68.337	Multiple R		0.961			
24	12.804	12.524	12.874	68.494						
105	14.02	14.055	14.291	69.627						
106	16.354	16.401	16.62	75.977						

columns A–D to see how we generated the data with the desired properties.) It is clear that the correlation between Height and either Right or Left is quite large, and the correlation between Right and Left is very close to 1 (see cells G7 to G9).

The regression output when both Right and Left are entered in the equation for Height appears at the bottom right in Figure 11.5. (We entered our own matrix formulas for the regression because we wanted them to be "live," unlike those in StatTools.) The output tells a somewhat confusing story. The multiple R and the corresponding R^2 are about as expected, given the correlations between Height and either Right or Left. In particular, the multiple R is close to the correlation between Height and either Right or Left. Also, the s_e value is quite good. It implies that predictions of height from this regression equation will typically be off by only about three inches.

Multicollinearity often causes regression coefficients to have the "wrong" sign, t-values to be too small, and p-values to be too large.

However, the coefficients of Right and Left are not at all what you might expect, given that the heights were generated as approximately 31.8 plus 3.2 times foot length. In fact, the coefficient of Right is the wrong sign—it is *negative*. Besides this "wrong" sign, the tip-off that there is a problem is that the *t*-value of Right is quite small and the corresponding *p*-value is quite large. Judging by this, you might conclude that Height and Right are either not related or are related negatively. But you know from the correlation in cell G9 that both of these conclusions are wrong. In contrast, the coefficient of Left has the "correct" sign, and its *t*-value and associated *p*-value do imply statistical significance. However, this happened mostly by chance. Slight changes in the data could change the results completely—the coefficient of Right could become negative and insignificant, or both coefficients could become insignificant. For example, the random numbers in Figure 11.6, generated from the same model, lead to regression output where *neither* Right nor Left is statistically significant.

Figure 11.6 Another Example of Height versus Foot Length

	A	B	C	D	E	F	G	H	I	J
1	Parameters of foot size distribution				Parameters of regression, given generic foot size					
2	Mean	12.95			Intercept	31.8				
3	Stdev1	3.1			Slope	3.2				
4	Stdev2	0.2			StErr of Est	3.0				
5										
6	Generic foot size	Left	Right	Height			Correlations	Squares		
7	12.207	12.36	12.301	68.985		Left vs Right	0.995			
8	13.343	13.369	13.29	75.615		Left vs Height	0.950	0.903		
9	10.981	11.183	11.185	59.805		Right vs Height	0.950	0.903		
10	10.757	10.592	10.756	69.754						
11	13.602	13.736	14.02	79.694		Regression equation				
12	11.688	11.932	11.692	65.166		Variable	Coeff	StErr	t-value	p-value
13	10.674	10.6	10.653	65.999		Constant	31.755	1.398	22.714	0.0000
14	12.731	12.766	12.55	68.061		Left	1.639	1.079	1.519	0.1321
15	16.981	17.155	16.996	85.618		Right	1.559	1.096	1.422	0.1581
16	14.417	14.434	13.931	77.947		Sum of coeffs	3.198			
17	15.369	15.57	15.408	82.511						
18	11.514	11.776	11.392	67.787		SSE	1010.758			
19	11.363	11.345	10.807	65.025		MSE	10.420			
20	14.768	14.977	14.522	85.902		StErr of est	3.228			
21	11.165	10.893	11.55	67.92						
22	8.823	9.107	9.039	65.852		R-square	0.905			
23	19.944	20.003	20.074	96.903		Multiple R	0.951			
24	15.832	15.546	15.721	79.923						
105	18.37	18.451	18.472	89.623						
106	13.584	13.78	13.424	78.05						

Multicollinearity typically causes unreliable estimates of regression coefficients, but it does not generally cause poor predictions.

The problem is that although both Right and Left are clearly related to Height, it is impossible for the least squares method to distinguish their *separate* effects. Note that the regression equation does estimate the combined effect fairly well—the sum of the coefficients of Right and Left in cell G16 in both figures is close to the coefficient 3.2 that was used to generate the data. Also, the estimated intercept is pretty close to the intercept 31.8 that was used to generate the data. Therefore, the estimated equation will work well for predicting heights. It just does not produce reliable estimates of the individual coefficients of Right and Left. ■

This example illustrates an extreme form of multicollinearity, where two explanatory variables are very highly correlated. In general, there are various degrees of multicollinearity. In each of them, there is a linear relationship between two or more explanatory variables, and this relationship makes it difficult to estimate the individual effects of the Xs on the dependent variable. The symptoms of multicollinearity can be "wrong" signs of the coefficients, smaller-than-expected t-values, and larger-than-expected (insignificant) p-values. In other words, variables that are really related to the dependent variable can look like they aren't related, based on their p-values. The reason is that their effects on Y are already explained by other Xs in the equation.

Moderate to extreme multicollinearity poses a problem in many regression applications. Unfortunately, there are usually no easy remedies.

Sometimes multicollinearity is easy to spot and treat. For example, it would be silly to include both Right and Left foot length in the equation for Height. They are obviously very highly correlated and either one suffices in the equation for Height. One of them—either one—should be excluded from the equation. However, multicollinearity is not usually this easy to treat or even diagnose.

Effect of Multicollinearity

Multicollinearity occurs when Xs are highly correlated with one another, and it is a problem in many real regression applications. It prevents you from separating the influences of these Xs on Y. In short, it prevents you from seeing clearly how the world works. However, multicollinearity is *not* a problem if you simply want to use a regression equation as a "black box" for predictions.

Suppose, for example, that you want to use regression to explain variations in salary. Three potentially useful explanatory variables are age, years of experience with the company, and years of experience in the industry. It is very likely that each of these is positively related to salary, and it is also very likely that they are very closely related to each other. However, it isn't clear which, if any, you should exclude from the regression equation. If you include all three, you are likely to find that at least one of them is insignificant (high p-value), in which case you might consider excluding it from the equation. If you do so, the s_e and R^2 values will probably not change very much—the equation will provide equally good predicted values—but the coefficients of the variables that remain in the equation could change considerably.

PROBLEMS

Level A

13. Using the data given in P10_10.xlsx, estimate a multiple regression equation to predict the price of houses in a given community. Employ all available explanatory variables. Is there evidence of multicollinearity in this model? Explain why or why not.

14. Consider the data for *Business Week*'s top U.S. MBA programs in the MBA Data sheet of the file P10_21.xlsx. Use these data to estimate a multiple regression model to assess whether there is a relationship between the enrollment and the following explanatory variables: (a) the percentage of international students, (b) the percentage of female students, (c) the percentage of Asian American students, (d) the percentage of minority students, and (e) the resident tuition and fees at these business schools.
  a. Determine whether each of the regression coefficients for the explanatory variables in this model is statistically different from zero at the 5% significance level. Summarize your findings.
  b. Is there evidence of multicollinearity in this model? Explain why or why not.

15. The manager of a commuter rail transportation system was recently asked by her governing board to determine the factors that have a significant impact on the demand for rides in the large city served by the transportation network. The system manager has collected data on variables that might be related to the number of weekly riders on the city's rail system. The file P10_20.xlsx contains these data.
  a. Estimate a multiple regression model using all of the available explanatory variables. Perform a test

of significance for each of the model's regression coefficients. Are the signs of the estimated coefficients consistent with your expectations?
  b. Is there evidence of multicollinearity in this model? Explain why or why not. If multicollinearity is present, explain what you would do to remedy this problem.

Level B

16. The file P10_05.xlsx contains salaries for a sample of DataCom employees, along with several variables that might be related to salary.
  a. Estimate the relationship between Y (Salary) and X (Years Employed) using simple linear regression. (For this problem, ignore the other potential explanatory variables.) Is there evidence to support the hypothesis that the coefficient for the number of years employed is statistically different from zero at the 5% significance level?
  b. Estimate a multiple regression model to explain annual salaries of DataCom employees with X and X^2 as explanatory variables. Perform relevant hypothesis tests to determine the significance of the regression coefficients of these two variables. Summarize your findings.
  c. How do you explain your findings in part **b** in light of the results found in part **a**?

17. The owner of a restaurant in Bloomington, Indiana, has recorded sales data for the past 19 years. He has also recorded data on potentially relevant variables. The data appear in the file P10_23.xlsx.
  a. Estimate a multiple regression equation that includes annual sales as the dependent variable

and the following explanatory variables: year, size of the population residing within 10 miles of the restaurant, annual advertising expenditures, and advertising expenditures in the *previous* year.

b. Which of the explanatory variables have significant effects on sales at the 10% significance level? Do any of these results surprise you? Explain why or why not.

c. Exclude all insignificant explanatory variables from the equation in part **a** and estimate the equation with the remaining variables. Comment on the significance of each remaining variable.

d. Based on your analysis of this problem, does multicollinearity appear to be present in the original or revised versions of the model? Explain.

11.5 INCLUDE/EXCLUDE DECISIONS

In this section we make further use of the *t*-values of regression coefficients. In particular, we explain how they can be used to make **include/exclude decisions** for explanatory variables in a regression equation. Section 11.3 explained how a *t*-value can be used to test whether a population regression coefficient is zero. But does this mean that you should automatically include a variable if its *t*-value is significant and automatically exclude it if its *t*-value is insignificant? The decision is not always this simple.

The bottom line is that you are always trying to get the best fit possible, and the principle of parsimony suggests using the fewest number of variables. This presents a trade-off, where there not always easy answers. On the one hand, more variables certainly increase R^2, and they usually reduce the standard error of estimate s_e. On the other hand, fewer variables are better for parsimony. To help with the decision, we present several guidelines. These guidelines are not hard and fast rules, and they are sometimes contradictory. In real applications there are often several equations that are equally good for all practical purposes, and it is rather pointless to search for a single "true" equation.

GUIDELINES FOR INCLUDING/EXCLUDING VARIABLES IN A REGRESSION EQUATION

1 Look at a variable's *t*-value and its associated *p*-value. If the *p*-value is above some accepted significance level, such as 0.05, this variable is a candidate for exclusion.

2 Check whether a variable's *t*-value is less than 1 or greater than 1 in magnitude. If it is less than 1, then it is a mathematical fact that s_e will decrease (and adjusted R^2 will increase) if this variable is excluded from the equation. If it is greater than 1, the opposite will occur. Because of this, some statisticians advocate excluding variables with *t*-values less than 1 and including variables with *t*-values greater than 1.

3 Look at *t*-values and *p*-values, rather than correlations, when making include/exclude decisions. An explanatory variable can have a fairly high correlation with the dependent variable, but because of *other* variables included in the equation, it might not be needed. This would be reflected in a low *t*-value and a high *p*-value, and this variable could possibly be excluded for reasons of parsimony. This often occurs in the presence of multicollinearity.

4 When there is a group of variables that are in some sense logically related, it is sometimes a good idea to include all of them or exclude all of them. In this case, their individual t-values are less relevant. Instead, a "partial F test" (discussed in section 11.7) can be used to make the include/exclude decision.

5 Use economic and/or physical theory to decide whether to include or exclude variables, and put less reliance on t-values and/or p-values. Some variables might really *belong* in an equation because of their theoretical relationship with the dependent variable, and their low t-values, possibly the result of an unlucky sample, should not necessarily disqualify them from being in the equation. Similarly, a variable that has no economic or physical relationship with the dependent variable might have a significant t-value just by chance. This does not necessarily mean that it should be included in the equation. You should not use a software package blindly to hunt for "good" explanatory variables. You should have some idea, before running the package, of which variables belong and which do not belong.

Again, these guidelines can give contradictory signals. Specifically, guideline 2 bases the include/exclude decision on whether the magnitude of the t-value is greater or less than 1. However, analysts who base the decision on statistical significance at the usual 5% level, as in guideline 1, typically exclude a variable from the equation unless its t-value is at least 2 (approximately). This latter approach is more stringent—fewer variables will be retained—but it is probably the more popular approach. However, either approach is likely to result in similar equations for all practical purposes.

In our experience, you should not agonize too much about whether to include or exclude a variable "at the margin." If you decide to exclude a variable that doesn't add much explanatory power, you get a somewhat cleaner equation, and you probably won't see any dramatic shifts in R^2 or s_e. On the other hand, if you decide to keep such a variable in the equation, the equation is less parsimonious and you have one more variable to interpret, but otherwise, there is no real penalty for including it.

We illustrate how these guidelines can be used in the following example.

EXAMPLE	**11.3 EXPLAINING SPENDING AMOUNTS AT HYTEX**

The file Catalog Marketing.xlsx contains data on 1000 customers who purchased mail-order products from the HyTex Company in the current year. (This is a slightly different version of the file that was used in Chapter 2.) HyTex is a direct marketer of stereo equipment, personal computers, and other electronic products. HyTex advertises entirely by mailing catalogs to its customers, and all of its orders are taken over the telephone. The company spends a great deal of money on its catalog mailings, and it wants to be sure that this is paying off in sales. For each customer there are data on the following variables:

- Age: age of the customer at the end of the current year
- Gender: coded as 1 for males, 0 for females
- OwnHome: coded as 1 if customer owns a home, 0 otherwise
- Married: coded as 1 if customer is currently married, 0 otherwise
- Close: coded as 1 if customer lives reasonably close to a shopping area that sells similar merchandise, 0 otherwise
- Salary: combined annual salary of customer and spouse (if any)
- Children: number of children living with customer
- PrevCust: coded as 1 if customer purchased from HyTex during the previous year, 0 otherwise

- PrevSpent: total amount of purchases made from HyTex during the previous year
- Catalogs: number of catalogs sent to the customer this year
- AmountSpent: total amount of purchases made from HyTex this year

Estimate and interpret a regression equation for AmountSpent based on all of these variables.

Objective   To see which potential explanatory variables are useful for explaining current year spending amounts at HyTex with multiple regression.

Solution

With this much data, 1000 observations, it is possible to set aside part of the data set for validation, as discussed in section 10.7. Although any split can be used, we decided to base the regression on the first 750 observations and use the other 250 for validation. Therefore, you should select only the range through row 751 when defining the StatTools data set.

You can begin by entering all of the potential explanatory variables. The goal is then to exclude variables that aren't necessary, based on their t-values and p-values. The multiple regression output with all explanatory variables appears in Figure 11.7. It indicates a fairly good fit. The R^2 value is 74.7% and s_e is about $491. Given that the actual amounts spent in the current year vary from a low of under $50 to a high of over $5500, with a median of about $950, a typical prediction error of around $491 is decent but not great.

From the p-value column, you can see that there are four variables, Age, Gender, OwnHome, and Married, that have p-values well above 0.05. These are the obvious candidates for exclusion from the equation. You could rerun the equation with all three of these variables excluded, but it is a better practice to exclude one variable at a time. It is possible that when one of these variables is excluded, another one of them will become significant (the Right–Left foot phenomenon).

Figure 11.7   Regression Output with All Explanatory Variables Included

	A	B	C	D	E	F	G
7		Multiple	R-Square	Adjusted	StErr of		
8	*Summary*	R		R-Square	Estimate		
9		0.8643	0.7470	0.7435	491.4513		
10							
11		Degrees of	Sum of	Mean of	F-Ratio	p-Value	
12	*ANOVA Table*	Freedom	Squares	Squares			
13	Explained	10	526916948.1	52691694.81	218.1631	< 0.0001	
14	Unexplained	739	178486506.7	241524.3663			
15							
16		Coefficient	Standard	t-Value	p-Value	Confidence Interval 95%	
17	*Regression Table*		Error			Lower	Upper
18	Constant	197.3915	85.8636	2.2989	0.0218	28.8259	365.9572
19	Age	0.6014	1.2596	0.4775	0.6332	-1.8715	3.0743
20	Gender	-57.4924	37.9022	-1.5169	0.1297	-131.9013	16.9165
21	OwnHome	23.3068	40.3559	0.5775	0.5638	-55.9191	102.5326
22	Married	8.6877	48.5435	0.1790	0.8580	-86.6119	103.9872
23	Close	-418.7341	45.2356	-9.2567	< 0.0001	-507.5397	-329.9284
24	Salary	0.0179	0.0012	15.5194	< 0.0001	0.0157	0.0202
25	Children	-161.4875	21.0032	-7.6887	< 0.0001	-202.7205	-120.2544
26	PrevCust	-546.0081	63.4794	-8.6013	< 0.0001	-670.6295	-421.3867
27	PrevSpent	0.2684	0.0528	5.0876	< 0.0001	0.1648	0.3719
28	Catalogs	43.9463	2.8618	15.3560	< 0.0001	38.3280	49.5646

Actually, this did not happen. We first excluded the variable with the largest p-value, Married, and reran the regression. At this point, Age, Gender, and OwnHome still had large p-values, so we excluded Age, the variable with the largest remaining p-value, and reran the regression. Next, we excluded OwnHome, the variable with the largest remaining p-value, and finally, we excluded Gender because its p-value was still large. The resulting output appears in Figure 11.8. The R^2 and s_e values of 74.6% and $491 are almost the same as they were with all variables included, and all of the p-values are very small.

Figure 11.8   Regression Output with Insignificant Variables Excluded

	A	B	C	D	E	F	G
7		Multiple	R-Square	Adjusted	StErr of		
8	Summary	R		R-Square	Estimate		
9		0.8636	0.7458	0.7438	491.2283		
10							
11		Degrees of	Sum of	Mean of	F-Ratio	p-Value	
12	ANOVA Table	Freedom	Squares	Squares			
13	Explained	6	526113683.9	87685613.98	363.3805	< 0.0001	
14	Unexplained	743	179289770.9	241305.2099			
15							
16		Coefficient	Standard	t-Value	p-Value	Confidence Interval 95%	
17	Regression Table		Error			Lower	Upper
18	Constant	205.0936	70.3152	2.9168	0.0036	67.0534	343.1338
19	Close	-416.2462	45.0846	-9.2326	< 0.0001	-504.7546	-327.7378
20	Salary	0.0180	0.0009	19.8773	< 0.0001	0.0162	0.0197
21	Children	-161.1577	20.4828	-7.8679	< 0.0001	-201.3688	-120.9466
22	PrevCust	-543.5948	63.2988	-8.5878	< 0.0001	-667.8606	-419.3290
23	PrevSpent	0.2724	0.0525	5.1844	< 0.0001	0.1692	0.3755
24	Catalogs	43.8067	2.8542	15.3481	< 0.0001	38.2034	49.4100

This final regression equation can be interpreted as follows:

Interpretation of Regression Equation

- The coefficient of Close implies that an average customer living close to stores with this type of merchandise spent about $416 less than an average customer living far from such stores.

- The coefficient of Salary implies that, on average, about 1.8 cents of every extra salary dollar was spent on HyTex merchandise.

- The coefficient of Children implies that about $161 *less* was spent for every extra child living at home.

- The PrevCust and PrevSpent terms are somewhat more difficult to interpret. First, both of these terms are zero for customers who didn't purchase from HyTex in the previous year. For those who did, the terms become $-544 + 0.27$PrevSpent. The coefficient 0.27 implies that each extra dollar spent the previous year can be expected to contribute an extra 27 cents in the current year. The -544 literally means that if you compare a customer who didn't purchase from HyTex last year to another customer who purchased only a tiny amount, the latter is expected to spend about $544 less than the former this year. However, none of the latter customers were in the data set. A look at the data shows that of all customers who purchased from HyTex last year, almost all spent at least $100 and most spent considerably more. In fact, the median amount spent by these customers last year was about $900 (the median of all positive values for the PrevSpent variable). If you substitute this median value into the expression −544 + 0.27PrevSpent, you obtain −298. Therefore, this "median" spender from last year can be expected to spend about $298 less this year than the previous year nonspender.

■ The coefficient of Catalogs implies that each extra catalog can be expected to generate about $44 in extra spending.

We conclude this example with a couple of cautionary notes. First, if you validate this final regression equation on the other 250 customers, using the procedure from section 10.7, you will find R^2 and s_e values of 73.2% and $486. These are very promising. They are very close to the values based on the original 750 customers. Second, we haven't tried all possibilities yet. We haven't tried nonlinear or interaction variables, nor have we looked at different coding schemes (such as treating Catalogs as a categorical variable and using dummy variables to represent it). Also, we haven't checked for nonconstant error variance (Figure 11.1 is based on this data set) or looked at the potential effects of outliers. ■

PROBLEMS

Level A

18. The Undergraduate Data sheet of the file P10_21.xlsx contains information on 101 undergraduate business programs in the U.S., including various rankings by *Business Week*. Use multiple regression to explore the relationship between the median starting salary and the following set of potential explanatory variables: annual cost, full-time enrollment, faculty-student ratio, average SAT score, and average ACT score. Which explanatory variables should be included in a final version of this regression equation? Justify your choices. Is multicollinearity a problem? Why or why not?

19. A manager of boiler drums wants to use regression analysis to predict the number of worker-hours needed to erect the drums in future projects. Consequently, data for 36 randomly selected boilers were collected. In addition to worker-hours (*Y*), the variables measured include boiler capacity, boiler design pressure, boiler type, and drum type. All of these measurements are listed in the file P10_27.xlsx. Estimate an appropriate multiple regression model to predict the number of worker-hours needed to erect given boiler drums using all available explanatory variables. Which explanatory variables should be included in a final version of this regression model? Justify your choices.

20. The file P02_35.xlsx contains data from a survey of 500 randomly selected households.
   a. In an effort to explain the variation in the size of the monthly home mortgage or rent payment,

estimate a multiple regression equation that includes all of the potential household explanatory variables.
   b. Using the regression output, determine which of the explanatory variables should be excluded from the regression equation. Justify your choices.
   c. Do you obtain substantially different results if you combine First Income and Second Income into a Total Income variable and then use the latter as the only income explanatory variable?

21. The file P02_07.xlsx includes data on 204 employees at the (fictional) company Beta Technologies.
   a. Estimate a multiple regression equation to explain the variation in employee salaries at Beta Technologies using all of the potential explanatory variables.
   b. Using the regression output, determine which of the explanatory variables, if any, should be excluded from the regression equation. Justify your choices.
   c. Regardless of your answer to part **b**, exclude the *least* significant variable (not counting the constant) and estimate the resulting equation. Would you conclude that this equation and the one from part **a** are equally good? Explain.

22. Stock market analysts are continually looking for reliable predictors of stock prices. Consider the problem of modeling the price per share of electric utility stocks (*Y*). Two variables thought to influence such a stock price are return on average equity (X_1) and annual dividend rate (X_2). The stock price, returns on equity, and dividend rates on a randomly selected day for 16 electric utility stocks are provided in the file P10_19.xlsx.

a. Estimate a multiple regression model using the given data. Include linear terms as well as an interaction term involving the return on average equity (X_1) and annual dividend rate (X_2).

b. Which of the three explanatory variables (X_1, X_2, and X_1X_2) should be included in a final version of this regression model? Explain. Does your conclusion make sense in light of your knowledge of corporate finance?

11.6 STEPWISE REGRESSION[4]

Multiple regression represents an improvement over simple regression because it allows any number of explanatory variables to be included in the analysis. Sometimes, however, the large number of potential explanatory variables makes it difficult to know which variables to include. Many statistical packages provide some assistance by including automatic equation-building options. These options estimate a series of regression equations by successively adding (or deleting) variables according to prescribed rules. Generically, the methods are referred to as **stepwise regression**.

Before discussing how stepwise procedures work, consider a naive approach to the problem. You have already looked at correlation tables for indications of linear relationships. Why not simply include all explanatory variables that have large correlations with the dependent variable? There are two reasons for not doing this. First, although a variable is highly correlated with the dependent variable, it might also be highly correlated with other explanatory variables. Therefore, this variable might not be needed in the equation once the other explanatory variables have been included. Perhaps surprisingly, this happens frequently.

Second, even if a variable's correlation with the dependent variable is small, its contribution when it is included with a number of other explanatory variables can be greater than anticipated. Essentially, this variable can have something unique to say about the dependent variable that none of the other variables provides, and this fact might not be apparent from the correlation table. This behavior doesn't happen as often, but it is possible.

For these reasons it is sometimes useful to let the software discover the best combination of variables by means of a stepwise procedure. There are a number of procedures for building equations in a stepwise manner, but they all share a basic idea. Suppose there is an existing regression equation and you want to add another variable to this equation from a set of variables not yet included. At this point, the variables already in the equation have explained a certain percentage of the variation of the dependent variable. The residuals represent the part still unexplained. Therefore, in choosing the next variable to enter the equation, you should pick the one that is most highly correlated with the current residuals. If none of the remaining variables is highly correlated with the residuals, you might decide to quit. This is the essence of stepwise regression. However, besides adding variables to the equation, a stepwise procedure might delete a variable. This is sometimes reasonable because a variable entered early in the procedure might no longer be needed, given the presence of other variables that have entered subsequently.

Stepwise regression (and its variations) can be helpful in discovering a useful regression model, but it should not be used mindlessly.

Many statistical packages have three types of equation-building procedures: forward, backward, and stepwise. A *forward* procedure begins with no explanatory variables in the equation and successively adds one at a time until no remaining variables make a significant contribution. A *backward* procedure begins with *all* potential explanatory variables in the equation and deletes them one at a time until further deletion would do more harm than

[4]This section can be omitted without any loss of continuity.

good. Finally, a true *stepwise* procedure is much like a forward procedure, except that it also considers possible deletions along the way. All of these procedures have the same basic objective—to find an equation with a small s_e and a large R^2 (or adjusted R^2). There is no guarantee that they will all produce exactly the same final equation, but in most cases their final results are very similar. The important thing to realize is that the equations estimated along the way, including the final equation, are estimated exactly as before—by least squares. Therefore, none of these procedures produces any new results. They merely take the burden off the user of having to decide ahead of time which variables to include in the equation.

StatTools implements each of the forward, backward, and stepwise procedures. To use them, select the dependent variable and a set of *potential* explanatory variables. Then specify the criterion for adding and/or deleting variables from the equation. This can be done in two ways, with an F-value or a p-value. We suggest using p-values because they are easier to understand, but either method is easy to use. In the p-value method, select a p-value such as the default value of 0.05. If the regression coefficient for a potential entering variable would have a p-value less than 0.05 (if it were entered), then it is a candidate for entering (if the forward or stepwise procedure is used). The procedure selects the variable with the *smallest* p-value as the next entering variable. Similarly, if any currently included variable has a p-value greater than some value such as the default value of 0.10, then (with the stepwise and backward procedures) it is a candidate for leaving the equation. The methods stop when there are no candidates (according to their p-values) for entering or leaving the current equation.

The following continuation of the HyTex mail-order example illustrates these stepwise procedures.

EXAMPLE | 11.3 EXPLAINING SPENDING AMOUNTS AT HYTEX (CONTINUED)

The analysis of the HyTex mail-order data (for the first 750 customers in the data set) resulted in a regression equation that included all potential explanatory variables except for Age, Gender, OwnHome, and Married. These were excluded because their t-values are large and their p-values are small (less than 0.05). Do forward, backward, and stepwise procedures produce the same regression equation for the amount spent in the current year?

Objective   To use StatTools's Stepwise Regression procedure to analyze the HyTex data.

Solution

Each of these options is found in the StatTools Regression dialog box. It is just a matter of choosing the appropriate option from the Regression Type dropdown list. (See Figure 11.9.) In each, specify AmountSpent as the dependent variable and select all of the other variables (besides Customer) as *potential* explanatory variables. Once you choose one of the stepwise types, the dialog box changes, as shown in Figure 11.10, to include a Parameters section and an "advanced" option to Include Detailed Step Information. We suggest the choices in Figure 11.10 for stepwise regression.

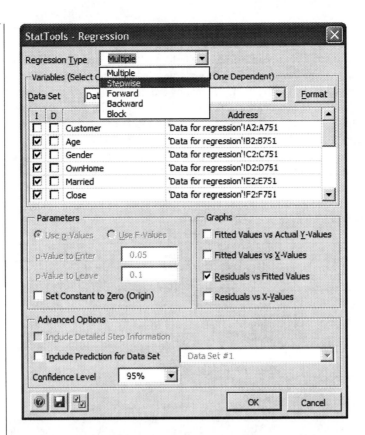

Figure 11.9
Regression Dialog
Box with Regression
Type Options

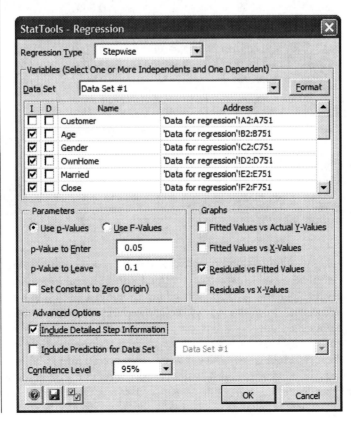

Figure 11.10
Dialog Box for
Stepwise Regression

It turns out that each stepwise procedure (stepwise, forward, and backward) produces the same *final* equation that we obtained previously, with all variables except Age, Gender, OwnHome, and Married included. This often happens, but not always. The stepwise and forward procedures add the variables in the order Salary, Catalogs, Close, Children, PrevCust, and PrevSpent. The backward procedure, which starts with *all* variables in the equation, eliminates variables in the order Age, Married, OwnHome, and Gender. A sample of the stepwise output appears in Figure 11.11. The variables that enter or exit the equation are listed at the bottom of the output. The usual regression output for the final equation also appears. Again, however, this final equation's output is *exactly* the same as when multiple regression is used with these particular variables.

Figure 11.11   Regression Output from Stepwise Procedure

	A	B	C	D	E	F	G
7		Multiple	R-Square	Adjusted	StErr of		
8	*Summary*	R		R-Square	Estimate		
9		0.8636	0.7458	0.7438	491.2283		
10							
11		Degrees of	Sum of	Mean of	F-Ratio	p-Value	
12	*ANOVA Table*	Freedom	Squares	Squares			
13	Explained	6	526113683.9	87685613.98	363.3805	< 0.0001	
14	Unexplained	743	179289770.9	241305.2099			
15							
16		Coefficient	Standard	t-Value	p-Value	Confidence Interval 95%	
17	*Regression Table*		Error			Lower	Upper
18	Constant	205.0936	70.3152	2.9168	0.0036	67.0534	343.1338
19	Salary	0.0180	0.0009	19.8773	< 0.0001	0.0162	0.0197
20	Catalogs	43.8067	2.8542	15.3481	< 0.0001	38.2034	49.4100
21	Close	-416.2462	45.0846	-9.2326	< 0.0001	-504.7546	-327.7378
22	Children	-161.1577	20.4828	-7.8679	< 0.0001	-201.3688	-120.9466
23	PrevCust	-543.5948	63.2988	-8.5878	< 0.0001	-667.8606	-419.3290
24	PrevSpent	0.2724	0.0525	5.1844	< 0.0001	0.1692	0.3755
25							
26		Multiple	R-Square	Adjusted	StErr of	Enter or	
27	*Step Information*	R		R-Square	Estimate	Exit	
28	Salary	0.6837	0.4674	0.4667	708.6821	Enter	
29	Catalogs	0.7841	0.6148	0.6138	603.0854	Enter	
30	Close	0.8192	0.6710	0.6697	557.7264	Enter	
31	Children	0.8477	0.7187	0.7171	516.1357	Enter	
32	PrevCust	0.8583	0.7366	0.7349	499.6982	Enter	
33	PrevSpent	0.8636	0.7458	0.7438	491.2283	Enter	

Stepwise regression or any of its variations can be very useful for narrowing down the set of all possible explanatory variables to a set that is useful for explaining a dependent variable. However, these procedures should not be used as a substitute for thoughtful analysis. With the availability of such procedures in statistical software packages, there is sometimes a tendency to turn the analysis over to the computer and accept its output. A good analyst does not just collect as much data as possible, throw it into a software package, and blindly report the results. There should always be some rationale, whether it is based on economic theory, business experience, or common sense, for the variables that are used to explain a given dependent variable. A thoughtless use of stepwise regression can sometimes capitalize on chance to obtain an equation with a reasonably large R^2 but no useful or practical interpretation. It is very possible that such an equation will not generalize well to new data.

Finally, keep in mind that if one stepwise procedure produces slightly different outputs than another (for example, one might include a variable, the other might exclude it), the differences are typically very small and are not worth agonizing about. The two equations typically have very similar R^2 values and standard errors of estimate, and they typically produce very similar predictions. If anything, most analysts prefer the smaller equation because of parsimony, but they realize that the differences are "at the margin."

PROBLEMS

Level A

23. The Undergraduate Data sheet of the file P10_21.xlsx contains information on 101 undergraduate business programs in the U.S., including various rankings by *Business Week*. Use forward, backward, and stepwise regression analysis to explore the relationship between the median starting salary and the following set of potential explanatory variables: annual cost, full-time enrollment, faculty-student ratio, average SAT score, and average ACT score. Do these three methods all lead to the same regression equation? If not, do you think any of the final equations are substantially better than any of the others?

24. The file P10_08.xlsx contains data on the top 200 professional golfers in each of the years 2003–2009. (The same data set was used in Example 3.4 in Chapter 3.)
  a. Create one large data set in a new sheet called All Years that has the data for all seven years stacked on top of one other. (This is possible because the variables are the same in each year.) In this combined data set, create a new column called Earnings per Round, the ratio of Earnings to Rounds. Similarly, create three other new variables, Eagles per Round, Birdies per Round, and Bogies per Round.
  b. Using the data set from part **a**, run a forward regression of Earnings per Round versus the following potential explanatory variables: Age, Yard/Drive, Driving Accuracy, Greens in Regulation, Putting Average, Sand Save Pct, Eagles per Round, Birdies per Round, and Bogies per Round. Given the results, comment on what seems to be important on the professional tour in terms of earnings per round. For any variable that does *not* end up in the equation, is it omitted because it is not related to Earnings per Round or because its effect is explained by other variables in the equation?
  c. Repeat part **b** with backward regression. Do you get the same, or basically the same, results?

25. In a study of housing demand, a county assessor is interested in developing a regression model to estimate the selling price of residential properties within her jurisdiction. She randomly selects 15 houses and records the selling price in addition to the following values: the size of the house (in hundreds of square feet), the total number of rooms in the house, the age of the house, and an indication of whether the house has an attached garage. These data are listed in the file P10_26.xlsx.
  a. Use stepwise regression to decide which explanatory variables should be included in the assessor's statistical model. Use the *p*-value method with a cutoff value of 0.05 for entering and leaving. Summarize your findings.
  b. How do the results in part **a** change when the critical *p*-value for entering and leaving is increased to 0.10? Explain any differences between the regression equation obtained here and the one found in part **a**.

26. Continuing Problem 2 with the data in the file P10_04.xlsx, employ stepwise regression to evaluate your conclusions regarding the specification of a regression model to predict the sales of deep-dish pizza by the Original Italian Pizza restaurant chain. Use the *p*-value method with a cutoff value of 0.05 for entering and leaving. Compare your conclusions in Problem 2 with those derived from a stepwise regression.

Level B

27. How sensitive are stepwise regression results to small changes in the data? This problem allows you to explore this. The file P11_27.xlsm can be used to generate 100 randomly chosen observations from a given population. It contains macros that help you do this. Specifically, the means, standard deviations, and correlations for the population of 10 *X*s and *Y* are given in rows 2–14. The macro has already been used to generate a "generic" row of data in row 16. It is done so that the *X*s and *Y* are normally distributed with the given means, standard deviations, and correlations. Press the F9 key a few times to see how the data in row 16 change. There is also a button you can click. When you do so, the generic row 16 is copied to rows 20–119 to generate new random data, and the new random data are frozen. Click on the button a few times to see how this works. Designate a StatTools data set in the range A19:L119 and run stepwise regression on the data. Then generate new data by clicking on the button and run stepwise regression again. Repeat this a few times. Then explain the results. Do all of the stepwise regressions produce about the same results? Are they consistent with the parameters in the top section, particularly the correlations involving Y in row 14?

28. Repeat the previous problem at least once, using means, standard deviations, and correlations of your choice. The interesting thing you will discover is that you can't arbitrarily enter just any correlations between -1 and $+1$. For many choices, the generic row will exhibit #VALUE! errors. This means that no population could possibly have the correlations you entered. Try to find correlations that do *not* produce the #VALUE! errors.

11.7 THE PARTIAL F TEST[5]

There are many situations where a set of explanatory variables form a logical group. It is then common to include all of the variables in the equation or exclude all of them. An example of this is when one of the explanatory variables is categorical with more than two categories. In this case you model it by including dummy variables—one fewer than the number of categories. If you decide that the categorical variable is worth including, you might want to keep all of the dummies (except of course for the reference dummy). Otherwise, you might decide to exclude all of them. We look at an example of this type subsequently.

For now, consider the following general situation. You have already estimated an equation that includes the variables X_1 through X_j, and you are proposing to estimate a larger equation that includes X_{j+1} through X_k in addition to the variables X_1 through X_j. That is, the larger equation includes all of the variables from the smaller equation, but it also includes $k - j$ extra variables. These extra variables are the ones that form a group. We assume that it makes logical sense to include all of them or none of them.

The complete equation always contains all of the explanatory variables in the reduced equation, plus some more. In other words, the reduced equation is a subset of the complete equation.

In this section we describe a test to determine whether the extra variables provide enough *extra* explanatory power as a group to warrant their inclusion in the equation. The test is called the partial F test. The original equation is called the *reduced* equation, and the larger equation is called the *complete* equation. In simple terms, the partial F test tests whether the complete equation is significantly better than the reduced equation.[6]

The test itself is intuitive. The output from the ANOVA tables of the reduced and complete equations is used to form an F-ratio. This ratio measures how much the sum of squared residuals, *SSE, decreases* by including the extra variables in the equation. It *must* decrease by some amount because the sum of squared residuals cannot increase when extra variables are added to an equation. But if it does not decrease sufficiently, the extra variables might not explain enough to warrant their inclusion in the equation, and they should probably be excluded. The F-ratio measures this. If it is sufficiently large, the extra variables are worth including; otherwise, they can safely be excluded.

To state the test formally, let β_{j+1} through β_k be the coefficients of the extra variables in the complete equation. Then the null hypothesis is that these extra variables have no effect on the dependent variable, that is, $H_0:\beta_{j+1} = \cdots = \beta_k = 0$. The alternative is that at least one of the extra variables has an effect on the dependent variable, so that at least one of these βs is not zero. The hypotheses are summarized in the box.

---

[5]This section is somewhat more advanced and can be omitted without any loss of continuity.
[6]StatTools does not run the partial F test, but it provides all of the ingredients to do so.

To run the test, estimate both the reduced and complete equations and look at the associated ANOVA tables. Let SSE_R and SSE_C be the sums of squared errors from the reduced and complete equations, respectively. Also, let MSE_C be the mean square error for the complete equation. All of these quantities appear in the ANOVA tables. Next, form the F-ratio in Equation (11.4).

Test Statistic for Partial F Test

$$F\text{-ratio} = \frac{(SSE_R - SSE_C)/(k - j)}{MSE_C} \tag{11.4}$$

The numerator includes the reduction in sum of squared errors discussed previously. If the null hypothesis is true, this F-ratio has an F distribution with $k - j$ and $n - k - 1$ degrees of freedom. If it is sufficiently large, H_0 can be rejected. As usual, the best way to run the test is to find the p-value corresponding to this F-ratio. This is the probability beyond the calculated F-ratio in the F distribution with $k - j$ and $n - k - 1$ degrees of freedom. In words, you can reject the hypothesis that the extra variables have no explanatory power if this p-value is sufficiently small—less than 0.05, say.

This F-ratio and corresponding p-value are *not* part of the StatTools regression output. However, they are fairly easy to obtain. To do so, run two regressions, one for the reduced equation and one for the complete equation, and use the appropriate values from their ANOVA tables to calculate the F-ratio in Equation (11.4). Then use Excel's FDIST function in the form **FDIST(F-ratio, $k - j$, $n - k - 1$)** to calculate the corresponding p-value. The procedure is illustrated in the following example. It uses the bank discrimination data from Example 10.3 of the previous chapter.

| EXAMPLE | **11.4 POSSIBLE GENDER DISCRIMINATION IN SALARY AT FIFTH NATIONAL BANK OF SPRINGFIELD** |

Recall from Example 11.3 that Fifth National Bank has 208 employees. The data for these employees are stored in the file Bank Salaries.xlsx. In the previous chapter we ran several regressions for Salary to see whether there is convincing evidence of salary discrimination against females. We will continue this analysis here. First, we regress Salary versus the Female dummy, YrsExper, and the interaction between Female and YrsExper, Interaction(YrsExper,Female). This is the reduced equation. Then we will see whether the EducLev dummies, EducLev=2 to EducLev=5, add anything significant to the reduced equation. If so, we will then see whether the JobGrade dummies, JobGrade=2 to JobGrade=6, add anything significant to what we already have. If so, we will finally see whether the interactions between the Female dummy and the education dummies, Interaction(Female,EducLev=2) to Interaction(Female,EducLev=5), add anything significant to what we already have.

Objective To use several partial F tests to see whether various groups of explanatory variables should be included in a regression equation for salary, given that other variables are already in the equation.

Solution

First, it is possible to create all of the dummies and interaction variables with StatTools's Data Utilities procedures. These could be entered directly with Excel functions, but StatTools makes the process much quicker and easier. Also, note that there are three sets of dummies: for gender, job grade, and education level. When these are used in a regression equation, the dummy for one category of each should always be excluded; it is the reference category. The reference categories we have used are male, job grade 1, and education level 1.

The output for the "smallest" equation, the one using Female, YrsExper, and Interaction(YrsExper,Female) as explanatory variables, appears in Figure 11.12. (This output is in a sheet called Regression1.) These three variables already explain 63.9% of the variation in Salary.

Figure 11.12   Reduced Equation for Bank Example

	A	B	C	D	E	F	G
7		Multiple	R-Square	Adjusted	StErr of		
8	Summary	R		R-Square	Estimate		
9		0.7991	0.6386	0.6333	6816.298		
10							
11		Degrees of	Sum of	Mean of	F-Ratio	p-Value	
12	ANOVA Table	Freedom	Squares	Squares			
13	Explained	3	16748875071	5582958357	120.1620	< 0.0001	
14	Unexplained	204	9478232160	46461922.35			
15							
16			Standard			Confidence Interval 95%	
17	Regression Table	Coefficient	Error	t-Value	p-Value	Lower	Upper
18	Constant	30430.028	1216.574	25.0129	< 0.0001	28031.356	32828.700
19	YrsExper	1527.762	90.460	16.8887	< 0.0001	1349.405	1706.119
20	Female	4098.252	1665.842	2.4602	0.0147	813.776	7382.727
21	Interaction(YrsExper,Female)	-1247.798	136.676	-9.1296	< 0.0001	-1517.277	-978.320

The output for the next equation, which adds the explanatory variables EducLev=2 to EducLev=5, appears in Figure 11.13. (This output is in a sheet called Regression2.) This equation appears to be much better. For example, R^2 has increased to 73.1%. You can check whether it is *significantly* better with the partial F test in rows 27 through 33. (This part of the output is not given by StatTools; you have to enter it manually.) The degrees of freedom in cell B28 is 4, the number of *extra* variables. The degrees of freedom in cell B29 is the same as the value in cell B14, the degrees of freedom for *SSE*. Then the F-ratio is calculated in cell B32 with the formula

=((Regression1!C13-C14)/B28)/D14

where Regression1!C13 refers to the *SSE* for the reduced equation from the Regression1 sheet. Finally, the corresponding *p*-value can be calculated in cell B33 with the formula

=FDIST(B30,B28,B29)

It is practically zero, so there is no doubt that the education dummies add significantly to the explanatory power of the equation.

Figure 11.13   Equation with Education Dummies Added

	A	B	C	D	E	F	G
7		Multiple	R-Square	Adjusted	StErr of		
8	Summary	R		R-Square	Estimate		
9		0.8552	0.7314	0.7220	5935.254		
10							
11		Degrees of	Sum of	Mean of	F-Ratio	p-Value	
12	ANOVA Table	Freedom	Squares	Squares			
13	Explained	7	19181659773	2740237110	77.7875	< 0.0001	
14	Unexplained	200	7045447458	35227237.29			
15							
16		Coefficient	Standard	t-Value	p-Value	Confidence Interval 95%	
17	Regression Table		Error			Lower	Upper
18	Constant	24780.996	1551.053	15.9769	< 0.0001	21722.480	27839.512
19	YrsExper	1456.388	79.761	18.2593	< 0.0001	1299.107	1613.669
20	Female	4898.656	1454.087	3.3689	0.0009	2031.347	7765.965
21	EducLev = 2	546.549	1418.139	0.3854	0.7004	-2249.874	3342.972
22	EducLev = 3	3587.341	1287.361	2.7866	0.0058	1048.798	6125.885
23	EducLev = 4	5862.894	2346.571	2.4985	0.0133	1235.700	10490.088
24	EducLev = 5	9428.090	1337.292	7.0501	< 0.0001	6791.089	12065.092
25	Interaction(YrsExper,Female)	-1029.858	121.924	-8.4467	< 0.0001	-1270.279	-789.437
26							
27	Partial F test for including EducLev dummies						
28	df numerator	4					
29	df denominator	200					
30	F ratio	68.863					
31	p-value	0.0000					

Do the job grade dummies add anything more? You can again use the partial F test, but now the previous *complete* equation becomes the new *reduced* equation, and the equation that includes the new job grade dummies becomes the new complete equation. The output for this new complete equation appears in Figure 11.14. (This output is in a sheet called Regression3.) The partial F test is performed in rows 32 through 36 exactly as before. For example, the formula for the F-ratio in cell B35 is

=(('Regression2'!C14-C14)/B33)/D14

Note how the SSE_R term in Equation (11.4) now comes from the Regression2 sheet because this sheet contains the current *reduced* equation. The terms *reduced* and *complete* are relative. The complete equation in one stage becomes the reduced equation in the next stage. In any case, the p-value in cell B36 is again extremely small, so there is no doubt that the job grade dummies add significantly to what was already in the equation. In fact, R^2 has increased from 73.1% to 81.5%.

Finally, you can add the interactions between Female and the education dummies. The resulting output is shown in Figure 11.15. (This output is in a sheet called Regression4.) Again, the terms *reduced* and *complete* are relative. This output now corresponds to the complete equation, and the previous output corresponds to the reduced equation. The formula in cell B39 for the F-ratio is now

=(('Regression3'!C14-C14)/B37)/D14

Its SSE_R value comes from the Regression3 sheet. Note that the increase in R^2 is from 81.5% to only 82.0%. Also, the p-value in cell B40 is *not* extremely small. According to the partial F test, it is not quite small enough to qualify for statistical significance at the 5% level. Based on this evidence, there is not much to gain from including the interaction terms in the equation, so you would probably elect to exclude them.

Figure 11.14 Regression Output with Job Dummies Added

	A	B	C	D	E	F	G
7		Multiple R	R-Square	Adjusted R-Square	StErr of Estimate		
8	Summary						
9		0.9028	0.8150	0.8036	4988.127		
10							
11		Degrees of Freedom	Sum of Squares	Mean of Squares	F-Ratio	p-Value	
12	ANOVA Table						
13	Explained	12	21375231697	1781269308	71.5904	< 0.0001	
14	Unexplained	195	4851875534	24881413			
15							
16		Coefficient	Standard Error	t-Value	p-Value	Confidence Interval 95%	
17	Regression Table					Lower	Upper
18	Constant	25624.820	1450.166	17.6703	< 0.0001	22764.798	28484.843
19	YrsExper	1109.889	105.608	10.5096	< 0.0001	901.610	1318.169
20	Female	6066.112	1267.472	4.7860	< 0.0001	3566.399	8565.825
21	EducLev = 2	-675.106	1204.702	-0.5604	0.5759	-3051.024	1700.812
22	EducLev = 3	447.269	1147.751	0.3897	0.6972	-1816.330	2710.868
23	EducLev = 4	525.063	2109.284	0.2489	0.8037	-3634.875	4685.001
24	EducLev = 5	1946.144	1394.627	1.3955	0.1645	-804.344	4696.633
25	JobGrade = 2	2245.355	1034.406	2.1707	0.0312	205.295	4285.414
26	JobGrade = 3	5552.070	1098.504	5.0542	< 0.0001	3385.596	7718.543
27	JobGrade = 4	9970.290	1314.585	7.5844	< 0.0001	7377.659	12562.921
28	JobGrade = 5	13235.194	1631.437	8.1126	< 0.0001	10017.667	16452.720
29	JobGrade = 6	14928.127	2695.706	5.5377	< 0.0001	9611.644	20244.610
30	Interaction(YrsExper,Female)	-1002.905	119.060	-8.4235	< 0.0001	-1237.716	-768.094
31							
32	Partial F test for including JobGrade dummies						
33	df numerator	5					
34	df denominator	195					
35	F ratio	17.632					
36	p-value	0.0000					

Before leaving this example, we make several comments. First, the partial test is *the* formal test of significance for an extra set of variables. Many users look only at the R^2 and/or s_e values to check whether extra variables are doing a "good job." For example, they might cite that R^2 went from 81.5% to 82.0% or that s_e went from 4988 to 4965 as evidence that extra variables provide a "significantly" better fit. Although these are important indicators, they are not the basis for a *formal* hypothesis test.

Second, if the partial F test shows that a block of variables is significant, it does not imply that each variable in this block is significant. Some of these variables can have low t-values. Consider Figure 11.13, for example. The education dummies as a whole are significant, but one of these dummies, EducLev=2, is clearly not significant. Some analysts favor excluding the *individual* variables that aren't significant, whereas others favor keeping the whole block or excluding the whole block. We lean toward the latter but recognize that either approach is valid. Fortunately, the results are often nearly the same either way.

Third, producing all of these outputs and doing the partial F tests is a lot of work. Therefore, a Block option is included in StatTools to simplify the analysis. To run the analysis in this example in one step, select the Block option from the Regression Type dropdown list. The dialog box then changes, as shown in Figure 11.16. Select four blocks and then check which variables are in which blocks (B1 to B4). Block 1 has Female, YrsExper, and Interaction(YrsExper,Female), block 2 has the education dummies, block 3 has the job grade dummies, and block 4 has the interactions between

Figure 11.15 Regression Output with Interaction Terms Added

	A	B	C	D	E	F	G
7		Multiple	R-Square	Adjusted	StErr of		
8	Summary	R		R-Square	Estimate		
9		0.9058	0.8204	0.8054	4965.729		
10							
11		Degrees of	Sum of	Mean of	F-Ratio	p-Value	
12	ANOVA Table	Freedom	Squares	Squares			
13	Explained	16	21517339674	1344833730	54.5384	< 0.0001	
14	Unexplained	191	4709767556	24658468.88			
15							
16		Coefficient	Standard	t-Value	p-Value	Confidence Interval 95%	
17	Regression Table		Error			Lower	Upper
18	Constant	19845.279	3263.760	6.0805	< 0.0001	13407.637	26282.922
19	YrsExper	1166.782	109.100	10.6946	< 0.0001	951.586	1381.977
20	Female	12424.015	3457.402	3.5935	0.0004	5604.421	19243.609
21	EducLev = 2	3114.496	3666.760	0.8494	0.3967	-4118.048	10347.040
22	EducLev = 3	6991.038	3257.025	2.1464	0.0331	566.681	13415.395
23	EducLev = 4	6394.234	4312.345	1.4828	0.1398	-2111.702	14900.170
24	EducLev = 5	7550.157	3268.374	2.3101	0.0220	1103.414	13996.900
25	JobGrade = 2	2142.469	1038.726	2.0626	0.0405	93.621	4191.316
26	JobGrade = 3	5629.803	1096.800	5.1329	< 0.0001	3466.406	7793.200
27	JobGrade = 4	10092.551	1312.448	7.6899	< 0.0001	7503.796	12681.305
28	JobGrade = 5	13038.574	1636.716	7.9663	< 0.0001	9810.215	16266.934
29	JobGrade = 6	13672.521	2762.533	4.9493	< 0.0001	8223.528	19121.513
30	Interaction(YrsExper,Female)	-1069.576	122.680	-8.7184	< 0.0001	-1311.558	-827.594
31	Interaction(Female EducLev = 2)	-3923.850	3882.671	-1.0106	0.3135	-11582.270	3734.570
32	Interaction(Female,EducLev = 3)	-7533.870	3448.578	-2.1846	0.0301	-14336.060	-731.680
33	Interaction(Female,EducLev = 4)	-6471.909	4864.678	-1.3304	0.1850	-16067.301	3123.484
34	Interaction(Female,EducLev = 5)	-6178.817	3368.287	-1.8344	0.0681	-12822.635	465.000
35							
36	Partial F test for including EducLev/Female interactions						
37	df numerator	4					
38	df denominator	191					
39	F ratio	1.441					

Female and the education dummies. Finally, specify 0.05 as the *p*-value to enter, which in this case indicates how significant the block *as a whole* must be to enter (for the partial *F* test).

The regression calculations are then done in stages. At each stage, the partial *F* test checks whether a block is significant. If it is, the variables in this block enter and the procedure goes to the next stage. If it is not, the procedure ends; neither this block nor any later blocks enter.

The output from this procedure appears in Figure 11.17. The middle part of the output shows the final regression equation. The output in rows 34 through 37 indicates summary measures after successive blocks have entered. Note that the final block, the interactions between Female and the education dummies, is not in the final equation. This block did not pass the partial *F* test at the 5% level.

For comparison, we ran the block procedure a second time, changing the order of the blocks. Now block 2 includes the job grade dummies, block 3 includes the education dummies, and block 4 includes the interactions between Female and the education dummies. The regression output appears in Figure 11.18. Note that *neither* of the last two blocks enters the equation this time. Once the job grade dummies are in the equation, the terms including education are no longer needed. The implication is that the order of the blocks can make a difference.

Figure 11.16
Dialog Box for Block Regression Option

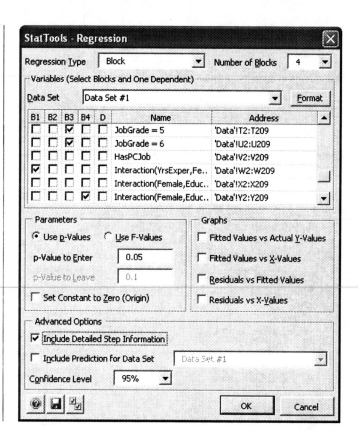

Figure 11.17 Block Regression Output

	A	B	C	D	E	F	G
7		Multiple R	R-Square	Adjusted R-Square	StErr of Estimate		
8	Summary						
9		0.9028	0.8150	0.8036	4988.127		
10							
11		Degrees of Freedom	Sum of Squares	Mean of Squares	F-Ratio	p-Value	
12	ANOVA Table						
13	Explained	12	21375231697	1781269308	70.1218	< 0.0001	
14	Unexplained	191	4851875534	25402489.71			
15							
16		Coefficient	Standard Error	t-Value	p-Value	Confidence Interval 95%	
17	Regression Table					Lower	Upper
18	Constant	25624.820	1450.166	17.670	< 0.0001	22764.424	28485.217
19	YrsExper	1109.889	105.608	10.510	< 0.0001	901.582	1318.196
20	Female	6066.112	1267.472	4.786	< 0.0001	3566.072	8566.152
21	Interaction(YrsExper,Female)	-1002.905	119.060	-8.424	< 0.0001	-1237.747	-768.063
22	EducLev = 2	-675.106	1204.702	-0.560	0.5759	-3051.335	1701.123
23	EducLev = 3	447.269	1147.751	0.390	0.6972	-1816.626	2711.164
24	EducLev = 4	525.063	2109.284	0.249	0.8037	-3635.419	4685.545
25	EducLev = 5	1946.144	1394.627	1.395	0.1645	-804.704	4696.993
26	JobGrade = 2	2245.355	1034.406	2.171	0.0312	205.028	4285.681
27	JobGrade = 3	5552.070	1098.504	5.054	< 0.0001	3385.313	7718.826
28	JobGrade = 4	9970.290	1314.585	7.584	< 0.0001	7377.320	12563.260
29	JobGrade = 5	13235.194	1631.437	8.113	< 0.0001	10017.247	16453.141
30	JobGrade = 6	14928.127	2695.706	5.538	< 0.0001	9610.948	20245.306
31							
32		Multiple R	R-Square	Adjusted R-Square	StErr of Estimate	Entry Number	
33	Step Information						
34	Block 1	0.7991	0.6386	0.6333	6816.298	1	
35	Block 2	0.8552	0.7314	0.7220	5935.254	2	
36	Block 3	0.9028	0.8150	0.8036	4988.127	3	
37	Block 4	Did Not Enter					

Figure 11.18 Block Regression Output with Order of Blocks Changed

	A	B	C	D	E	F	G
7		Multiple	R-Square	Adjusted	StErr of		
8	Summary	R		R-Square	Estimate		
9		0.9005	0.8109	0.8033	4991.635		
10							
11		Degrees of	Sum of	Mean of	F-Ratio	p-Value	
12	ANOVA Table	Freedom	Squares	Squares			
13	Explained	8	21268738998	2658592375	104.5557	< 0.0001	
14	Unexplained	195	4958368233	25427529.4			
15							
16		Coefficient	Standard	t-Value	p-Value	Confidence Interval 95%	
17	Regression Table		Error			Lower	Upper
18	Constant	26104.223	1105.443	23.614	< 0.0001	23924.064	28284.381
19	YrsExper	1070.883	102.013	10.497	< 0.0001	869.692	1272.074
20	Female	6063.328	1266.322	4.788	< 0.0001	3565.883	8560.773
21	Interaction(YrsExper,Female)	-1021.051	118.726	-8.600	< 0.0001	-1255.202	-786.900
22	JobGrade = 2	2596.493	1010.122	2.570	0.0109	604.325	4588.660
23	JobGrade = 3	6221.394	998.177	6.233	< 0.0001	4252.784	8190.003
24	JobGrade = 4	11071.954	1172.588	9.442	< 0.0001	8759.371	13384.537
25	JobGrade = 5	14946.576	1340.249	11.152	< 0.0001	12303.332	17589.821
26	JobGrade = 6	17097.372	2390.671	7.152	< 0.0001	12382.481	21812.262
27							
28		Multiple	R-Square	Adjusted	StErr of	Entry	
29	Step Information	R		R-Square	Estimate	Number	
30	Block 1	0.7991	0.6386	0.6333	6816.298	1	
31	Block 2	0.9005	0.8109	0.8033	4991.635	2	
32	Block 3	Did Not Enter					
33	Block 4	Did Not Enter					

Finally, although we have concentrated on the partial F test and statistical significance in this example, we don't want you to lose sight of the bigger picture. Once you have decided on a "final" regression equation such as the one in Figure 11.14, you need to analyze its implications for the problem at hand. In this case the bank is interested in possible salary discrimination against females, so you should interpret this final equation in these terms. We will not go through this exercise again here—we did similar interpretations in the previous chapter. Our point is simply that you shouldn't get so immersed in the details of statistical significance that you lose sight of the original purpose of the analysis. ∎

PROBLEMS

Level A

29. A regional express delivery service company recently conducted a study to investigate the relationship between the cost of shipping a package (Y), the package weight (X_1), and the distance shipped (X_2). Twenty packages were randomly selected from among the large number received for shipment and a detailed analysis of the shipping cost was conducted for each package. These sample observations are given in the file P10_22.xlsx.
    a. Estimate a multiple regression equation involving the two given explanatory variables. What do the

results in the ANOVA table indicate about this regression?
    b. Is it worthwhile to add the terms X^2_1 and X^2_2 to the regression equation in part a? Base your decision here on a partial F test and a 5% significance level.
    c. Is it worthwhile to add the term X_1X_2 to the most appropriate reduced equation determined in part b? Again, perform a partial F test with a 5% significance level.
    d. What regression equation should this company use in predicting the cost of shipping a package? Defend your recommendation.

30. Continuing Problem 6 with the data in the file P10_18.xlsx, refer to the original multiple regression model (the one that includes the age of the auctioned item and the number of bidders as explanatory variables) as the *reduced* equation. Suppose now that the antique collector believes that the *rate of increase* of the auction price with the age of the item will be driven upward by a large number of bidders.

  a. Revise the reduced regression equation to model this additional feature of the problem. Estimate this larger regression equation, called the *complete* equation.

  b. Using a 5% significance level, perform a partial F test to check whether the complete equation is significantly better than the reduced equation. Briefly explain your findings.

31. Many companies manufacture products that are at least partially produced using chemicals (for example, paint, gasoline, and steel). In many cases, the quality of the finished product is a function of the temperature and pressure at which the chemical reactions take place. Suppose that a particular manufacturer wants to model the quality (Y) of a product as a function of the temperature (X_1) and the pressure (X_2) at which it is produced. The file P10_39.xlsx contains data obtained from a designed experiment involving these variables. Note that the quality score can range from a minimum of 0 to a maximum of 100 for each product.

  a. Estimate a multiple regression equation that includes the two given explanatory variables. What do the results in the ANOVA table indicate about this regression?

  b. Use a partial F test with a 5% significance level to decide whether it is worthwhile to add second-order terms (X_1^2, X_2^2, and X_1X_2) to the regression equation in part **a**.

  c. Which regression equation is the most appropriate one for modeling the quality of the product? Keep in mind that a good statistical model is usually parsimonious.

Level B

32. Continuing Problem 27 with the simulated data in the file P11_27.xlsm, suppose the analyst believes that the variables $X4$ and $X6$ are the most important variables, $X2$, $X8$, and $X9$ are next most important, and the rest are of questionable importance. (Perhaps this is based on economic considerations.) Run stepwise regression on this data set. Then use the block regression procedure in StatTools, using the analyst's three blocks, and compare the block results to the stepwise results. Why are they different? Then repeat the whole comparison several more times, each time clicking on the button first to generate new data for the regressions. Do you get the same results (about which blocks enter and which don't) on each run?

33. The file P02_35.xlsx contains data from a survey of 500 randomly selected households.

  a. To explain the variation in the size of the Monthly Payment variable, estimate a multiple regression equation that includes the *numerical* variables Family Size, Total Income (sum of First Income and Second Income), Utilities, and Debt. What do the results in the ANOVA table indicate about this regression?

  b. Determine whether the *categorical* Location and Ownership variables add significantly to explaining Monthly Payment. Do this by using a partial F test, at the 5% significance level, for the group of extra variables that includes Ownership and the dummies corresponding to Location. Do the results depend on which Location dummy is used as the reference category? Experiment to find out.

11.8 OUTLIERS

In all of the regression examples so far, we have ignored the possibility of outliers. Unfortunately, outliers cannot be ignored in many real applications. They are often present, and they can often have a substantial effect on the results. In this section we briefly discuss outliers in the context of regression—how to detect them and what to do about them.

You probably tend to think of an **outlier** as an observation that has an extreme value for at least one variable. For example, if salaries in a data set are mostly in the $40,000 to $80,000 range, but one salary is $350,000, this observation is clearly an outlier with respect to salary. However, in a regression context outliers are not always this obvious. In fact, an observation can be considered an outlier for several reasons, and some types of outliers can be difficult to detect. An observation can be an outlier for one or more of the following reasons.

Potential Characteristics of an Outlier

Outliers can come in several forms, as indicated in this list.

1. It has an extreme value for one or more variables.

2. Its value of the dependent variable is much larger or smaller than predicted by the regression line, and its residual is abnormally large in magnitude. An example appears in Figure 11.19. The line in this scatterplot fits most of the points, but it misses badly on the one obvious outlier. This outlier has a large positive residual, but its Y value is not abnormally large. Its Y value is only large relative to points with the same X value that it has.

Figure 11.19   Outlier with a Large Residual

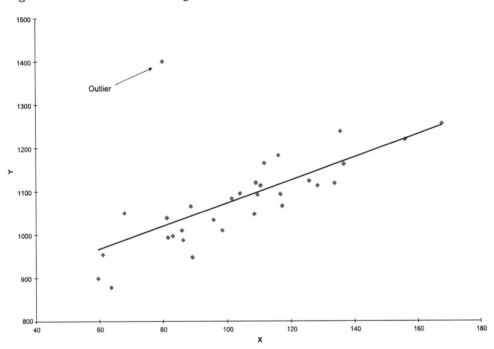

3. Its residual is not only large in magnitude, but this point "tilts" the regression line toward it. An example appears in Figure 11.20. The two lines shown are the regression lines with the outlier and without it. The outlier makes a big difference in the slope and intercept of the regression line. This type of outlier is called an **influential point**, for the obvious reason.

4. Its values of individual explanatory variables are not extreme, but they fall outside the general pattern of the other observations. An example appears in Figure 11.21. Here, we assume that the two variables shown, YrsExper (years of experience) and Rating (an employee's performance rating) are both explanatory variables for some other dependent variable (Salary) that isn't shown in the plot. The obvious outlier does not have an abnormal value of either YrsExper or Rating, but it falls well outside the pattern of most employees.

Once outliers have been identified, there is still the dilemma of what to do with them. In most cases the regression output will look "nicer" if you delete outliers, but this is not necessarily appropriate. If you can argue that the outlier isn't really a member of the relevant population, then it is appropriate and probably best to delete it. But if no such

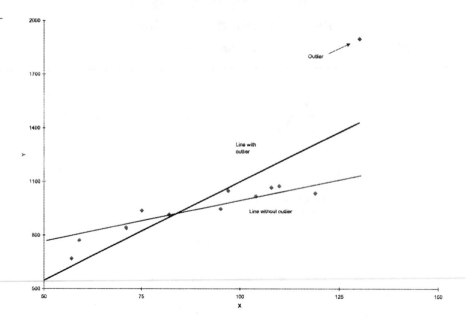

Figure 11.20

Outlier That Tilts the Regression Line

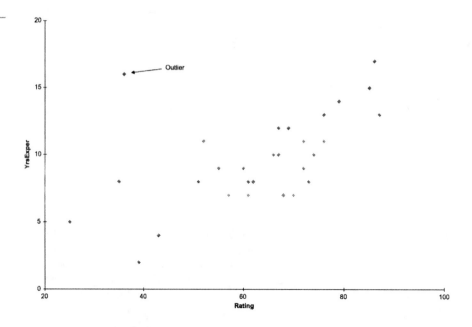

Figure 11.21

Outlier Outside the Pattern of Explanatory Variables

argument can be made, then it is not really appropriate to delete the outlier just to make the analysis come out better. Perhaps the best advice in this case is the advice we gave in the previous chapter: Run the analysis with the outliers and run it again without them. If the key outputs do not change much, then it does not really matter whether the outliers are included or not. If the key outputs change substantially, then report the results both with and without the outliers, along with a verbal explanation.

We illustrate this procedure in the following continuation of the bank discrimination example.

Of the 208 employees at Fifth National Bank, are there any obvious outliers? In what sense are they outliers? Does it matter to the regression results, particularly those concerning gender discrimination, whether the outliers are removed?

Objective To locate possible outliers in the bank salary data, and to see to what extent they affect the regression model.

Solution

There are several places to look for outliers. An obvious place is the Salary variable. The box plot in Figure 11.22 shows that there are several employees making substantially more in salary than most of the employees. You could consider these outliers and remove them, arguing perhaps that these are senior managers who shouldn't be included in the discrimination analysis. We leave it to you to check whether the regression results are any different with these high-salary employees than without them.

Figure 11.22

Box Plot of Salaries for Bank Data

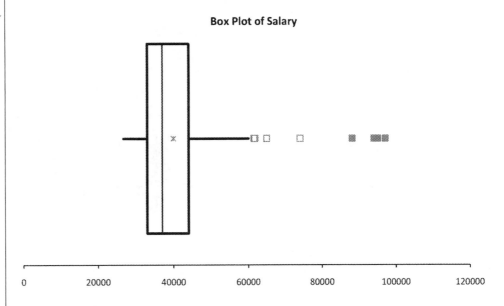

Another place to look is at a scatterplot of the residuals versus the fitted values. This type of plot (offered as an option by StatTools) shows points with abnormally large residuals. For example, we ran the regression with Female, YrsExper, Interaction(YrsExper,Female), and four education dummies, and we obtained the output and scatterplot in Figures 11.23 and 11.24. This scatterplot has several points that could be considered outliers, but we focus on the point identified in the figure. The residual for this point is approximately $-23,000$. Given that s_e for this regression is approximately 5900, this residual is about four standard errors below zero—quite a lot. If you examine this point more closely, you will see that it corresponds to employee 208, who is a 62-year-old female employee in the highest job grade. She has 33 years of experience with Fifth National, she has a graduate degree, and she earns only $30,000. She is clearly an unusual employee, and there are probably special circumstances that can explain her small salary, although we can only guess at what they are.

Figure 11.23   Regression Output with Outlier Included

	A	B	C	D	E	F	G
7		Multiple	R-Square	Adjusted	StErr of		
8	Summary	R		R-Square	Estimate		
9		0.8552	0.7314	0.7220	5935.254		
10							
11		Degrees of	Sum of	Mean of	F-Ratio	p-Value	
12	ANOVA Table	Freedom	Squares	Squares			
13	Explained	7	19181659773	2740237110	77.7875	< 0.0001	
14	Unexplained	200	7045447458	35227237.29			
15							
16		Coefficient	Standard	t-Value	p-Value	Confidence Interval 95%	
17	Regression Table		Error			Lower	Upper
18	Constant	24780.996	1551.053	15.9769	< 0.0001	21722.480	27839.512
19	YrsExper	1456.388	79.761	18.2593	< 0.0001	1299.107	1613.669
20	Female	4898.656	1454.087	3.3689	0.0009	2031.347	7765.965
21	EducLev = 2	546.549	1418.139	0.3854	0.7004	-2249.874	3342.972
22	EducLev = 3	3587.341	1287.361	2.7866	0.0058	1048.798	6125.885
23	EducLev = 4	5862.894	2346.571	2.4985	0.0133	1235.700	10490.088
24	EducLev = 5	9428.090	1337.292	7.0501	< 0.0001	6791.089	12065.092
25	Interaction(YrsExper,Female)	-1029.858	121.924	-8.4467	< 0.0001	-1270.279	-789.437

Figure 11.24

Scatterplot of Residuals Versus Fitted Values with Outlier Identified

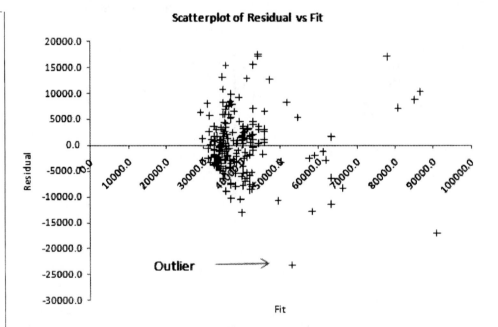

In any case, if you delete this employee and rerun the regression with the same variables, you will obtain the output in Figure 11.25.[7] Now, recalling that gender discrimination is the key issue in this example, you can compare the coefficients of Female and Interaction (YrsExper,Female) in the two outputs. The coefficient of Female has dropped from 4899 to 3774. In words, the Y-intercept for the female regression line used to be about $4900 higher than for the male line; now it is only about $3800 higher. More importantly, the coefficient of Interaction(YrsExper,Female) has changed from -1030 to -858. This

[7]As it turns out, this employee is the last observation in the data set. An easy way to run the regression (with StatTools) without this employee is to redefine the StatTools data set so that it doesn't include this last row.

Figure 11.25   Regression Output with Outlier Excluded

	A	B	C	D	E	F	G
7		Multiple	R-Square	Adjusted	StErr of		
8	Summary	R		R-Square	Estimate		
9		0.8690	0.7551	0.7465	5670.503		
10							
11		Degrees of	Sum of	Mean of	F-Ratio	p-Value	
12	ANOVA Table	Freedom	Squares	Squares			
13	Explained	7	19729421790	2818488827	87.6543	< 0.0001	
14	Unexplained	199	6398765306	32154599.53			
15							
16		Coefficient	Standard	t-Value	p-Value	Confidence Interval 95%	
17	Regression Table		Error			Lower	Upper
18	Constant	24056.616	1490.643	16.1384	< 0.0001	21117.132	26996.100
19	YrsExper	1449.596	76.218	19.0190	< 0.0001	1299.297	1599.896
20	Female	3774.315	1411.667	2.6737	0.0081	990.569	6558.060
21	EducLev = 2	777.542	1355.860	0.5735	0.5670	-1896.154	3451.239
22	EducLev = 3	4118.332	1235.623	3.3330	0.0010	1681.737	6554.926
23	EducLev = 4	6366.633	2244.711	2.8363	0.0050	1940.161	10793.105
24	EducLev = 5	10547.475	1301.794	8.1023	< 0.0001	7980.393	13114.556
25	Interaction(YrsExper,Female)	-858.202	122.613	-6.9993	< 0.0001	-1099.989	-616.415

coefficient indicates how much less steep the female line for Salary versus YrsExper is than the male line. So a change from -1030 to -858 indicates *less* discrimination against females now than before. In other words, this unusual female employee accounts for a good bit of the discrimination argument—although a strong argument still exists even without her. ∎

PROBLEMS

Level A

34. The file P11.34.xlsx contains data on the top 40 golfers in 2008. (It is a subset of the data examined in earlier chapters.) This was the year when Tiger Woods won the U.S. Open in June and then had year-ending surgery directly afterward. Using all 40 golfers, run a forward stepwise regression of Earnings per Round versus the potential explanatory variables in columns B–G. (Don't use Earnings in column H.) Then create a second data set that omits Tiger Woods and repeat the regression on this smaller data set. Are the results about the same? Explain the effect, if any, of the Tiger Woods outlier on the regression.

35. The file P02_07.xlsx includes data on 204 employees at the (fictional) company Beta Technologies.
  a. Run a forward stepwise regression of Annual Salary versus Gender, Age, Prior Experience, Beta Experience, and Education. Would you say this equation does a good job of explaining the variation in salaries?

  b. Add a new employee to the end of the data set, a top-level executive. The values of Gender through Annual Salary for this person are, respectively, 0, 56, 10, 15, 6, and $500,000. Run the regression in part **a** again, including this executive. Are the results much different? Is it "fair" to exclude this executive when analyzing the salary structure at this company?

Level B

36. Statistician Frank J. Anscombe created a data set to illustrate the importance of doing more than just examining the standard regression output. These data are provided in the file P10_64.xlsx.
  a. Regress Y_1 on X. How well does the estimated equation fit the data? Is there evidence of a linear relationship between Y_1 and X at the 5% significance level?
  b. Regress Y_2 on X. How well does the estimated equation fit the data? Is there evidence of a linear

relationship between Y_2 and X at the 5% significance level?

c. Regress Y_3 on X. How well does the estimated equation fit the data? Is there evidence of a linear relationship between Y_3 and X at the 5% significance level?

d. Regress Y_4 on X_4. How well does the estimated equation fit the data? Is there evidence of a linear relationship between Y_4 and X_4 at the 5% significance level?

e. Compare these four simple linear regression equations (1) in terms of goodness of fit and (2) in terms of overall statistical significance.

f. How do you explain these findings, considering that each of the regression equations is based on a *different* set of variables?

g. What role, if any, do outliers have on each of these estimated regression equations?

11.9 VIOLATIONS OF REGRESSION ASSUMPTIONS

Much of the theoretical research in the area of regression has dealt with violations of the regression assumptions discussed in section 11.2. There are three issues: how to detect violations of the assumptions, what goes wrong if the violations are ignored, and what to do about them if they are detected. Detection is usually relatively easy. You can look at scatterplots, histograms, and time series graphs for visual signs of violations, and there are a number of numerical measures (many not covered here) that have been developed for diagnostic purposes. The second issue, what goes wrong if the violations are ignored, depends on the type of violation and its severity. The third issue is the most difficult to resolve. There are some relatively easy fixes and some that are well beyond the level of this book. In this section we briefly discuss some of the most common violations and a few possible remedies for them.

11.9.1 Nonconstant Error Variance

The second regression assumption states that the variance of the errors should be *constant* for all values of the explanatory variables. This is a lot to ask, and it is almost always violated to some extent. Fortunately, mild violations do not have much effect on the validity of the regression output, so you can usually ignore them.

A fan shape can cause an incorrect value for the standard error of estimate, so that confidence intervals and hypothesis tests for the regression coefficients are not valid.

However, one particular form of nonconstant error variance occurs fairly often and should be dealt with. This is the fan shape shown earlier in the scatterplot of AmountSpent versus Salary in Figure 11.1. As salaries increase, the variability of amounts spent also increases. Although this fan shape appears in the scatterplot of the dependent variable AmountSpent versus the explanatory variable Salary, it also appears in the scatterplot of residuals versus fitted values if you regress AmountSpent versus Salary. If you ignore this nonconstant error variance, the standard error of the regression coefficient of Salary is inaccurate, and a confidence interval for this coefficient or a hypothesis test concerning it can be misleading.

There are at least two ways to deal with this fan-shape phenomenon. The first is to use a different estimation method than least squares. It is called *weighted least squares,* and it is an option available in some statistical software packages. However, it is fairly advanced and it is not available with StatTools, so we will not discuss it here.

A logarithmic transformation of Y can sometimes cure the fan-shape problem.

The second method is simpler. When you see a fan shape, where the variability increases from left to right in a scatterplot, you can try a logarithmic transformation of the dependent variable. The reason this often works is that the logarithmic transformation squeezes the large values closer together and pulls the small values farther apart. The scatterplot of the log of AmountSpent versus Salary is in Figure 11.26. Clearly, the fan shape evident in Figure 11.1 is gone.

This logarithmic transformation is not a magical cure for all instances of nonconstant error variance. For example, it appears to have introduced some curvature into the plot in

Figure 11.26

Scatterplot without
Fan Shape

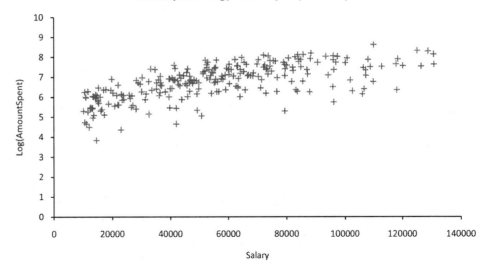

Scatterplot of Log(AmountSpent) vs Salary

Figure 11.26. However, as we discussed in the previous chapter, when the distribution of the dependent variable is heavily skewed to the right, as it often is, the logarithmic transformation is worth exploring.

11.9.2 Nonnormality of Residuals

The third regression assumption states that the error terms are normally distributed. You can check this assumption fairly easily by forming a histogram of the residuals. You can even perform a formal test of normality of the residuals by using the procedures discussed in section 9.5 of Chapter 9. However, unless the distribution of the residuals is severely nonnormal, the inferences made from the regression output are still approximately valid. In addition, one form of nonnormality often encountered is skewness to the right, and this can often be remedied by the same logarithmic transformation of the dependent variable that remedies nonconstant error variance.

11.9.3 Autocorrelated Residuals

The fourth regression assumption states that the error terms are probabilistically independent. This assumption is usually valid for cross-sectional data, but it is often violated for time series data. The problem with time series data is that the residuals are often correlated with nearby residuals, a property called **autocorrelation**. The most frequent type of autocorrelation is positive autocorrelation. For example, if residuals separated by one month are correlated—called **lag 1 autocorrelation**—in a positive direction, then an overprediction in January, say, will likely lead to an overprediction in February, and an underprediction in January will likely lead to an underprediction in February. If this autocorrelation is large, serious prediction errors can occur if it isn't dealt with appropriately.

A numerical measure has been developed to check for lag 1 autocorrelation. It is called the **Durbin–Watson statistic** (after the two statisticians who developed it), and it is quoted automatically in the regression output of many statistical software packages. The Durbin–Watson (DW) statistic is scaled to be between 0 and 4. Values close to 2 indicate very little lag 1 autocorrelation, values below 2 indicate positive autocorrelation, and values above 2 indicate negative autocorrelation.

Because *positive* autocorrelation is the usual culprit, the question becomes how much below 2 the DW statistic must be before you should react. There is a formal hypothesis test for answering this question, and a set of tables appears in some statistics texts. Without going into the details, we simply state that when the number of time series observations, n, is about 30 and the number of explanatory variables is fairly small, say, 1 to 5, then any DW statistic less than 1.2 should get your attention. If n increases to around 100, then you shouldn't be concerned unless the DW statistic is below 1.5.

If e_i is the ith residual, the formula for the DW statistic is

$$DW = \frac{\sum_{i=2}^{n}(e_i - e_{i-1})^2}{\sum_{i=1}^{n} e_i^2}$$

This is obviously not very attractive for hand calculation, so the StatDurbinWatson function is included in StatTools. To use it, run any regression and check the option to create a graph of residuals versus fitted values. This automatically creates columns of fitted values and residuals. Then enter the formula

=StatDurbinWatson(*ResidRange*)

in any cell, substituting the actual range of residuals for "ResidRange."

The following continuation of Example 11.1 with the Bendrix manufacturing data—the only time series data set we have analyzed with regression—checks for possible lag 1 autocorrelation.

EXAMPLE | 11.1 EXPLAINING OVERHEAD COSTS AT BENDRIX (CONTINUED)

Is there any evidence of lag 1 autocorrelation in the Bendrix data when Overhead is regressed on MachHrs and ProdRuns?

Objective To use the Durbin–Watson statistic to check whether there is any lag 1 autocorrelation in the residuals from the Bendrix regression model for overhead costs.

Solution

You should run the usual multiple regression and check that you want a graph of residuals versus fitted values. The results are shown in Figure 11.27. The residuals are listed in column D. Each represents how much the regression overpredicts (if negative) or underpredicts (if positive) the overhead cost for that month. You can check for lag 1 autocorrelation in two ways, with the DW statistic and by examining the time series graph of the residuals in Figure 11.28.

Figure 11.27   **Regression Output with Residuals and DW Statistic**

	A	B	C	D	E	F
44	*Graph Data*	Overhead	Fit	Residual		Durbin-Watson for residuals
45	1	99798	98391.35059	1406.649409		1.313
46	2	87804	85522.33322	2281.666779		
47	3	93681	92723.59538	957.4046174		
48	4	82262	82428.09201	-166.0920107		
49	5	106968	100227.9028	6740.097234		

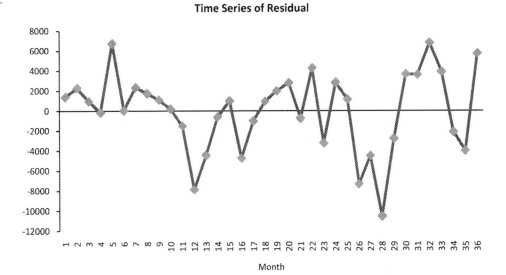

Figure 11.28

Time Series Graph of Residuals

The DW statistic is calculated in cell F45 of Figure 11.27 with the formula

$=$StatDurbinWatson(D45:D80)

(Remember that StatDurbinWatson is *not* a built-in Excel function. It is available only if StatTools is loaded.) Based on our guidelines for DW values, 1.3131 suggests positive autocorrelation—it is less than 2—but not enough to cause concern.[8] This general conclusion is supported by the time series graph. Serious autocorrelation of lag 1 would tend to show longer runs of residuals alternating above and below the horizontal axis—positives would tend to follow positives, and negatives would tend to follow negatives. There is some indication of this behavior in the graph but not an excessive amount. ∎

What should you do if the DW statistic signals significant autocorrelation? Unfortunately, the answer to this question would take us much more deeply into time series analysis than we can go in this book. Suffice it to say that time series analysis in the context of regression can become very complex, and there are no easy fixes for the autocorrelation that often occurs.

PROBLEMS

Level A

37. A company produces electric motors for use in home appliances. One of the company's production managers is interested in examining the relationship between the dollars spent per month in inspecting finished motor products (X) and the number of motors produced during that month that were returned by dissatisfied customers (Y). He has collected the data in the file P10_03.xlsx to explore this relationship for the past 36 months.

a. Estimate a simple linear regression equation using the given data and interpret it. What does the ANOVA table indicate for this model?

b. Examine the residuals of the regression equation. Do you see evidence of any violations of the regression assumptions?

c. Conduct a Durbin–Watson test on the model's residuals. Interpret the result of this test.

d. In light of your result in part **c**, do you recommend modifying the original regression model? If so, how would you revise it?

---

[8]A more formal test, using Durbin–Watson tables, supports this conclusion.

38. Examine the relationship between the average utility bills for homes of a particular size (Y) and the average monthly temperature (X). The data in the file P10_07.xlsx include the average monthly bill and temperature for each month of the past year.

a. Use the given data to estimate a simple linear regression equation. How well does the estimated regression model fit the given data? What does the ANOVA table indicate for this model?

b. Examine the residuals of the regression equation. Do you see evidence of any violations of the regression assumptions?

c. Conduct a Durbin–Watson test on the model's residuals. Interpret the result of this test.

d. In light of your result in part **c**, do you recommend modifying the original regression model? If so, how would you revise it?

39. The manager of a commuter rail transportation system was recently asked by her governing board to predict the demand for rides in the large city served by the transportation network. The system manager has collected data on variables thought to be related to the number of weekly riders on the city's rail system. The file P10_20.xlsx contains these data.

a. Estimate a multiple regression equation using all of the available explanatory variables. What does the ANOVA table indicate for this model?

b. Is there evidence of autocorrelated residuals in this model? Explain why or why not.

11.10 PREDICTION

Once you have estimated a regression equation from a set of data, you might want to use this equation to predict the value of the dependent variable for *new* observations. As an example, suppose that a retail chain is considering opening a new store in one of several proposed locations. It naturally wants to choose the location that will result in the largest revenues. The problem is that the revenues for the new locations are not yet known. They can be observed only after stores are opened in these locations, and the chain cannot afford to open more than one store at the current time. An alternative is to use regression analysis. Using data from *existing* stores, the chain can run a regression of the dependent variable revenue on several explanatory variables such as population density, level of wealth in the vicinity, number of competitors nearby, ease of access given the existing roads, and so on.

Assuming that the regression equation has a reasonably large R^2 and, even more important, a reasonably small s_e, the chain can then use this equation to predict revenues for the proposed locations. Specifically, it will gather values of the explanatory variables for each of the proposed locations, substitute these into the regression equation, and look at the predicted revenue for each proposed location. All else being equal, the chain will probably choose the location with the highest predicted revenue.

As another example, suppose that you are trying to explain the starting salaries for undergraduate college students. You want to predict the *mean* salary of all graduates with certain characteristics, such as all male marketing majors from state-supported universities. To do this, you first gather salary data from a sample of graduates from various universities. Included in this data set are relevant explanatory variables for each graduate in the sample, such as the type of university, the student's major, GPA, years of work experience, and so on. You then use these data to estimate a regression equation for starting salary and substitute the relevant values of the explanatory variables into the regression equation to obtain the required prediction.

Regression can be used to predict Y for a single observation, or it can be used to predict the mean Y for many observations, all with the same X values.

These two examples illustrate two types of prediction problems in regression. The first problem, illustrated by the retail chain example, is the more common of the two. Here the objective is to predict the value of the dependent variable for one or more *individual* members of the population. In this specific example you are trying to predict the future revenue for several potential locations of the new store. In the second problem, illustrated by the salary example, the objective is to predict the *mean* of the dependent variable for all members of the population with certain values of the explanatory variables. In the first problem you are predicting an individual value; in the second problem you are predicting a mean.

The second problem is inherently easier than the first in the sense that the resulting prediction is bound to be more accurate. The reason is intuitive. Recall that the mean of the dependent variable for any fixed values of the explanatory variables lies on the population regression line. Therefore, if you can accurately estimate this line—that is, if you can accurately estimate the regression coefficients—you can accurately predict the required mean. In contrast, most individual points do *not* lie on the population regression line. Therefore, even if your estimate of the population regression line is perfectly accurate, you still cannot predict exactly where an individual point will fall.

Stated another way, when you predict a mean, there is a single source of error: the possibly inaccurate estimates of the regression coefficients. But when you predict an individual value, there are two sources of error: the inaccurate estimates of the regression coefficients and the inherent variation of individual points around the regression line. This second source of error often dominates the first.

We illustrate these comments in Figure 11.29. For the sake of illustration, the dependent variable is salary and the single explanatory variable is years of experience with the company. Let's suppose that you want to predict either the salary for a particular employee with 10 years of experience or the mean salary of all employees with 10 years of experience. The two lines in this graph represent the population regression line (which in reality is unobservable) and the estimated regression line. For each prediction problem the point prediction—the best guess—is the value above 10 on the estimated regression line. The error in predicting the mean occurs because the two lines in the graph are not the same—that is, the estimated line is not quite correct. The error in predicting the individual value (the point shown in the graph) occurs because the two lines are not the same and also because this point does not lie on the population regression line.

Figure 11.29

Prediction Errors for an Individual Value and a Mean

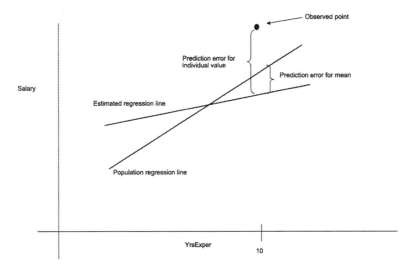

One general aspect of prediction becomes apparent by looking at this graph. If we let Xs denote the explanatory variables, predictions for values of the Xs close to their means are likely to be more accurate than predictions for Xs far from their means. In the graph, the mean of YrsExper is about 7. (This is approximately where the two lines cross.) Because the slopes of the two lines are different, they get farther apart as YrsExper gets farther away from 7 (on either side). As a result, predictions tend to become less accurate.

This phenomenon shows up as higher standard errors of prediction as the Xs get farther away from their means. However, for extreme values of the Xs, there is another problem. Suppose, for example, that all values of YrsExper in the data set are between 1 and 15, and you attempt to predict the salary for an employee with 25 years of experience. This is called *extrapolation*; you are attempting to predict beyond the limits of the sample.

The problem here is that there is no guarantee, and sometimes no reason to believe, that the relationship within the range of the sample is valid outside of this range. It is perfectly possible that the effect of years of experience on salary is considerably different in the 25-year range than in the range of the sample. If it is, then extrapolation is bound to yield inaccurate predictions. In general, you should avoid extrapolation whenever possible. If you really want to predict the salaries of employees with 25-plus years of experience, you should include some employees of this type in the original sample.

We now discuss how to make predictions and how to estimate their accuracy, both for individual values and for means. To keep it simple, we first assume that there is a single explanatory variable X. We choose a fixed "trial" value of X, labeled X_0, and predict the value of a single Y or the mean of all Ys when X equals X_0. For both prediction problems the **point prediction**, or best guess, is found by substituting into the right side of the estimated regression equation. Graphically, this is the height of the estimated regression line above X_0.

> To calculate a **point prediction**, substitute the given values of the Xs into the estimated regression equation.

The standard error of prediction for a single Y is approximately equal to the standard error of estimate.

To measure the accuracy of these point predictions, you calculate a standard error for each prediction. These standard errors can be interpreted in the usual way. For example, you are about 68% certain that the actual values will be within one standard error of the point predictions, and you are about 95% certain that the actual values will be within two standard errors of the point predictions. For the individual prediction problem, the standard error is labeled s_{ind} and is given by Equation (11.5). As indicated by the approximate equality on the right, when the sample size n is large and X_0 is fairly close to $\overline{X}$, the last two terms inside the square root are relatively small, and this standard error of prediction can be approximated by s_e, the standard error of estimate.

Standard Error of Prediction for a Single Y

$$s_{\text{ind}} = s_e\sqrt{1 + \frac{1}{n} + \frac{(X_0 - \overline{X})^2}{\sum_{i=1}^{n}(X_i - \overline{X})^2}} \simeq s_e \qquad \textbf{(11.5)}$$

For the prediction of the mean, the standard error is labeled s_{mean} and is given by Equation (11.6). Here, if X_0 is fairly close to $\overline{X}$, the last term inside the square root is relatively small, and this standard error of prediction is approximately equal to the expression on the right.

Standard Error of Prediction for the Mean Y

$$s_{\text{mean}} = s_e\sqrt{\frac{1}{n} + \frac{(X_0 - \overline{X})^2}{\sum_{i=1}^{n}(X_i - \overline{X})^2}} \simeq s_e/\sqrt{n} \qquad \textbf{(11.6)}$$

These standard errors can be used to calculate a 95% prediction interval for an individual value and a 95% confidence interval for a mean value. Exactly as in Chapter 8, you go out a *t*-multiple of the relevant standard error on either side of the point prediction. The *t*-multiple is the value that cuts off 0.025 probability in the right-hand tail of a *t* distribution with $n - 2$ degrees of freedom.

The term *prediction interval* (rather than confidence interval) is used for an individual value because an individual value of *Y* is not a population *parameter*; it is an individual point. However, the interpretation is basically the same. If you calculate a 95% prediction interval for many members of the population, you can expect their actual *Y* values to fall within the corresponding prediction intervals about 95% of the time.

To see how all of this can be implemented in Excel, we revisit the Bendrix example of predicting overhead expenses.

EXAMPLE | **11.1 PREDICTING OVERHEAD AT BENDRIX (CONTINUED)**

W e have already used regression to analyze overhead expenses at Bendrix, based on 36 months of data. Suppose Bendrix expects the values of MachHrs and ProdRuns for the next three months to be 1430, 1560, 1520, and 35, 45, 40, respectively. What are their point predictions and 95% prediction intervals for Overhead for these three months?

Objective   To predict Overhead at Bendrix for the next three months, given anticipated values of MachHrs and ProdRuns.

Solution

StatTools has the capability to provide predictions and 95% prediction intervals, but you must set up a second data set to capture the results. This second data set can be placed next to (or below) the original data set. It should have the same variable name headings, and it should include values of the explanatory variable to be used for prediction. (It can also have LowerLimit95 and UpperLimit95 headings, but these are optional and will be added by StatTools if they do not already exist.) For this example we called the original data set Original Data and the new data set Data for Prediction. The regression dialog box and results in Data for Prediction appear in Figures 11.30 and 11.31. In the dialog box, note that the Prediction option is checked, and the second data set is specified in the corresponding dropdown list.

The text box in Figure 11.31 explains how the second data set range should be set up. Initially, you should enter the given values in the Month, MachHrs, and ProdRuns columns. Then when the regression is run (with the Prediction option checked), the values in the Overhead, LowerLimit95, and UpperLimit95 columns will be filled in. (Again, if you do not create LowerLimit95 and UpperLimit95 columns as part of the second data set, StatTools will do it for you.)

The Overhead values in column I are the point predictions for the next three months, and the LowerLimit95 and UpperLimit95 values in column J and K indicate the 95% prediction intervals. You can see from the wide prediction intervals how much uncertainty remains. The reason is the relatively large standard error of estimate, s_e. If you could halve the value of s_e, the length of the prediction interval would be only half as large. Contrary to what you might expect, this is not a sample size problem. That is, a larger sample size would probably *not* produce a smaller value of s_e. The whole problem is that MachHrs and

Figure 11.30

Regression Dialog Box with Predictions Checked

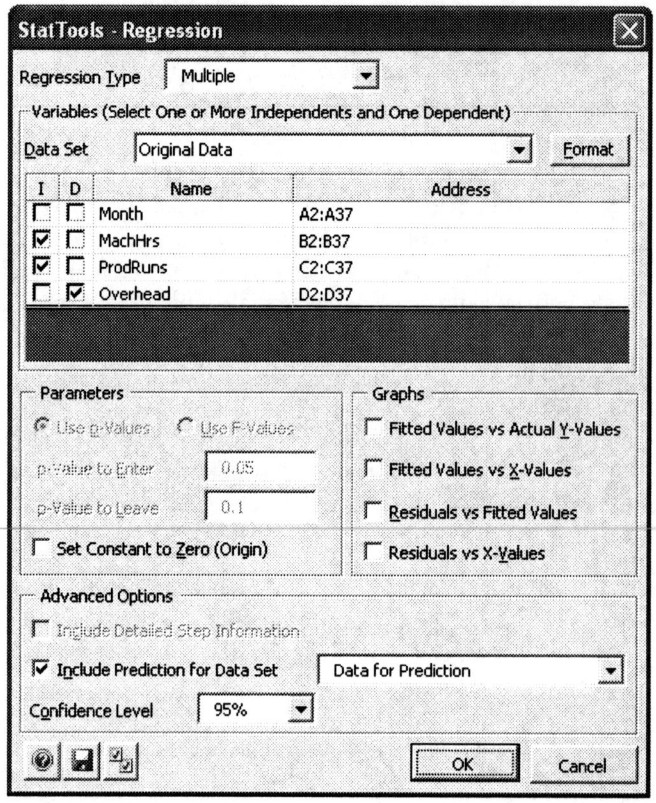

Figure 11.31

Prediction of Overhead

	F	G	H	I	J	K	L
1	Month	MachHrs	ProdRuns	Overhead	LowerLimit95	UpperLimit95	
2	37	1430	35	97180.35	88700.80	105659.91	
3	38	1560	45	111676.27	103002.95	120349.58	
4	39	1520	40	105516.72	96993.16	114040.28	
5							
6	Above is the data set for prediction. It is best to set this up ahead of time,						
7	entering all of the column headings, entering the values of the explanatory						
8	variables you want to test, and defining this entire range as a new StatTools data						
9	set. The values in the last three columns can be blank or have values, but when						
10	regression is run with the prediction options, they will be filled in or overwritten.						
11	Also, if you don't include the last two columns in your StatTools data set,						
12	StatTools will create them for you.						
13							

ProdRuns are not perfectly correlated with Overhead. The only way to decrease s_e and get more accurate predictions is to find other explanatory variables that are more closely related to Overhead. ▪

StatTools provides prediction intervals for individual values, as you have just seen, but it does not provide confidence intervals for the mean of Y, given a set of Xs. To obtain such a confidence interval, you can use Equation (11.6) to get the required standard error of prediction (for simple regression only), or you can approximate it by $s_e/\sqrt{n}$.

Level A

40. The file P10_05.xlsx contains salaries for a sample of DataCom employees, along with several variables that might be related to salary.
  a. Estimate an appropriate multiple regression equation to predict the annual salary of a given DataCom employee.
  b. Given the estimated regression model, predict the annual salary of a male employee who served in a similar department at another company for five years prior to coming to work at DataCom. This man, a graduate of a four-year collegiate business program, has been supervising six subordinates in the sales department since joining the organization seven years ago.
  c. Find a 95% prediction interval for the salary earned by the employee in part **b**.
  d. Find a 95% confidence interval for the mean salary earned by all DataCom employees sharing the characteristics provided in part **b**.
  e. How can you explain the difference between the widths of the intervals in parts **c** and **d**?

41. The owner of a restaurant in Bloomington, Indiana, has recorded sales data for the past 19 years. He has also recorded data on potentially relevant variables. The data appear in the file P10_23.xlsx.
  a. Estimate a regression equation for sales as a function of population, advertising in the current year, and advertising in the previous year. Can you expect predictions of sales in *future* years to be very accurate if they are based on this regression equation? Explain.
  b. The company would like to predict sales in the next year (year 20). It doesn't know what the population

will be in year 20, so it assumes no change from year 19. Its planned advertising level for year 20 is $30,000. Find a prediction and a 95% prediction interval for sales in year 20.

42. A power company located in southern Alabama wants to predict the peak power load (i.e., Y, the maximum amount of power that must be generated each day to meet demand) as a function of the daily high temperature (X). A random sample of 25 summer days is chosen, and the peak power load and the high temperature are recorded on each day. The file P10_40.xlsx contain these observations.
  a. Use the given data to estimate a simple linear regression equation. How well does the regression equation fit the given data?
  b. Examine the residuals of the estimated regression equation. Do you see evidence of any violations of the assumptions regarding the errors of the regression model?
  c. Calculate the Durbin–Watson statistic on the model's residuals. What does it indicate?
  d. Given your result in part **d**, do you recommend modifying the original regression model in this case? If so, how would you revise it?
  e. Use the final version of your regression equation to predict the peak power load on a summer day with a high temperature of 90 degrees.
  f. Find a 95% prediction interval for the peak power load on a summer day with a high temperature of 90 degrees.
  h. Find a 95% confidence interval for the *average* peak power load on all summer days with a high temperature of 90 degrees.

11.11 CONCLUSION

In these two chapters on regression, you have seen how useful regression analysis can be for a variety of business applications and how statistical software such as StatTools enables you to obtain relevant output—both graphical and numerical—with very little effort. However, you have also seen that there are many concepts that you must understand well before you can use regression analysis appropriately. Given that user-friendly software is available, it is all too easy to generate enormous amounts of regression output and then misinterpret or misuse much of it.

At the very least, you should (1) be able to interpret the standard regression output, including statistics on the regression coefficients, summary measures such as R^2 and s_e, and the ANOVA table, (2) know what to look for in the many scatterplots available, (3) know how to use dummy variables, interaction terms, and nonlinear transformations to improve a fit, and (4) be able to spot clear violations of the regression assumptions. However, we haven't covered everything. Indeed, many entire books are devoted exclusively to regression analysis. Therefore, you should recognize when you *don't* know enough to handle a regression problem such as nonconstant error variance or autocorrelation appropriately. In this case, you should consult a statistical expert.

Summary of Key Terms

Term	Symbol	Explanation	Excel	Page	Equation
Statistical model		A theoretical model including several assumptions that must be satisfied, at least approximately, for inferences from regression output to be valid		603	11.1
Error	ε	The difference between the actual Y value and the predicted value from the population regression line		604	
Homoscedasticity (and heteroscedasticity)		Equal (and unequal) variance of the dependent variable for different values of the explanatory variables		605	
Parsimony		The concept of explaining the most with the least		608	
Standard error of regression coefficient	s_b	Measures how much the estimates of a regression coefficient vary from sample to sample	StatTools/ Regression & Classification/ Regression	609	
Confidence interval for regression coefficient		An interval likely to contain the population regression coefficient	StatTools/ Regression & Classification/ Regression	610	
t-value for regression coefficient	t	The ratio of the estimate of a regression coefficient to its standard error, used to test whether the coefficient is 0	StatTools/ Regression& Classification/ Regression	611	11.3
Hypothesis test for regression coefficient		Typically, a two-tailed test, where the null hypothesis is that the regression coefficient is 0	StatTools/ Regression & Classification/ Regression	611	
ANOVA table for regression		Used to test whether the explanatory variables, as a whole, have any significant explanatory power	StatTools/ Regression & Classification/ Regression	612	
Multicollinearity		Occurs when there is a fairly strong linear relationship between explanatory variables		616	
Include/exclude decisions		Guidelines for deciding whether to include or exclude potential explanatory variables		620	
Stepwise regression		A class of automatic equation-building methods, where variables are added (or deleted) in order of their importance	StatTools/ Regression & Classification/ Regression	625	

(continued)

Term	Symbol	Explanation	Excel	Page	Equation
Partial F test		Tests whether a set of extra explanatory variables adds any explanatory power to an existing regression equation	Must be done manually, using StatTools regression outputs	631	11.4
Outliers		Observations that lie outside the general pattern of points and can have a substantial effect on the regression model		638	
Influential point		A point that can "tilt" the regression line		639	
Autocorrelation of residuals		Lack of independence in the series of residuals, especially relevant for time series data		645	
Durbin–Watson statistic		A measure of the autocorrelation between residuals, especially useful for time series data	=StatDurbin Watson(range), a StatTools function	645	
Point prediction		The predicted value of Y from the regression equation		650	
Standard errors of prediction	s_{ind}, s_{mean}	Measures of the accuracy of prediction when predicting Y for an individual observation, or predicting the mean of all Y's, for fixed values of the explanatory variables	StatTools/ Regression & Classification/ Regression	650	11.5, 11.6

PROBLEMS

Conceptual Questions

C.1. Suppose a regression output produces the following 99% confidence interval for one of the regression coefficients: $[-32.47, -16.88]$. Given this information, should an analyst reject the null hypothesis that this population regression coefficient is equal to zero? Explain your answer.

C.2. Explain why it is not possible to estimate a linear regression model that contains *all* dummy variables associated with a particular categorical explanatory variable.

C.3. Suppose you have a data set that includes *all* of the professional athletes in a given sport over a given period of time, such as all NFL football players during the 2008–2010 seasons, and you use regression to estimate a variable of interest. Are the inferences discussed in this chapter relevant? Recall that we have been assuming that the data represent a random sample of some larger population. In this sports example, what is the larger population—or is there one?

C.4. Distinguish between the test of significance of an individual regression coefficient and the ANOVA test. When, if ever, are these two statistical tests essentially equivalent?

C.5. Which of these intervals based on the same estimated regression equation with fixed values of the explanatory variables would be *wider*: (1) a 95% prediction interval for an individual value of Y or (2) a 95% confidence interval for the mean value of Y? Explain your answer. How do you interpret the wider of these two intervals in words?

C.6. Regression outputs from virtually all statistical packages look the same. In particular, the section on coefficients lists the coefficients, their standard errors, their t-values, their p-values, and (possibly) 95% confidence intervals for them. Explain how all of these are related.

C.7. If you are building a regression equation in a forward stepwise manner, that is, by adding one variable at a time, explain why it is useful to monitor the adjusted R^2 and the standard error of estimate. Why is it not as useful to monitor R^2?

C.8. You run a regression with two explanatory variables and notice that the p-value in the ANOVA table is extremely small but the *p*-values of both explanatory variables are larger than 0.10. What is the probable reason? Can you conclude that neither explanatory variable does a good job in predicting the dependent variable?

C.9. Why are outliers sometimes called *influential* observations? What *could* happen to the slope of a regression of *Y* versus a single *X* when an outlier is included versus when it is not included? Will this necessarily happen when a point is an outlier? Answer by giving a couple of examples.

C.10. The Durbin-Watson test is for detecting lag 1 autocorrelation in the residuals. Which values of DW signal *positive* autocorrelation? If you observe such a DW value but ignore it, what might go wrong with predictions based on the regression equation? Specifically, if the data are time series data, and your goal is to predict the next six months, what might go wrong with the predictions?

Level A

43. For 12 straight weeks you have observed the sales (in number of cases) of canned tomatoes at Mr. D's super-market. Each week you kept track of the following:
- Was a promotional notice placed in all shopping carts for canned tomatoes?
- Was a coupon given for canned tomatoes?
- Was a price reduction (none, 1, or 2 cents off) given?

The file P11_43.xlsx contains these data.
  a. Use multiple regression to determine how these factors influence sales.
  b. Discuss how you can tell whether autocorrelation, heteroscedasticity, or multicollinearity might be a problem.
  c. Predict sales of canned tomatoes during a week in which Mr. D's uses a shopping cart notice, a coupon, and a one-cent price reduction.

44. The file P11_44.xlsx contains quarterly data on pork sales. Price is in dollars per hundred pounds, quantity sold is in billions of pounds, per capita income is in dollars, U.S. population is in millions, and GDP is in billions of dollars.
  a. Use the data to develop a regression equation that could be used to predict the quantity of pork sold during future periods. Discuss how you can tell whether heteroscedasticity, autocorrelation, or multicollinearity might be a problem.
  b. Suppose that during each of the next two quarters, price is 45, U.S. population is 240, GDP is 2620, and per capita income is 10,000. (These are in the units described previously.) Predict the quantity of pork sold during each of the next two quarters.

45. The file P11_45.xlsx contains monthly sales for a photography studio and the price charged per portrait during each month. Use regression to estimate an equation for predicting the current month's sales from last month's sales and the current month's price.
  a. If the price of a portrait during month 21 is $30, predict month 21 sales.
  b. Discuss how you can tell whether autocorrelation, multicollinearity, or heteroscedasticity might be a problem.

46. The file P11_46.xlsx contains data on a motel chain's revenue and advertising. Note that column C is simply column B "pushed down" a row.
  a. If the goal is to get the best-fitting regression equation for Revenue, which of the Advertising variables should be used? Or is it better to use both?
  b. Using the best-fitting equation from part **a**, make predictions for the motel chain's revenues during the next four quarters. Assume that advertising during each of the next four quarters is $50,000.
  c. Does autocorrelation of the residuals from the best-fitting equation appear to be a problem?

47. The file P11_47.xlsx contains the quarterly revenues (in millions of dollars) of a utility company for a seven-year period. The goal is to use these data to build a multiple regression model that can be used to forecast future revenues.
  a. Which variables should be included in the regression? Explain your rationale for including or excluding variables. (Look at a time series graph for clues.)
  b. Interpret the coefficients of your final equation.
  c. Make a forecast for revenues during the next quarter, quarter 29. Also, estimate the probability that revenue in the next quarter will be at least $150 million. (*Hint*: Use the standard error of prediction and the fact that the errors are approximately normally distributed.)

48. The belief that larger majorities for a president in a presidential election help the president's party increase its representation in the House and Senate is called the *coattail* effect. The file P11_48.xlsx lists the percentage by which each president since 1948 won the election and the number of seats in the House and Senate gained (or lost) during each election by the elected president's party. Are these data consistent with the idea of presidential coattails?

49. When potential workers apply for a job that requires extensive manual assembly of small intricate parts, they are initially given three different tests to measure their manual dexterity. The ones who are hired are then periodically given a performance rating on a 0 to 100 scale that combines their speed and accuracy in performing the required assembly operations. The file P11_49.xlsx lists the test scores and performance ratings for a randomly selected group of employees. It also lists their seniority (months with the company) at the time of the performance rating.

a. Look at a matrix of correlations. Can you say with certainty (based only on these correlations) that the R^2 value for the regression will be at least 35%? Why or why not?

b. Is there any evidence (from the correlation matrix) that multicollinearity will be a problem? Why or why not?

c. Run the regression of Performance Rating versus all four explanatory variables. List the equation, the value of R^2, and the value of s_e. Do all of the coefficients have the signs (negative or positive) you would expect? Briefly explain.

d. Referring to the equation in part c, if a worker (outside of the 80 in the sample) has 15 months of seniority and test scores of 57, 71, and 63, find a prediction and an approximate 95% prediction interval for this worker's Performance Rating score.

e. One of the t-values for the coefficients in part c is less than 1. Explain briefly why this occurred. Does it mean that this variable is not related to Performance Rating?

f. Arguably, the three test measures provide overlapping (or redundant) information. For the sake of parsimony (explaining "the most with the least"), it might be sensible to regress Performance Rating versus only two explanatory variables, Seniority and Average Test, where Average Test is the average of the three test scores—that is, Average Test = (Test1 + Test2 + Test3)/3. Run this regression and report the same measures as in part c: the equation itself, R^2, and s_e. Can you argue that this equation is just as good as the equation in part c? Explain briefly.

50. Nicklaus Electronics manufactures electronic components used in the computer and space industries. The annual rate of return on the market portfolio and the annual rate of return on Nicklaus Electronics stock for the last 36 months are listed in the file P11_50.xlsx. The company wants to calculate the *systematic risk* of its common stock. (It is systematic in the sense that it represents the part of the risk that Nicklaus shares with the market as a whole.) The rate of return Y_t in period t on a security is hypothesized to be related to the rate of return m_t on a market portfolio by the equation

$$Y_t = \alpha + \beta m_t + \varepsilon_t$$

Here, α is the risk-free rate of return, β is the security's systematic risk, and ε_t is an error term. Estimate the systematic risk of the common stock of Nicklaus Electronics. Would you say that Nicklaus stock is a risky investment? Why or why not?

51. The auditor of Kaefer Manufacturing uses regression analysis during the analytical review stage of the firm's annual audit. The regression analysis attempts to uncover relationships that exist between various account balances. Any such relationship is subsequently used as a preliminary test of the reasonableness of the reported account balances. The auditor wants to determine whether a relationship exists between the balance of accounts receivable at the end of the month and that month's sales. The file P11_51.xlsx contains data on these two accounts for the last 36 months. It also shows the sales levels two months before month 1.

a. Is there any statistical evidence to suggest a relationship between the monthly sales level and accounts receivable?

b. Referring to part a, would the relationship be described any better by including this month's sales and the previous month's sales (called *lagged sales*) in the equation for accounts receivable? What about adding the sales from more than a month ago to the equation? For this problem, why might it make accounting sense to include lagged sales variables in the equation? How do you interpret their coefficients?

c. During month 37, which is a fiscal year-end month, the sales were $1,800,000. The reported accounts receivable balance was $3,000,000. Does this reported amount seem consistent with past experience? Explain.

52. A company gives prospective managers four separate tests for judging their potential. For a sample of 30 managers, the test scores and the subsequent job effectiveness ratings (Rating) given one year later are listed in the file P11_52.xlsx.

a. Look at scatterplots and the table of correlations for these five variables. Does it appear that a multiple regression equation for Rating, with the test scores as explanatory variables, will be successful? Can you foresee any problems in obtaining accurate estimates of the individual regression coefficients?

b. Estimate the regression equation that includes all four test scores, and find 95% confidence intervals for the coefficients of the explanatory variables. How can you explain the negative coefficient of Test3, given that the correlation between Rating and Test3 is positive?

c. Can you reject the null hypothesis that these test scores, as a whole, have no predictive ability for job effectiveness at the 1% level? Why or why not?

d. If a new prospective manager has test scores of 83, 74, 65, and 77, what do you predict his job effectiveness rating will be in one year? What is the standard error of this prediction?

53. Confederate Express is attempting to determine how its monthly shipping costs depend on the number of units shipped during a month. The file P11_53.xlsx contains the number of units shipped and total shipping costs for the last 15 months.

   a. Use regression to determine a relationship between units shipped and monthly shipping costs.

   b. Plot the errors for the predictions in order of time sequence. Is there any unusual pattern?

   c. You have now been told that there was a trucking strike during months 11 through 15, and you believe that this might have influenced shipping costs. How can the analysis in part **a** be modified to account for the effects of the strike? After accounting for the effects of the strike, does the unusual pattern in part **b** disappear?

54. The file P11_54.xlsx contains monthly data on fatal automobile crashes in the U.S. in each of eight three-hour intervals. Suppose you didn't have the data on the midnight to 3AM time interval. How well could multiple regression be used to predict the data for this interval? Which time intervals are most useful in this prediction? Is multicollinearity a problem?

Level B

55. You want to determine the variables that influence bus usage in major American cities. For 24 cities, the following data are listed in the file P11_55.xlsx:

   ■ Bus travel (annual, in thousands of hours)

   ■ Income (average per capita income)

   ■ Population (in thousands)

   ■ Land area (in square miles)

   a. Use these data to fit the multiplicative equation

$$\text{BusTravel} = \alpha\text{Income}^{\beta_1}\text{Population}^{\beta_2}\text{LandArea}^{\beta_3}$$

   b. Are all variables significant at the 5% level?

   c. Interpret the estimated values of β_1, β_2, and β_3.

56. The file P11_56.xlsx contains data on 80 managers at a large (fictitious) corporation. The variables are Salary (current annual salary), YrsExper (years of experience in the industry), YrsHere (years of experience with this company), and MglLevel (current level in the company, coded 1 to 4). You want to regress Salary on the potential explanatory variables. What is the best way to do so? Specifically, how should you handle MglLevel? Should you include both YrsExper and YrsHere or only one of them, and if only one, which one? Present your results, and explain them and your reasoning behind them.

57. A toy company has assigned you to analyze the factors influencing the sales of its most popular doll. The number of these dolls sold during the last 23 years is given in the file P11_57.xlsx. The following factors are thought to influence sales of these dolls:

   ■ Was there a recession?

   ■ Were the dolls on sale at Christmas?

   ■ Was there an upward trend over time?

   a. Determine an equation that can be used to predict annual sales of these dolls. Make sure that all variables in your equation are significant at the 10% level.

   b. Interpret the coefficients in your equation.

   c. Are there any outliers?

   d. Is heteroscedasticity or autocorrelation of residuals a problem?

   e. During the current year (year 24), a recession is predicted and the dolls will be put on sale at Christmas. There is a 1% chance that sales of the dolls will exceed what value? You can assume here that heteroscedasticity and autocorrelation are *not* a problem. (*Hint:* Use the standard error of prediction and the fact that the errors are approximately normally distributed.)

58. The file P11_58.xlsx shows the "yield curve" (at monthly intervals). For example, in January 1985 the annual rate on a three-month T-bill was 7.76% and the annual rate on a 30-year government bond was 11.45%. Use regression to determine which interest rates tend to move together most closely. (Source: International Investment and Exchange Database. Developed by Craig Holden, Indiana University School of Business)

59. The Keynesian school of macroeconomics believes that increased government spending leads to increased growth. The file P11_59.xlsx contains the following annual data:

   ■ Government spending as percentage of GDP (gross domestic product)

   ■ Percentage annual growth in annual GDP

Are these data consistent with the Keynesian school of economics? (Source: *Wall Street Journal*)

60. The June 1997 issue of *Management Accounting* gave the following rule for predicting your current salary if you are a managerial accountant. Take $31,865. Next, add $20,811 if you are top management, add $3604 if you are senior management, or subtract $11,419 if you are entry management. Then add $1105 for every year you have been a managerial accountant. Add $7600 if you have a master's degree or subtract $12,467 if you have no college degree. Add $11,257 if you have a professional certification. Finally, add $8667 if you are male.

   a. How do you think the journal derived this method of predicting an accountant's current salary? Be specific.

   b. How could a managerial accountant use this information to determine whether he or she is significantly underpaid?

61. A business school committee was charged with studying admissions criteria to the school. Until that time, only juniors were admitted. Part of the committee's task was to see whether freshman courses would be equally good predictors of success as freshman and sophomore courses combined. Here, we take "success" to mean doing well in I-core (the integrated core, a combination of the junior level finance, marketing, and operations courses, F301, M301, and P301). The file P11_61.xlsx contains data on 250 students who had just completed I-core. For each student, the file lists their grades in the following courses:

- M118 (freshman)—finite math
- M119 (freshman)—calculus
- K201 (freshman)—computers
- W131 (freshman)—writing
- E201, E202 (sophomore)—micro- and macroeconomics
- L201 (sophomore)—business law
- A201, A202 (sophomore)—accounting
- E270 (sophomore)—statistics
- I-core (junior)—finance, marketing, and operations

Except for I-core, each value is a grade point for a specific course (such as 3.7 for an A−). For I-core, each value is the average grade point for the three courses comprising I-core.

a. The I-core grade point is the eventual dependent variable in a regression analysis. Look at the correlations between all variables. Is multicollinearity likely to be a problem? Why or why not?

b. Run a multiple regression using all of the potential explanatory variables. Now, eliminate the variables as follows. (This is a reasonable variation of the procedures discussed in the chapter.) Look at 95% confidence intervals for their coefficients (as usual, not counting the intercept term). Any variable whose confidence interval contains the value zero is a candidate for exclusion. For all such candidates, eliminate the variable with the t-value lowest in magnitude. Then rerun the regression, and use the same procedure to possibly exclude another variable. Keep doing this until 95% confidence intervals of the coefficients of all remaining variables do *not* include zero. Report this final equation, its R^2 value, and its standard error of estimate s_e.

c. Give a quick summary of the properties of the final equation in part **b**. Specifically, (1) do the variables have the "correct" signs, (2) which courses tend to be the best predictors, (3) are the predictions from this equation likely to be much good, and (4) are there any obvious violations of the regression assumptions?

d. Redo part **b**, but now use as your potential explanatory variables only courses taken in the freshman year. As in part **b**, report the final equation, its R^2, and its standard error of estimate s_e.

e. Briefly, do you think there is enough predictive power in the freshman courses, relative to the freshman and sophomore courses combined, to change to a sophomore admit policy? (Answer only on the basis of the regression results; don't get into other merits of the argument.)

62. The file P11_62.xlsx has (somewhat old) data on several countries. The variables are listed here.

- Country: name of country
- GNPCapita: GNP per capita
- PopGrowth: average annual percentage change in population, 1980–1990
- Calorie: daily per capita calorie content of food used for domestic consumption
- LifeExp: average life expectancy of newborn given current mortality conditions
- Fertility: births per woman given current fertility rates

With data such as these, cause and effect are difficult to determine. For example, does low LifeExp cause GNPCapita to be low, or vice versa? Therefore, the purpose of this problem is to experiment with the following sets of dependent and explanatory variables. In each case, look at scatterplots (and use economic reasoning) to find and estimate the best form of the equation, using only linear and logarithmic variables. Then interpret precisely what each equation is saying.

a. Dependent: LifeExp; Explanatories: Calorie, Fertility

b. Dependent: LifeExp; Explanatories: GNPCapita, PopGrowth

c. Dependent: GNPCapita; Explanatories: PopGrowth, Calorie, Fertility

63. Suppose that an economist has been able to gather data on the relationship between demand and price for a particular product. After analyzing scatterplots and using economic theory, the economist decides to estimate an equation of the form $Q = aP^b$, where Q is quantity demanded and P is price. An appropriate regression analysis is then performed, and the estimated parameters turn out to be $a = 1000$ and $b = -1.3$. Now consider two scenarios: (1) the price increases from $10 to $12.50; (2) the price increases from $20 to $25.

a. Do you predict the percentage decrease in demand to be the same in scenario 1 as in scenario 2? Why or why not?

b. What is the predicted percentage decrease in demand in scenario 1? What about scenario 2? Be as exact as possible. (*Hint*: Remember from economics that an elasticity shows directly what happens for a "small" percentage change in price. These changes aren't that small, so you'll have to do some calculating.)

64. A human resources analyst believes that in a particular industry, the wage rate ($/hr) is related to seniority by an equation of the form $W = ae^{bS}$, where W equals wage rate and S equals seniority (in years). However, the analyst suspects that both parameters, a and b, might depend on whether the workers belong to a union. Therefore, the analyst gathers data on a number of workers, both union and nonunion, and estimates the following equation with regression:

$$\ln(W) = 2.14 + 0.027S + 0.12U + 0.006SU$$

Here $\ln(W)$ is the natural log of W, U is 1 for union workers and 0 for nonunion workers, and SU is the product of S and U.

a. According to this model, what is the predicted wage rate for a nonunion worker with 0 years of seniority? What is it for a union worker with 0 years of seniority?

b. Explain exactly what this equation implies about the predicted effect of seniority on wage rate for a nonunion worker and for a union worker.

65. A company has recorded its overhead costs, machine hours, and labor hours for the past 60 months. The data are in the file P11_65.xlsx. The company decides to use regression to explain its overhead hours linearly as a function of machine hours and labor hours. However, recognizing good statistical practice, it decides to estimate a regression equation for the first 36 months and then validate this regression with the data from the last 24 months. That is, it will substitute the values of machine and labor hours from the last 24 months into the regression equation that is based on the first 36 months and see how well it does.

a. Run the regression for the first 36 months. Explain briefly why the coefficient of labor hours is not significant.

b. For this part, use the regression equation from part **a** with both variables still in the equation (even though one was insignificant). Fill in the fitted and residual columns for months 37 through 60. Then do relevant calculations to see whether the R^2 (or multiple R) and the standard error of estimate s_e are as good for these 24 months as they are for the first 36 months. Explain your results briefly. (*Hint*: Remember the meaning of the multiple R and the standard error of estimate.)

66. Pernavik Dairy produces and sells a wide range of dairy products. Because most of the dairy's costs and prices are set by a government regulatory board, most of the competition between the dairy and its competitors takes place through advertising. The controller of Pernavik has developed the sales and advertising levels for the last 52 weeks. These appear in the file P11_66.xlsx. Note that the advertising levels for the three weeks prior to week 1 are also listed. The controller wonders whether Pernavik is spending too much money on advertising. He argues that the company's contribution-margin ratio is about 10%. That is, 10% of each sales dollar goes toward covering fixed costs. This means that each advertising dollar has to generate at least $10 of sales or the advertising is not cost-effective. Use regression to determine whether advertising dollars are generating this type of sales response. (*Hint*: It is very possible that the sales value in any week is affected not only by advertising this week, but also by advertising levels in the past one, two, or three weeks. These are called *lagged* values of advertising. Try regression models with lagged values of advertising included, and see whether you get better results.)

67. The Pierce Company manufactures drill bits. The production of the drill bits occurs in lots of 1000 units. Due to the intense competition in the industry and the correspondingly low prices, Pierce has undertaken a study of the manufacturing costs of each of the products it manufactures. One part of this study concerns the overhead costs associated with producing the drill bits. Senior production personnel have determined that the number of lots produced, the direct labor hours used, and the number of production runs per month might help to explain the behavior of overhead costs. The file P11_67.xlsx contains the data on these variables for the past 36 months.

a. How well can you can predict overhead costs on the basis of these variables with a linear regression equation? Why might you be disappointed with the results?

b. A production supervisor believes that labor hours and the number of production run setups affect overhead because Pierce uses a lot of supplies when it is working on the machines and because the machine setup time for each run is charged to overhead. As he says, "When the rate of production increases, we use overtime until we can train the additional people that we require for the machines. When the rate of production falls, we incur idle time until the surplus workers are transferred to other parts of the plant. So it would seem to me that there will be an additional overhead cost whenever the level of production changes. I would also say that because of the nature of this rescheduling process, the bigger the change in production, the greater the effect of the change in production on the increase in overhead." How might you use this information to find a better regression equation than in part **a**? (*Hint*: Develop a new explanatory variable, and assume that the number of lots produced in the month preceding month 1 was 5964.)

68. Danielson Electronics manufactures color television sets for sale in a highly competitive marketplace. Recently Ron Thomas, the marketing manager of Danielson Electronics, has been complaining that the company is losing market share because of a poor-quality image, and he has asked that the company's major product, the 25-inch console model, be redesigned to incorporate a higher quality level. The company general manager, Steve Hatting, is considering the request to improve the product quality but is not convinced that consumers will be willing to pay the additional expense for improved quality. As the company controller, you are in charge of determining the cost-effectiveness of improving the quality of the television sets. With the help of the marketing staff, you have obtained a summary of the average retail price of the company's television set and the prices of 29 competitive sets. In addition, you have obtained from *The Shoppers' Guide,* a magazine that evaluates and reports on various consumer products, a quality rating of the television sets produced by Danielson Electronics and its competitors. The file P11_68.xlsx summarizes these data. According to *The Shoppers' Guide,* the quality rating, which varies from 0 to 10 (10 being the highest level of quality), considers such factors as the quality of the picture, the frequency of repair, and the cost of repairs. Discussions with the product design group suggest that the cost of manufacturing this type of television set is $125 + Q^2$, where Q is the quality rating.

a. Regress Average Price versus Quality Rating. Does the regression equation imply that customers are willing to pay a premium for quality? Explain.

b. Given the results from part **a**, is there a preferred level of quality for this product? Assume that the quality level will affect only the price charged and not the level of sales of the product.

c. How might you answer part **b** if the level of sales is also affected by the quality level (or alternatively, if the level of sales is affected by price)?

69. The file P11_69.xlsx contains data on gasoline consumption and several economic variables. The variables are gasoline consumption for passenger cars (GasUsed), service station price excluding taxes (SSPrice), retail price of gasoline including state and federal taxes (RPrice), Consumer Price Index for all items (CPI), Consumer Price Index for public transportation (CPIT), number of registered passenger cars (Cars), average miles traveled per gallon (MPG), and real per capita disposable income (DispInc).

a. Regress GasUsed linearly versus CPIT, Cars, MPG, DispInc, and DefRPrice, where DefRPrice is the deflated retail price of gasoline (RPrice divided by CPI). What signs would you expect the coefficients to have? Do they have these signs? Which of the coefficients are statistically significant at the 5% significance level?

b. Suppose the government makes the claim that for every one cent of tax on gasoline, there will be a $1 billion increase in tax revenue. Use the estimated equation in part **a** to support or refute the government's claim.

70. On October 30, 1995, the citizens of Quebec went to the polls to decide the future of their province. They were asked to vote "Yes" or "No" on whether Quebec, a predominantly French-speaking province, should secede from Canada and become a sovereign country. The "No" side was declared the winner, but only by a thin margin. Immediately following the vote, however, allegations began to surface that the result was closer than it should have been. (Source: Cawley and Sommers (1996)). In particular, the ruling separatist Parti Québécois, whose job was to decide which ballots were rejected, was accused by the "No" voters of systematic electoral fraud by voiding thousands of "No" votes in the predominantly allophone and anglophone electoral divisions of Montreal. (An *allophone* refers to someone whose first language is neither English nor French. An *anglophone* refers to someone whose first language is English.)

Cawley and Sommers examined whether electoral fraud had been committed by running a regression, using data from the 125 electoral divisions in the October 1995 referendum. The dependent variable was REJECT, the percentage of rejected ballots in the electoral division. The explanatory variables were as follows:

- ALLOPHONE: percentage of allophones in the electoral division
- ANGLOPHONE: percentage of anglophones in the electoral division
- REJECT94: percentage of rejected votes from that electoral division during a similar referendum in 1994
- LAVAL: dummy variable equal to 1 for electoral divisions in the Laval region, 0 otherwise
- LAV_ALL: interaction (i.e., product) of LAVAL and ALLOPHONE

The estimated regression equation (with *t*-values in parentheses) is

$$\text{Prediced REJECT} = \underset{(5.68)}{1.112} + \underset{(4.34)}{0.020 \text{ ALLOPHONE}}$$

$$+ \underset{(0.12)}{0.001 \text{ ANGLOPHONE}} + \underset{(2.64)}{0.223 \text{ REJECT94}}$$

$$- \underset{(-8.61)}{3.773 \text{ LAVAL}} + \underset{(15.62)}{0.387 \text{ LAV\_ALL}}$$

The R^2 value was 0.759. Based on this analysis, Cawley and Sommers state that, "The evidence presented here suggests that there were voting irregularities in the October 1995 Quebec referendum, especially in Laval." Discuss how they came to this conclusion.

71. Suppose you are trying to explain variations in salaries for technicians in a particular field of work. The file P11_71.xlsx contains annual salaries for 200 technicians.

It also shows how many years of experience each technician has, as well as his or her education level. There are four education levels, as explained in the comment in cell D1. Three suggestions are put forth for the relationship between Salary and these two explanatory variables:

- You should regress Salary linearly versus the two given variables, YrsExper and EducLev.
- All that really matters in terms of education is whether the person got a college degree or not. Therefore, you should regress Salary linearly versus YrsExper and a dummy variable indicating whether he or she got a college degree.
- Each level of education might result in different jumps in salary. Therefore, you should regress Salary linearly versus YrsExper and dummy variables for the different education levels.

a. Run the indicated regressions for each of these three suggestions. Then (1) explain what each equation is saying and how the three are different (focus here on the coefficients), (2) which you prefer, and (3) whether (or how) the regression results in your preferred equation contradict the average salary results shown in the Pivot Table sheet of the file.

b. Consider the four workers shown on the Prediction sheet of the file. (These are four new workers, not among the original 200.) Using your preferred equation, calculate a predicted salary and a 95% prediction interval for each of these four workers.

c. It turns out (you don't have to check this) that the interaction between years of experience and education level is *not* significant for this data set. In general, however, argue why you might expect an interaction between them for salary data of technical workers. What form of interaction would you suspect? (There is not necessarily one right answer, but argue convincingly one way or the other for a positive or a negative interaction.)

72. The file P03_55.xlsx contains baseball data on all MLB teams from during the years 2004–2009. For each year and team, the total salary and the number of (regular-season) wins are listed.

a. Rearrange the data so that there are six columns: Team, Year, Salary Last Year, Salary This Year, Wins Last Year, and Wins This Year. You don't need rows for 2004 rows, because the data for 2003 isn't available for Salary Last Year and Wins Last Year. Your ending data set should have 5*30 rows of data.

b. Run a multiple regression for Wins This Year versus the other variables (besides Team). Then run a forward stepwise regression with these same

variables. Compare the two equations, and explain exactly what the coefficients of the equation from the forward method imply about wins.

c. The Year variable *should* be insignificant. Is it? Why would it be contradictory for the "true" coefficient of Year to be anything other than zero?

d. Statistical inference from regression equations is all about inferring from the given data to a larger population. Does it make sense to talk about a larger population in this situation? If so, what is the larger population?

73. Do the previous problem, but use the basketball data on all NBA teams in the file P03_56.xlsx.

74. Do the previous problem, but use the football data on all NFL teams in the file P03_57.xlsx.

75. The file P03_65.xlsx contains basketball data on all NBA teams for five seasons. The SRS (simple rating system) variable is a measure of how good a team is in any given year. (It is explained in more detail in the comment in cell F3.)

a. Given the explanation of SRS, it makes sense to use multiple regression, with PTS and O_PTS as the explanatory variables, to predict SRS. Do you get a good fit?

b. Suppose instead that the goal is to predict Wins. Try multiple regression, using the variables in columns G–AH or variables calculated from them. For example, instead of FG and FGA, you could try FG/FGA, the fraction of attempted field goals made. You will have to guard against exact multicollinearity. For example, PTS can be calculated exactly from FG, 3P, and FT. This is a good time to use some form of stepwise regression. How well is your best equation able to predict Wins?

76. Do the preceding problem, but now use the football data in the file P03_66.xlsx. (This file contains offensive and defensive ratings in the OSRS and DSRS variables, but you can ignore them for this problem. Focus only on the SRS rating in part **a**.)

77. The file P03_63.xlsx contains 2009 data on R&D expenses and many financial variables for 85 U.S. publicly traded companies in the computer and electronic product manufacturing industry. The question is whether R&D expenses can be predicted from any combination of the potential variables. Use scatterplots, correlations (possibly on nonlinear transformations of variables) to search for promising relationships. Eventually, find a regression that seems to provide the best explanatory power for R&D expenses. Interpret this best equation and indicate how good a fit it provides.

The Artsy Corporation has been sued in U.S. Federal Court on charges of sex discrimination in employment under Title VII of the Civil Rights Act of 1964.[10] The litigation at contention here is a class-action lawsuit brought on behalf of all females who were employed by the company, or who had applied for work with the company, between 1979 and 1987. Artsy operates in several states, runs four quite distinct businesses, and has many different types of employees. The allegations of the plaintiffs deal with issues of hiring, pay, promotions, and other "conditions of employment."

In such large class-action employment discrimination lawsuits, it has become common for statistical evidence to play a central role in the determination of guilt or damages. In an interesting twist on typical legal procedures, a precedent has developed in these cases that plaintiffs may make a prima facie case purely in terms of circumstantial statistical evidence. If that statistical evidence is reasonably strong, the burden of proof shifts to the defendants to rebut the plaintiffs' statistics with other data, other analyses of the same data, or nonstatistical testimony. In practice, statistical arguments often dominate the proceedings of such Equal Employment Opportunity (EEO) cases. Indeed, in this case the statistical data used as evidence filled numerous computer tapes, and the supporting statistical analysis comprised thousands of pages of printouts and reports. We work here with a typical subset that pertains to one contested issue at one of the company's locations.

The data in the file Artsy Lawsuit.xlsx relate to the pay of 256 employees on the hourly payroll at one of the company's production facilities. The data include an identification number (ID) that would identify the person by name or social security number; the person's gender (Gender), where 0 denotes female and 1 denotes male; the person's job grade in 1986 (Grade); the length of time (in years) the person had been in that job grade as of December 31, 1986 (TInGrade); and the person's weekly pay rate as of December 31, 1986 (Rate). These data permit a statistical examination of one of the issues in the case—fair pay for female employees. We deal with one of three pay classes of employees—those on the biweekly payroll at one of the company's locations at Pocahantas, Maine.

The plaintiffs' attorneys have proposed settling the pay issues in the case for this group of female employees for a "back pay" lump payment to female employees of 25% of their pay during the period 1979 to 1987. It is your task to examine the data statistically for evidence in favor of, or against, the charges. You are to advise the lawyers for the company on how to proceed. Consider the following issues as they have been laid out to you by the attorneys representing the firm:

1. Overall, how different is pay by gender? Are the differences in pay statistically significant? Does a statistical significance test have meaning in a case like this? If so, how should it be performed? Lay out as succinctly as possible the arguments that you anticipate the plaintiffs will make with this data set.

2. The company wishes to argue that a legitimate explanation of the pay-rate differences may be the difference in job grades. (In this analysis, we will tacitly assume that each person's job grade is, in fact, appropriate for him or her, even though the plaintiffs' attorneys have charged that females have been unfairly kept in the lower grades. Other statistical data, not available here, are used in that analysis.) The lawyers ask, "Is there a relatively easy way to understand, analyze, and display the pay differences by job grade? Is it easy enough that it could be presented to an average jury without confusing them?" Again, use the data to anticipate the possible arguments of the plaintiffs. To what extent does job grade appear to explain the pay-rate differences between the genders? Propose and carry out appropriate hypothesis tests or confidence intervals to check whether the difference in pay between genders is statistically significant within each of the grades.

[9]This case was contributed by Peter Kolesar from Columbia University.
[10]Artsy is an actual corporation, and the data given in this case are real, but the name has been changed to protect the firm's true identity.

3. In the actual case, the previous analysis suggested to the attorneys that differences in pay rates are due, at least in part, to differences in job grades. They had heard that in another EEO case, the dependence of pay rate on job grade had been investigated with regression analysis. Perform a simple linear regression of pay rate on job grade for them. Interpret the results fully. Is the regression significant? How much of the variability in pay does job grade account for? Carry out a full check of the quality of your regression. What light does this shed on the pay fairness issue? Does it help or hurt the company? Is it fair to the female employees?

4. It is argued that seniority within a job grade should be taken into account because the company's written pay policy explicitly calls for the consideration of this factor. How different are times in grade by gender? Are they enough to matter?

5. The Artsy legal team wants an analysis of the simultaneous influence of grade and time in grade on pay. Perform a multiple regression of pay rate versus grade and time in grade. Is the regression significant? How much of the variability in pay rates is explained by this model? Will this analysis help your clients? Could the plaintiffs effectively attack it? Consider residuals in your analysis of these issues.

6. Organize your analyses and conclusions in a brief report summarizing your findings for your client, the Artsy Corporation. Be complete but succinct. Be sure to advise them on the settlement issue. Be as forceful as you can be in arguing "the Artsy Case" without misusing the data or statistical theory. Apprise your client of the risks they face, by showing them the forceful and legitimate counterargument the female plaintiffs could make. ■

Dupree Fuels Company is facing a difficult problem. Dupree sells heating oil to residential customers. Given the amount of competition in the industry, both from other home heating oil suppliers and from electric and natural gas utilities, the price of the oil supplied and the level of service are critical in determining a company's success. Unlike electric and natural gas customers, oil customers are exposed to the risk of running out of fuel. Home heating oil suppliers therefore have to guarantee that the customer's oil tank will not be allowed to run dry. In fact, Dupree's service pledge is, "50 free gallons on us if we let you run dry." Beyond the cost of the oil, however, Dupree is concerned about the perceived reliability of his service if a customer is allowed to run out of oil.

To estimate customer oil use, the home heating oil industry uses the concept of a *degree-day*, equal to the difference between the average daily temperature and 68 degrees Fahrenheit. So if the average temperature on a given day is 50, the degree-days for that day will be 18. (If the degree-day calculation results in a negative number, the degree-day number is recorded as 0.) By keeping track of the number of degree-days since the customer's last oil fill, knowing the size of the customer's oil tank, and estimating the customer's oil consumption as a function of the number of degree-days, the oil supplier can estimate when the customer is getting low on fuel and then resupply the customer.

Dupree has used this scheme in the past but is disappointed with the results and the computational burdens it places on the company. First, the system requires that a consumption-per-degree-day figure be estimated for each customer to reflect that customer's consumption habits, size of home, quality of home insulation, and family size. Because Dupree has more than 1500 customers, the computational burden of keeping track of all of these customers is enormous. Second, the system is crude and unreliable. The consumption per degree-day for each customer is computed by dividing the oil consumption during the preceding year by the degree-days during the preceding year. Customers have tended to use less fuel than estimated during the colder months and more fuel than estimated during the warmer months. This means that Dupree is making more deliveries than necessary during the colder months and customers are running out of oil during the warmer months.

Dupree wants to develop a consumption estimation model that is practical and more reliable. The following data are available in the file **Dupree Fuels.xlsx**:

- The number of degree-days since the last oil fill and the consumption amounts for 40 customers.

- The number of people residing in the homes of each of the 40 customers. Dupree thinks that this might be important in predicting the oil consumption of customers using oil-fired water heaters because it provides an estimate of the hot-water requirements of each customer. Each of the customers in this sample uses an oil-fired water heater.

- An assessment, provided by Dupree sales staff, of the home type of each of these 40 customers. The home type classification, which is a number between 1 and 5, is a composite index of the home size, age, exposure to wind, level of insulation, and furnace type. A low index implies a lower oil consumption per degree-day, and a high index implies a higher consumption of oil per degree-day. Dupree thinks that the use of such an index will allow them to estimate a consumption model based on a sample data set and then to apply the same model to predict the oil demand of each of his customers.

Use regression to see whether a statistically reliable oil consumption model can be estimated from the data. ■

---

[11]Case Studies 11.2 through 11.4 are based on problems from *Advanced Management Accounting*, 2nd edition, by Robert S. Kaplan and Anthony A. Atkinson, 1989, Upper Saddle River, NJ: Prentice Hall. We thank them for allowing us to adapt their problems.

The Gunderson Plant manufactures the industrial product line of FGT Industries. Plant management wants to be able to get a good, yet quick, estimate of the manufacturing overhead costs that can be expected each month. The easiest and simplest method to accomplish this task is to develop a flexible budget formula for the manufacturing overhead costs. The plant's accounting staff has suggested that simple linear regression be used to determine the behavior pattern of the overhead costs. The regression data can provide the basis for the flexible budget formula. Sufficient evidence is available to conclude that manufacturing overhead costs vary with direct labor hours. The actual direct labor hours and the corresponding manufacturing overhead costs for each month of the last three years have been used in the linear regression analysis.

The three-year period contained various occurrences not uncommon to many businesses. During the first year, production was severely curtailed during two months due to wildcat strikes. In the second year, production was reduced in one month because of material shortages, and increased significantly (scheduled overtime) during two months to meet the units required for a one-time sales order. At the end of the second year, employee benefits were raised significantly as the result of a labor agreement. Production during the third year was not affected by any special circumstances. Various members of Gunderson's accounting staff raised some issues regarding the historical data collected for the regression analysis. These issues were as follows.

■ Some members of the accounting staff believed that the use of data from all 36 months would provide a more accurate portrayal of the cost behavior. While they recognized that any of the monthly data could include efficiencies and inefficiencies, they believed these efficiencies and inefficiencies would tend to balance out over a longer period of time.

■ Other members of the accounting staff suggested that only those months that were considered normal should be used so that the regression would not be distorted.

■ Still other members felt that only the most recent 12 months should be used because they were the most current.

■ Some members questioned whether historical data should be used at all to form the basis for a flexible budget formula.

The accounting department ran two regression analyses of the data—one using the data from all 36 months and the other using only the data from the last 12 months. The information derived from the two linear regressions is shown below (t-values shown in parentheses). The 36-month regression is

$$OH_t = 123,810 + 1.60 \, DLH_t, \quad R^2 = 0.32$$
$$(1.64)$$

The 12-month regression is

$$OH_t = 109,020 + 3.00 \, DLH_t, \quad R^2 = 0.48$$
$$(3.01)$$

Questions

1. Which of the two results (12 months versus 36 months) would you use as a basis for the flexible budget formula?

2. How would the four specific issues raised by the members of Gunderson's accounting staff influence your willingness to use the results of the statistical analyses as the basis for the flexible budget formula? Explain your answer. ■

Wagner Printers performs all types of printing, including custom work, such as advertising displays, and standard work, such as business cards. Market prices exist for standard work, and Wagner Printers must match or better these prices to get the business. The key issue is whether the existing market price covers the cost associated with doing the work. On the other hand, most of the custom work must be priced individually. Because all custom work is done on a job-order basis, Wagner routinely keeps track of all the direct labor and direct materials costs associated with each job. However, the overhead for each job must be estimated. The overhead is applied to each job using a predetermined (normalized) rate based on estimated overhead and labor hours. Once the cost of the prospective job is determined, the sales manager develops a bid that reflects both the existing market conditions and the estimated price of completing the job.

In the past, the normalized rate for overhead has been computed by using the historical average of overhead per direct labor hour. Wagner has become increasingly concerned about this practice for two reasons. First, it hasn't produced accurate forecasts of overhead in the past. Second, technology has changed the printing process, so that the labor content of jobs has been decreasing, and the normalized rate of overhead per direct labor hour has steadily been increasing. The file **Wagner Printers.xlsx** shows the overhead data that Wagner has collected for its shop for the past 52 weeks. The average weekly overhead for the last 52 weeks is $54,208, and the average weekly number of labor hours worked is 716. Therefore, the normalized rate for overhead that will be used in the upcoming week is about $76 (= 54208/716) per direct labor hour.

Questions

1. Determine whether you can develop a more accurate estimate of overhead costs.

2. Wagner is now preparing a bid for an important order that may involve a considerable amount of repeat business. The estimated requirements for this project are 15 labor hours, 8 machine hours, $150 direct labor cost, and $750 direct material cost. Using the existing approach to cost estimation, Wagner has estimated the cost for this job as $2040 (= 150 + 750 + (76 × 15)). Given the existing data, what cost would you estimate for this job? ■

Time Series Analysis and Forecasting

Monkeybusinessimages/Dreamstime.com

REVENUE MANAGEMENT AT HARRAH'S CHEROKEE CASINO & HOTEL

Real applications of forecasting are almost never done in isolation. They are typically one part—a crucial part—of an overall quantitative solution to a business problem. This is certainly the case at Harrah's Cherokee Casino & Hotel in North Carolina, as explained in an article by Metters et al. (2008). This particular casino uses revenue management (RM) on a daily basis to increase its revenue from its gambling customers. As customers call to request reservations at the casino's hotel, the essential problem is to decide which reservations to accept and which to deny. The idea is that there is an opportunity cost from accepting early requests from lower-valued customers because higher-valued customers might request the same rooms later on.

As the article explains, there are several unique features about casinos, and this casino in particular, that make a quantitative approach to RM successful. First, the detailed behaviors of customers can be tracked, via electronic cards they use while placing bets in the electronic gambling machines, so that the casino can create a large database of individual customers' gambling patterns. This allows the casino to segment the customers into different groups, based on how much they typically bet in a given night. For example, one segment might contain all customers who bet between $500 and $600 per night. When a customer calls for a room reservation and provides his card number, the casino can immediately look up his information in the database and see which segment he is in.

A second reason for the successful use of RM is that customers differ substantially in the price they are willing to pay for the same commodity, a stay at the casino's hotel. Actually, many don't pay anything for the room or the food—these are frequently complimentary from the casino—but they pay by losing money at gambling. Some customers typically gamble thousands of dollars per night while others gamble much less. (This is quite different from the disparities in other hotels or in air travel, where a business traveler might pay twice as much as a vacationer, but not much more.) Because some customers are much more valuable than others, there are real opportunity costs from treating all customers alike.

A third reason for the success of RM at this casino is that the casino can afford to hold out for the best-paying customers until the last minute. The reason is that a significant percentage of the customers from all segments wait until the last minute to make their reservations. In fact, they often make them while driving, say, from Atlanta to the casino. Therefore, the casino can afford to deny requests for reservations to lower-valued customers made a day or two in advance, knowing that last-minute reservations, very possibly from higher-valued customers, will fill up the casino's rooms. Indeed, the occupancy rate is virtually always 98% or above.

The overall RM solution includes (1) data collection and customer segmentation, as explained above, (2) forecasting demand for reservations from each customer segment, (3) a linear programming (LP) optimization model that is run frequently to decide which reservations to accept, and (4) a customer relationship management model to entice loyal customers to book rooms on nights with lower demand. The forecasting model is very similar to the Winters' exponential smoothing model discussed in this chapter. Specifically, the model uses the large volume of historical data to forecast customer demand by each customer segment for any particular night in the future. These forecasts include information about time-related or seasonal patterns (weekends are busier, for example) and any special events that are scheduled. Also, the forecasts are updated daily as the night in question approaches. These forecasts are then used in an LP optimization model to determine which requests to approve. For example, the LP model might indicate that, given the current status of bookings and three nights to go, requests for rooms on the specified night should be accepted only for the four most valuable customer segments. As the given night approaches and the number of booked rooms changes, the LP model is rerun many times and provides staff with the necessary information for real-time decisions. (By the way, a customer who is refused a room at the casino is often given a free room at another nearby hotel. After all, this customer can still be valuable enough to offset the price of the room at the other hotel.)

It is difficult to measure the effect of this entire RM system because it has always been in place since the casino opened. But there is no doubt that it is effective. Despite the fact that it serves no alcohol and has only electronic games, not the traditional gaming tables, the casino has nearly full occupancy and returns a 60% profit margin on gross revenue—double the industry norm. ■

12.1 INTRODUCTION

Many decision-making applications depend on a forecast of some quantity. Here are several examples.

Examples of Forecasting Applications

* When a service organization, such as a fast-food restaurant, plans its staffing over some time period, it must forecast the customer demand as a function of time. This might be done at a very detailed level, such as the demand in successive 15-minute periods, or at a more aggregate level, such as the demand in successive weeks.

* When a company plans its ordering or production schedule for a product it sells to the public, it must forecast the customer demand for this product so that it can stock appropriate quantities—neither too many nor too few.

* When an organization plans to invest in stocks, bonds, or other financial instruments, it typically attempts to forecast movements in stock prices and interest rates.

* When government officials plan policy, they attempt to forecast movements in macroeconomic variables such as inflation, interest rates, and unemployment.

Unfortunately, forecasting is a very difficult task, both in the short run and in the long run. Typically, forecasts are based on historical data. Analysts search for patterns or relationships in the historical data, and then make forecasts. There are two problems with this approach. The first is that it is not always easy to uncover historical patterns or relationships. In particular, it is often difficult to separate the noise, or random behavior, from the underlying patterns. Some forecasts can even overdo it, by attributing importance to patterns that are in fact random variations and are unlikely to repeat themselves.

The second problem is that there are no guarantees that past patterns will continue in the future. A new war could break out somewhere in the world, a company's competitor could introduce a new product into the market, the bottom could fall out of the stock market, and so on. Each of these shocks to the system being studied could drastically alter the future in a highly unpredictable way. This partly explains why forecasts are almost always wrong. Unless they have inside information to the contrary, analysts must assume that history will repeat itself. But we all know that history does *not* always repeat itself. Therefore, there are many famous forecasts that turned out to be way off the mark, even though the analysts made reasonable assumptions and used standard forecasting techniques. Nevertheless, forecasts are required throughout the business world, so fear of failure is no excuse for not giving it our best effort.

12.2 FORECASTING METHODS: AN OVERVIEW

There are many forecasting methods available, and all practitioners have their favorites. To say the least, there is little agreement among practitioners or academics as to the best forecasting method. The methods can generally be divided into three groups: (1) *judgmental* methods, (2) *extrapolation* (or *time series*) methods, and (3) *econometric* (or *causal*) methods. The first of these is basically nonquantitative and will not be discussed here; the last two are quantitative. In this section we describe extrapolation and econometric methods in some generality. In the rest of the chapter, we go into more detail, particularly about the extrapolation methods.

12.2.1 Extrapolation Methods

Extrapolation methods are quantitative methods that use past data of a time series variable—and nothing else, except possibly time itself—to forecast future values of the variable. The idea is that past movements of a variable, such as company sales or U.S. exports to Japan, can be used to forecast future values of the variable. Many extrapolation methods are available, including trend-based regression, autoregression, moving averages, and exponential smoothing. Some of these methods are relatively simple, both conceptually and in terms of the calculations required, whereas others are quite complex. Also, as the names imply, some of these methods use the same regression methods from the previous two chapters, whereas others do not.

All of these extrapolation methods search for *patterns* in the historical series and then extrapolate these patterns into the future. Some try to track long-term upward or downward trends and then project these. Some try to track the seasonal patterns (such as sales up in November and December, down in other months) and then project these. Basically, the more complex the method, the more closely it tries to track historical patterns. Researchers have long believed that good forecasting methods should be able to track the ups and downs—the zigzags on a graph—of a time series. This has led to voluminous research and increasingly complex methods. But is complexity always better?

Surprisingly, empirical evidence shows that complexity is *not* always better. This is documented in a quarter-century review article by Armstrong (1986) and an article by Schnarrs and Bavuso (1986). They document a number of empirical studies on literally thousands of time series forecasts where complex methods fared no better, and sometimes even worse, than simple methods. In fact, the Schnarrs and Bavuso article presents evidence that a naive forecast from a "random walk" model sometimes outperforms all of the more sophisticated extrapolation methods. This naive model forecasts that next period's value will be the same as this period's value. So if today's closing stock price is 51.375, it forecasts that tomorrow's closing stock price will be 51.375. This method is certainly simple, and it sometimes works quite well. We discuss random walks in more detail in section 12.5.

The evidence in favor of simpler models is not accepted by everyone, particularly not those who have spent years investigating complex models, and complex models continue to be studied and used. However, there is a very plausible reason why simple models can provide reasonably good forecasts. The whole goal of extrapolation methods is to extrapolate historical patterns into the future. But it is often difficult to determine which patterns are real and which represent noise—random ups and downs that are not likely to repeat themselves. Also, if something important changes (a competitor introduces a new product or there is an oil embargo, for example), it is certainly possible that historical patterns will change. A potential problem with complex methods is that they can track a historical series *too* closely. That is, they sometimes track patterns that are really noise. Simpler methods, on the other hand, track only the most basic underlying patterns and therefore can be more flexible and accurate in forecasting the future.

12.2.2 Econometric Models

Econometric models, also called **causal** or **regression-based** models, use regression to forecast a time series variable by using other explanatory time series variables. For example, a company might use a causal model to regress future sales on its advertising level, the population income level, the interest rate, and possibly others. In one sense, regression analysis involving time series variables is similar to the regression analysis discussed in the previous two chapters. The same least squares approach and the same multiple regression software can be used in many time series regression models. In fact, several examples and problems in the previous two chapters used time series data.

However, causal regression models for time series data present new mathematical challenges that go well beyond the level of this book. To get a glimpse of the potential difficulties, suppose a company wants to use a regression model to forecast its monthly sales for some product, using two other time series variables as predictors: its monthly advertising levels for the product and its main competitor's monthly advertising levels for a competing product. The resulting regression equation has the form

$$\text{Predicted } Y_t = a + b_1 X_{1t} + b_2 X_{2t} \tag{12.1}$$

Here, Y_t is the company's sales in month t, and X_{1t} and X_{2t} are, respectively, the company's and the competitor's advertising levels in month t. This regression model might provide some useful results, but there are some issues that must be faced.

One issue is that the appropriate "lags" for the regression equation must be determined. Do sales this month depend only on advertising levels *this* month, as specified in Equation (12.1), or also on advertising levels in the previous month, the previous two months, and so on? A second issue is whether to include lags of the *sales* variable in the regression equation as explanatory variables. Presumably, sales in one month might depend on the level of sales in previous months (as well as on advertising levels). A third issue is that the two advertising variables can be autocorrelated and cross-correlated. *Autocorrelation* means correlated with itself. For example, the company's advertising level in one month might depend on its advertising levels in previous months. *Cross-correlation* means being correlated with a lagged version of another variable. For example, the company's advertising level in one month might be related to the competitor's advertising levels in previous months, or the competitor's advertising in one month might be related to the company's advertising levels in previous months.

These are difficult issues, and the way in which they are addressed can make a big difference in the usefulness of the regression model. We will examine several regression-based models in this chapter, but we won't discuss situations such as the one just described, where one time series variable Y is regressed on one or more time series of Xs. [Pankratz (1991) is a good reference for these latter types of models. Unfortunately, the level of mathematics is considerably beyond the level in this book.]

12.2.3 Combining Forecasts

There is one other general forecasting method that is worth mentioning. In fact, it has attracted a lot of attention in recent years, and many researchers believe that it has potential for increasing forecast accuracy. The method is simple—it combines two or more forecasts to obtain the final forecast. The reasoning behind this method is also simple: The forecast errors from different forecasting methods might cancel one another. The forecasts that are combined can be of the same general type—extrapolation forecasts, for example—or they can be of different types, such as judgmental and extrapolation.

The *number* of forecasts to combine and the *weights* to use in combining them have been the subject of several research studies. Although the findings are not entirely consistent, it appears that the marginal benefit from each individual forecast after the first two or three is minor. Also, there is not much evidence to suggest that the simplest weighting scheme—weighting each forecast equally, that is, averaging them—is any less accurate than more complex weighting schemes.

12.2.4 Components of Time Series Data

In Chapter 2 we discussed time series graphs, a useful graphical way of displaying time series data. We now use these time series graphs to help explain and identify four important components of a time series. These components are called the *trend* component, the *seasonal* component, the *cyclic* component, and the *random* (or *noise*) component.

We start by looking at a very simple time series. This is a time series where every observation has the same value. Such a series is shown in Figure 12.1. The graph in this figure shows time (t) on the horizontal axis and the observed values (Y) on the vertical axis. We assume that Y is measured at regularly spaced intervals, usually days, weeks, months, quarters, or years, with Y_t being the value of the observation at time period t. As indicated in Figure 12.1, the individual observation points are usually joined by straight lines to make any patterns in the time series more apparent. Because all observations in this time series are equal, the resulting time series graph is a horizontal line. We refer to this time series as the *base* series. We will now illustrate more interesting time series built from this base series.

Figure 12.1

The Base Series

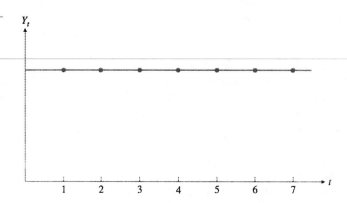

If the observations increase or decrease regularly through time, we say that the time series has a **trend**. The graphs in Figure 12.2 illustrate several possible trends. The *linear* trend in Figure 12.2a occurs if a company's sales increase by the same amount from period to period. This constant per period change is then the slope of the linear trend line. The curve in Figure 12.2b is an *exponential* trend. It occurs in a business such as the personal computer business, where sales have increased at a tremendous rate (at least during the 1990s, the boom years). For this type of curve, the *percentage* increase in Y_t from period to period remains constant. The curve in Figure 12.2c is an *S-shaped* trend. This type of trend is appropriate for a new product that takes a while to catch on, then exhibits a rapid increase in sales as the public becomes aware of it, and finally tapers off to a fairly constant

Figure 12.2 Series with Trends

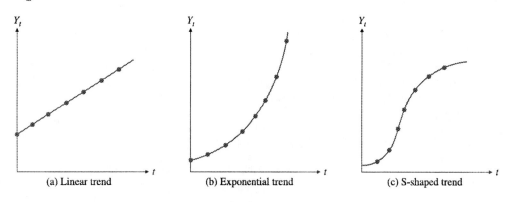

(a) Linear trend   (b) Exponential trend   (c) S-shaped trend

level because of market saturation. The series in Figure 12.2 all represent *upward* trends. Of course, there are *downward* trends of the same types.

Many time series have a **seasonal** component. For example, a company's sales of swimming pool equipment increase every spring, then stay relatively high during the summer, and then drop off until next spring, at which time the yearly pattern repeats itself. An important aspect of the seasonal component is that it tends to be predictable from one year to the next. That is, the *same* seasonal pattern tends to repeat itself every year.

Figure 12.3 illustrates two possible seasonal patterns. In Figure 12.3a there is nothing but the seasonal component. That is, if there were no seasonal variation, the series would be the base series in Figure 12.1. Figure 12.3b illustrates a seasonal pattern superimposed on a linear trend line.

Figure 12.3

Series with Seasonality

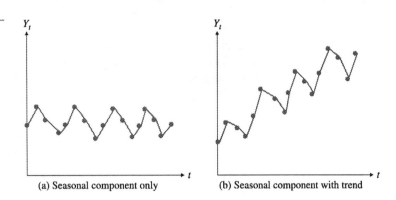

(a) Seasonal component only

(b) Seasonal component with trend

The third component of a time series is the **cyclic** component. By studying past movements of many business and economic variables, it becomes apparent that there are business cycles that affect many variables in similar ways. For example, during a recession housing starts generally go down, unemployment goes up, stock prices go down, and so on. But when the recession is over, all of these variables tend to move in the opposite direction. Unfortunately, the cyclic component is more difficult to predict than the seasonal component. The reason is that seasonal variation is much more regular. For example, swimming pool supplies sales *always* start to increase during the spring. Cyclic variation, on the other hand, is more irregular because the length of the business cycle varies, sometimes considerably. A further distinction is that the length of a seasonal cycle is generally one year; the length of a business cycle is generally longer than one year and its actual length is difficult to predict.

The graphs in Figure 12.4 illustrate the cyclic component of a time series. In Figure 12.4a cyclic variation is superimposed on the base series in Figure 12.1. In Figure 12.4b this same

Figure 12.4

Series with Cyclic Component

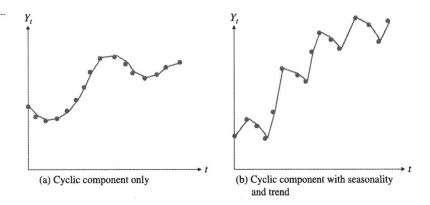

(a) Cyclic component only

(b) Cyclic component with seasonality and trend

cyclic variation is superimposed on the series in Figure 12.3b. The resulting graph has trend, seasonal variation, and cyclic variation.

The final component in a time series is called **random variation**, or simply **noise**. This unpredictable component gives most time series graphs their irregular, zigzag appearance. Usually, a time series can be determined only to a certain extent by its trend, seasonal, and cyclic components. Then other factors determine the rest. These other factors may be inherent randomness, unpredictable "shocks" to the system, the unpredictable behavior of human beings who interact with the system, and possibly others. These factors combine to create a certain amount of unpredictability in almost all time series.

Figures 12.5 and 12.6 show the effect that noise can have on a time series graph. The graph on the left of each figure shows the random component only, superimposed on the base series. Then on the right of each figure, the random component is superimposed on the trend-with-seasonal-component graph from Figure 12.3b. The difference between Figures 12.5 and 12.6 is the relative magnitude of the noise. When it is small, as in Figure 12.5, the other components emerge fairly clearly; they are not disguised by the noise. But if the noise is large in magnitude, as in Figure 12.6, the noise makes it very difficult to distinguish the other components.

Figure 12.5

Series with Noise

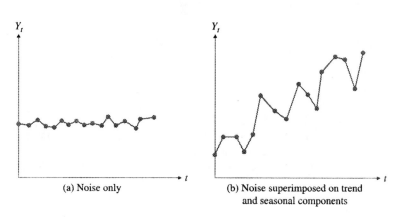

(a) Noise only

(b) Noise superimposed on trend and seasonal components

Figure 12.6

Series with More Noise

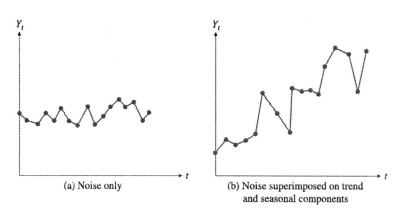

(a) Noise only

(b) Noise superimposed on trend and seasonal components

12.2.5 Measures of Accuracy

We now introduce some notation and discuss aspects common to most forecasting methods. In general, we let Y denote the variable of interest. Then Y_t denotes the observed value of Y at time t. Typically, the first observation (the most distant one) corresponds to period $t = 1$, and the last observation (the most recent one) corresponds to period $t = T$, where T denotes the number of historical observations of Y. The periods themselves might be days, weeks, months, quarters, years, or any other convenient unit of time.

Suppose that Y_{t-k} has just been observed and you want to make a "k-period-ahead" forecast; that is, you want to use the information through time $t - k$ to forecast Y_t. The resulting forecast is denoted by $F_{t-k,t}$. The first subscript indicates the period in which the forecast is made, and the second subscript indicates the period being forecast. As an example, if the data are monthly and September 2009 corresponds to $t = 67$, then a forecast of Y_{69}, the value in November 2009, would be labeled $F_{67,69}$. The **forecast error** is the difference between the actual value and the forecast. It is denoted by E with appropriate subscripts. Specifically, the forecast error associated with $F_{t-k,t}$ is

$$E_{t-k,t} = Y_t - F_{t-k,t}$$

This double-subscript notation is necessary to specify when the forecast is being made and which period is being forecast. However, the former is often clear from context. Therefore, to simplify the notation, we usually drop the first subscript and write F_t and E_t to denote the forecast of Y_t and the error in this forecast.

You first develop a model to fit the historical data. Then you use this model to forecast the future.

There are actually two steps in any forecasting procedure. The first step is to build a model that fits the historical data well. The second step is to use this model to forecast the future. Most of the work goes into the first step. For any trial model you see how well it "tracks" the known values of the time series. Specifically, the one-period-ahead forecasts, F_t (or more precisely, $F_{t-1,t}$) are calculated from the model, and these are compared to the known values, Y_t, for each t in the historical time period. The goal is to find a model that produces small forecast errors, E_t. Presumably, if the model tracks the *historical* data well, it will also forecast *future* data well. Of course, there is no guarantee that this is true, but it is often a reasonable assumption.

Forecasting software packages typically report several summary measures of the forecast errors. The most important of these are **MAE (mean absolute error)**, **RMSE (root mean square error)**, and **MAPE (mean absolute percentage error)**. These are defined in equations (12.2), (12.3), and (12.4). Fortunately, models that make any one of these measures small tend to make the others small, so you can choose whichever measure you want to minimize. In the following formulas, N denotes the number of terms in each sum. This value is typically slightly less than T, the number of historical observations, because it is usually not possible to provide a forecast for each historical period.

Mean Absolute Error

$$\text{MAE} = \left(\sum_{t=1}^{N} |E_t| \right) / N \tag{12.2}$$

Root Mean Square Error

$$\text{RMSE} = \sqrt{\left(\sum_{t=1}^{N} E_t^2 \right) / N} \tag{12.3}$$

Mean Absolute Percentage Error

$$\text{MAPE} = 100\% \times \left(\sum_{t=1}^{N} |E_t / Y_t| \right) / N \tag{12.4}$$

A model that makes any one of these error measures small tends to make the other two small as well.

RMSE is similar to a standard deviation in that the errors are squared; because of the square root, it is in the same units as those of the forecast variable. The MAE is similar to the RMSE, except that absolute values of errors are used instead of squared errors. The MAPE is probably the most easily understood measure because it does not depend on the units of the forecast variable; it is always stated as a percentage. For example, the statement that the forecasts are off on average by 2% has a clear meaning, even if you do not know the units of the variable being forecast.

Some forecasting software packages choose the best model from a given class (such as the best exponential smoothing model) by minimizing MAE, RMSE, or MAPE. However, small values of these measures guarantee only that the model tracks the *historical* observations well. There is still no guarantee that the model will forecast *future* values accurately.

One other measure of forecast errors is the *average* of the errors. (It is not reported by StatTools, but it is easy to calculate.) Recall from the regression chapters that the residuals from any regression equation, which are analogous to forecast errors, always average to zero. This is a mathematical property of the least-squares method. However, there is no such guarantee for forecasting errors based on nonregression methods. For example, it is very possible that most of the forecast errors, and the corresponding average, are *negative*. This would imply a *bias*, where the forecasts tend to be too high. Or the average of the forecast errors could be *positive*, in which case the forecasts tend to be too low. If you choose an "appropriate" forecasting method, based on the evidence from a time series graph, this type of bias is not likely to be a problem, but it is easy to check. Furthermore, if a company realizes that its forecasting method produces forecasts that are consistently, say, 5% below the actual values, it could simply multiply its forecasts by 1/0.95 to remove the bias.

We now examine a number of useful forecasting models. You should be aware that more than one of these models can be appropriate for any particular time series data. For example, a random walk model and an autoregression model could be equally effective for forecasting stock price data. (Remember also that forecasts from more than one model can be combined to obtain a possibly better forecast.) We try to provide some insights into choosing the best type of model for various types of time series data, but ultimately the choice depends on the experience of the analyst.

FUNDAMENTAL INSIGHT

Extrapolation and Noise

There are two important things to remember about extrapolation methods. First, by definition, all such methods try to extrapolate historical patterns into the future. If history doesn't essentially repeat itself, for whatever reason, these methods are doomed to fail. In fact, if you *know* that something has changed fundamentally, you probably should not use an extrapolation method. Second, it does no good to track noise and then forecast it into the future. For this reason, most extrapolation methods try to smooth out the noise, so that the underlying pattern is more apparent.

12.3 TESTING FOR RANDOMNESS

All forecasting models have the general form shown in Equation (12.5). The fitted value in this equation is the part calculated from past data and any other available information (such as the season of the year), and it is used as a forecast for Y. The residual is the forecast error, the difference between the observed value of Y and its forecast:

$$Y_t = \text{Fitted Value} + \text{Residual} \qquad (12.5)$$

In a time series context the terms residual and forecast error are used interchangeably.

For time series data, there is a residual for each historical period, that is, for each value of t. We want this time series of residuals to be random noise, as discussed in section 12.2.4. The reason is that if this series of residuals is not noise, it can be modeled further. For example, if the residuals trend upwardly, then the forecasting model can be modified to include this trend component in the *fitted* value. The point is that the fitted value should include all components of the original series that can possibly be forecast, and the leftover residuals should be unpredictable noise.

We now discuss ways to determine whether a time series of residuals is random noise (which we usually abbreviate to "random".) The simplest method, but not always a reliable one, is to examine time series graphs of residuals visually. Nonrandom patterns are sometimes easy to detect. For example, the time series graphs in Figures 12.7 through 12.11 illustrate some common nonrandom patterns. In Figure 12.7, there is an upward trend. In Figure 12.8, the variance increases through time (larger zigzags to the right). Figure 12.9 exhibits seasonality, where observations in certain months are consistently larger than those in other months. There is a meandering pattern in Figure 12.10, where large observations tend to be followed by other large observations, and small observations tend to be followed by other small observations. Finally, Figure 12.11 illustrates the opposite behavior, where there are *too many* zigzags—large observations tend to follow small observations and vice versa. None of the time series in these figures is random.

Figure 12.7

A Series with Trend

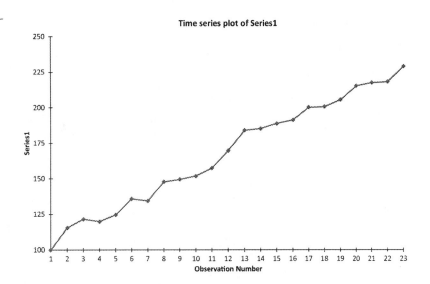

Figure 12.8

A Series with Increasing Variance Through Time

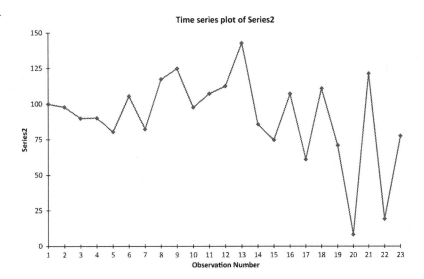

Figure 12.9

A Series with
Seasonality

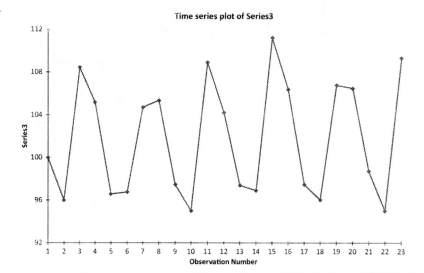

Figure 12.10

A Series That
Meanders

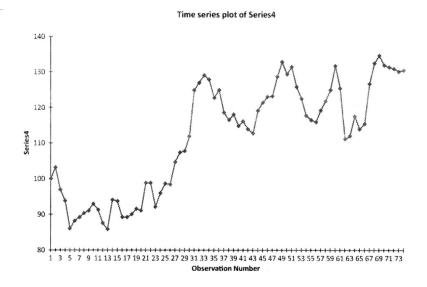

Figure 12.11

A Series That
Oscillates Frequently

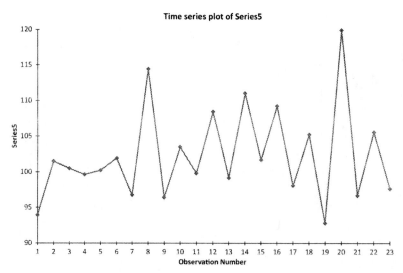

12.3.1 The Runs Test

It is not always easy to detect randomness or the lack of it from the visual inspection of a graph. Therefore, we discuss two quantitative methods that test for randomness. The first is called the *runs test*. You first choose a base value, which could be the average value of the series, the median value, or even some other value. Then a **run** is defined as a consecutive series of observations that remain on one side of this base level. For example, if the base level is 0 and the series is 1, 5, 3, –3, –2, –4, –1, 3, 2, there are three runs: 1, 5, 3; –3, –2, –4, –1; and 3, 2. The idea behind the runs test is that a random series should have a number of runs that is neither too large nor too small. If the series has too few runs, it could be trending (as in Figure 12.7) or it could be meandering (as in Figure 12.10). If the series has too many runs, it is zigzagging too often (as in Figure 12.11).

This runs test can be used on any time series, not just a series of residuals.

> The **runs test** is a formal test of the null hypothesis of randomness. If there are too many or too few runs in the series, the null hypothesis of randomness can be rejected.

We do not provide the mathematical details of the runs test, but we illustrate how it is implemented in StatTools in the following example.

EXAMPLE 12.1 Forecasting Monthly Stereo Sales

Monthly sales for a chain of stereo retailers are listed in the file Stereo Sales.xlsx. They cover the period from the beginning of 2006 to the end of 2009, during which there was no upward or downward trend in sales and no clear seasonality. This behavior is apparent in the time series graph of sales in Figure 12.12. Therefore, a simple forecast model of sales is to use the *average* of the series, 182.67, as a forecast of sales for each month. Do the resulting residuals represent random noise?

Objective   To use StatTools's Runs Test procedure to check whether the residuals from this simple forecasting model represent random noise.

Figure 12.12

Time Series Graph of Stereo Sales

Solution

The residuals for this forecasting model are found by subtracting the average, 182.67, from each observation. Therefore, the plot of the residuals, shown in Figure 12.13, has exactly the same shape as the plot of sales. The only difference is that it is shifted down by 182.67 and has mean 0. The runs test can now be used to check whether there are too many or too few runs around the base value of 0 in this residual plot. To do so, select Runs Test for Randomness from the StatTools Time Series and Forecasting dropdown, choose Residual as the variable to analyze, and choose Mean of Series as the cutoff value. (This corresponds to the horizontal line at 0 in Figure 12.13.) The resulting output in shown in Figure 12.14.

Figure 12.13

Time Series Graph of Residuals

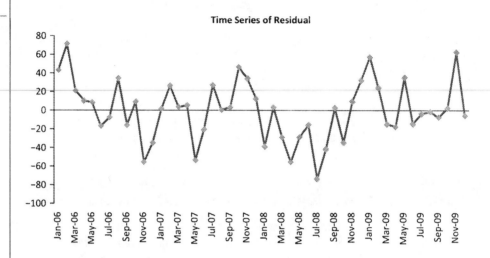

Figure 12.14

Runs Test for Randomness

	I	J
7		Residual
8	*Runs Test for Randomness*	Data Set #1
9	Observations	48
10	Below Mean	22
11	Above Mean	26
12	Number of Runs	20
13	Mean	0.00
14	E(R)	24.8333
15	StdDev(R)	3.4027
16	Z-Value	-1.4204
17	P-Value (two-tailed)	0.1555

The important elements of this output are the following:

- The number of observed runs is 20, in cell J12.

- The number of runs *expected* under an assumption of randomness is 24.833, in cell J14. (This follows from a probability argument not shown here.) Therefore, the series of residuals has too *few* runs. Positive values tend to follow positive values, and negative values tend to follow negative values.

A small p-value in the runs test provides evidence of nonrandomness.

- The z-value in cell J16, −1.42, indicates how many standard errors the observed number of runs is below the expected number of runs. The corresponding *p*-value indicates how extreme this z-value is. It can be interpreted just like other p-values for hypothesis tests. If it is small, say, less than 0.05, then the null hypothesis of randomness can be rejected. In this case, the conclusion is that the series of residuals is not random noise. However, the p-value for this example is only 0.1555. Therefore, there is not convincing evidence of nonrandomness in the residuals. In other words, it is reasonable to conclude that the residuals represent noise. ■

12.3.2 Autocorrelation

Like the runs test, autocorrelations can be calculated for any time series, not just a series of residuals.

In this section we discuss another way to check for randomness of a time series of residuals—we examine the **autocorrelations** of the residuals. The "auto" means that successive observations are correlated with one another. For example, in the most common form of autocorrelation, *positive* autocorrelation, large observations tend to follow large observations, and small observations tend to follow small observations. In this case the runs test is likely to pick it up because there will be fewer runs than expected. Another way to check for the same nonrandomness property is to calculate the autocorrelations of the time series.

An **autocorrelation** is a type of correlation used to measure whether values of a time series are related to their own past values.

To understand autocorrelations, it is first necessary to understand what it means to *lag* a time series. This concept is easy to illustrate in a spreadsheet. We again use the monthly stereo sales data in the Stereo Sales.xlsx file. To lag by one month, you simply "push down" the series by one row. See column D of Figure 12.15. Note that there is a blank cell at the top of the lagged series (in cell D2). You can continue to push the series down one row at a time to obtain other lags. For example, the lag 3 version of the series appears in column F. Now there are three missing observations at the top. Note that in December 2006, say, the first, second, and third lags correspond to the observations in November 2006, October 2006, and September 2006, respectively. That is, lags are simply previous observations, removed by a certain number of periods from the present time. These lagged columns can be obtained by copying and pasting the original series or by selecting Lag from the StatTools Data Utilities dropdown menu.

Figure 12.15

Lags for Stereo Sales

	A	B	C	D	E	F
1	Month	Sales	Residual	Lag1(Residual)	Lag2(Residual)	Lag3(Residual)
2	Jan-06	226	43.333			
3	Feb-06	254	71.333	43.333		
4	Mar-06	204	21.333	71.333	43.333	
5	Apr-06	193	10.333	21.333	71.333	43.333
6	May-06	191	8.333	10.333	21.333	71.333
7	Jun-06	166	-16.667	8.333	10.333	21.333
8	Jul-06	175	-7.667	-16.667	8.333	10.333
9	Aug-06	217	34.333	-7.667	-16.667	8.333
10	Sep-06	167	-15.667	34.333	-7.667	-16.667
11	Oct-06	192	9.333	-15.667	34.333	-7.667
12	Nov-06	127	-55.667	9.333	-15.667	34.333
13	Dec-06	148	-34.667	-55.667	9.333	-15.667
14	Jan-07	184	1.333	-34.667	-55.667	9.333
15	Feb-07	209	26.333	1.333	-34.667	-55.667
16	Mar-07	186	3.333	26.333	1.333	-34.667

Then the autocorrelation of lag k, for any integer k, is essentially the correlation between the original series and the lag k version of the series. For example, in Figure 12.15 the lag 1 autocorrelation is the correlation between the observations in columns C and D. Similarly, the lag 2 autocorrelation is the correlation between the observations in columns C and E.[1]

We have shown the lagged versions of Sales in Figure 12.15, and we have explained autocorrelations in terms of these lagged variables, to help motivate the concept of autocorrelation. However, you can use StatTools's Autocorrelation procedure directly, *without* forming the lagged variables, to calculate autocorrelations. This is illustrated in the following continuation of Example 12.1.

EXAMPLE | **12.1 FORECASTING MONTHLY STEREO SALES (CONTINUED)**

The runs test on the stereo sales data suggests that the pattern of sales is not completely random. There is some tendency for large values to follow large values, and for small values to follow small values. Do autocorrelations support this evidence?

Objective   To examine the autocorrelations of the residuals from the forecasting model for evidence of nonrandomness.

Solution

To answer this question, use StatTools's Autocorrelation procedure, found on the StatTools Time Series and Forecasting dropdown list. It requires you to specify the time series variable (Residual), the number of lags you want (the StatTools default value was accepted here), and whether you want a chart of the autocorrelations. This chart is called a **correlogram**. The resulting autocorrelations and correlogram appear in Figure 12.16. A typical autocorrelation of lag k indicates the relationship between observations k periods apart. For example, the autocorrelation of lag 3, 0.0814, indicates that there is very little relationship between residuals separated by three months.

How large is a "large" autocorrelation? Under the assumption of randomness, it can be shown that the standard error of any autocorrelation is approximately $1/\sqrt{T}$, in this case $1/\sqrt{48} = 0.1443$. (Recall that T denotes the number of observations in the series.) If the series is truly random, then only an occasional autocorrelation will be larger than two standard errors in magnitude. Therefore, any autocorrelation that *is* larger than two standard errors in magnitude is worth your attention. All significantly nonzero autocorrelations are boldfaced in the StatTools output. For this example, the only "large" autocorrelation for the residuals is the first, or lag 1, autocorrelation of 0.3492. The fact that it is *positive* indicates once again that there is some tendency for large residuals to follow large residuals and for small to follow small. The autocorrelations for other lags are less than two standard errors in magnitude and can safely be ignored.

[1]We ignore the exact details of the calculations here. Just be aware that the formula for autocorrelations that is usually used differs slightly from the correlation formula in Chapter 3. However, the difference is very slight and of no practical importance.

Figure 12.16

Correlogram and
Autocorrelations of
Residuals

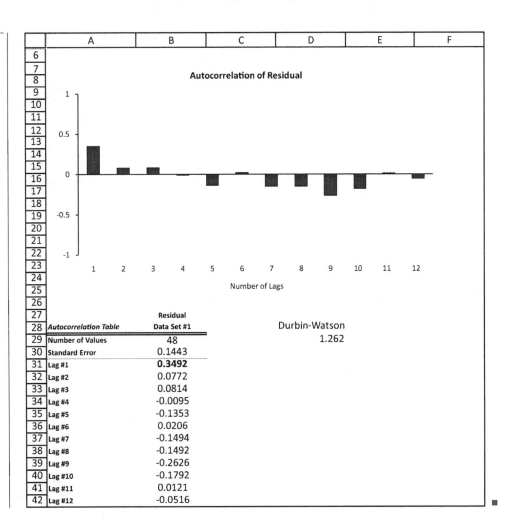

	A	B	C	D	E	F
			Residual			
28	*Autocorrelation Table*	Data Set #1		Durbin-Watson		
29	Number of Values	48		1.262		
30	Standard Error	0.1443				
31	Lag #1	**0.3492**				
32	Lag #2	0.0772				
33	Lag #3	0.0814				
34	Lag #4	-0.0095				
35	Lag #5	-0.1353				
36	Lag #6	0.0206				
37	Lag #7	-0.1494				
38	Lag #8	-0.1492				
39	Lag #9	-0.2626				
40	Lag #10	-0.1792				
41	Lag #11	0.0121				
42	Lag #12	-0.0516				

Typically, you can ask for autocorrelations up to as many lags as you like. However, there are several practical considerations to keep in mind. First, it is common practice to ask for no more lags than 25% of the number of observations. For example, if there are 48 observations, you should ask for no more than 12 autocorrelations (lags 1 to 12). (StatTools chooses this number of lags if you accept its Auto setting.)

Second, the first few lags are typically the most important. Intuitively, if there is any relationship between successive observations, it is likely to be between nearby observations. The June 2009 observation is more likely to be related to the May 2009 observation than to the October 2008 observation. Sometimes there is a fairly large spike in the correlogram at some large lag, such as lag 9. However, this can often be dismissed as a random blip unless there is some obvious reason for its occurrence. A similarly large autocorrelation at lag 1 or 2 is usually taken more seriously. The one exception to this is a *seasonal* lag. For example, an autocorrelation at lag 12 for monthly data corresponds to a relationship between observations a year apart, such as May 2009 and May 2008. If this autocorrelation is significantly large, it probably should not be ignored.

As discussed briefly in the previous chapter, one measure of the lag 1 autocorrelation, often the most important autocorrelation, is provided by the Durbin-Watson (DW) statistic. (See section 11.9.3.) This statistic can be calculated with the StatTools function StatDurbinWatson. Its value for the residuals in this example is 1.262, as shown in

Figure 12.16. The DW statistic is always between 0 and 4. A DW value of 2 indicates *no* lag 1 autocorrelation, a DW value less than 2 indicates *positive* autocorrelation, and a DW value greater than 2 indicates *negative* autocorrelation. The current DW value, 1.262, is considerably less than 2, another indication that the lag 1 autocorrelation of the residuals is positive and possibly significant. There are tables of significance levels for DW statistics (how much less than 2 must DW be to be significant?), but they are not presented here.

Autocorrelation analysis is somewhat advanced. However, it is the basis for many useful forecasting methods.

We will not examine autocorrelations much further in this book. However, many advanced forecasting techniques are based largely on the examination of the autocorrelation structure of time series. This autocorrelation structure indicates how a series is related to its own past values through time, which can be very valuable information for forecasting *future* values.

PROBLEMS

Note: Student solutions for problems whose numbers appear within a colored box are available for purchase at www.cengagebrain.com.

Level A

1. The file P12_01.xlsx contains the monthly number of airline tickets sold by a travel agency. Is this time series *random*? Perform a runs test and find a few autocorrelations to support your answer.

2. The file P12_02.xlsx contains the weekly sales at a local bookstore for each of the past 25 weeks. Is this time series *random*? Perform a runs test and find a few autocorrelations to support your answer.

3. The number of employees on the payroll at a food-processing plant is recorded at the start of each month. These data are provided in the file P12_03.xlsx. Perform a runs test and find a few autocorrelations to determine whether this time series is random.

4. The quarterly numbers of applications for home mortgage loans at a branch office of Northern Central Bank are recorded in the file P12_04.xlsx. Perform a runs test and find a few autocorrelations to determine whether this time series is random.

5. The number of reported accidents at a manufacturing plant located in Flint, Michigan, was recorded at the start of each month. These data are provided in the file P12_05.xlsx. Is this time series *random*? Perform a runs test and find a few autocorrelations to support your answer.

6. The file P12_06.xlsx contains the weekly sales at the local outlet of West Coast Video Rentals for each of the past 36 weeks. Perform a runs test and find a few autocorrelations to determine whether this time series is random.

Level B

7. Determine whether the RAND() function in Excel actually generates a random stream of numbers. Generate at least 100 random numbers to test their randomness with a runs test and with autocorrelations. Summarize your findings.

8. Use a runs test and calculate autorrelations to decide whether the random series explained in each part of this problem (a–c) are random. For each part, generate at least 100 random numbers in the series.
   a. A series of independent normally distributed values, each with mean 70 and standard deviation 5.
   b. A series where the first value is normally distributed with mean 70 and standard deviation 5, and each succeeding value is normally distributed with mean equal to the *previous* value and standard deviation 5. (For example, if the fourth value is 67.32, then the fifth value will be normally distributed with mean 67.32.)
   c. A series where the first value, Y_1, is normally distributed with mean 70 and standard deviation 5, and each succeeding value, Y_t, is normally distributed with mean $(1 + a_t)Y_{t-1}$ and standard deviation $5(1 + a_t)$, where the a_t values are independent and normally distributed with mean 0 and standard deviation 0.2. (For example, if $Y_{t-1} = 67.32$ and $a_t = -0.2$, then Y_t will be normally distributed with mean $0.8(67.32) = 53.856$ and standard deviation $0.8(5) = 4$.)

12.4 REGRESSION-BASED TREND MODELS

Many time series follow a long-term trend except for random variation. This trend can be upward or downward. A straightforward way to model this trend is to estimate a regression equation for Y_t, using time t as the *single* explanatory variable. In this section we discuss the two most frequently used trend models, *linear* trend and *exponential* trend.

12.4.1 Linear Trend

A linear trend means that the time series variable changes by a constant *amount* each time period. The relevant equation is Equation (12.6), where, as in previous regression equations, a is the intercept, b is the slope, and e_t is an error term.[2]

Linear Trend Model

$$Y_t = a + bt + e_t \tag{12.6}$$

The interpretation of b is that it represents the expected change in the series from one period to the next. If b is positive, the trend is upward; if b is negative, the trend is downward. The intercept term a is less important. It literally represents the expected value of the series at time $t = 0$. If time t is coded so that the first observation corresponds to $t = 1$, then a is where the series was one period before the observations began. However, it is possible that time is coded in another way. For example, if the data are annual, starting in 1997, the first value of t might be entered as 1997, which means that the intercept a then corresponds to a period 1997 years earlier. Clearly, its value should not be taken literally in this case.

As always, a graph of the time series is a good place to start. It indicates whether a **linear trend** is likely to provide a good fit. Generally, the graph should rise or fall at approximately a constant rate through time, without too much random variation. But even if there is a lot of random variation—a lot of zigzags—a linear trend to the data might still be a good starting point. Then the *residuals* from this trend line, which should have no remaining trend, could possibly be modeled by some other method in this chapter.

EXAMPLE | **12.2 MONTHLY U.S. POPULATION**

The file US Population.xlsx contains monthly population data for the United States from January 1952 to October 2009 (in thousands). During this period, the population has increased steadily from about 156 million to about 308 million. The time series graph of these data appears in Figure 12.17. How well does a linear trend fit these data? Are the residuals from this fit random?

Objective To fit a linear trend line to monthly population and examine its residuals for randomness.

---

[2]It is traditional in the regression literature to use Greek letters for population parameters and Roman letters for estimates of them. However, we decided to use only Roman letters in the regression sections of this chapter. For a book at this level, they are less intimidating.

Figure 12.17   Time Series Graph of U.S. Population

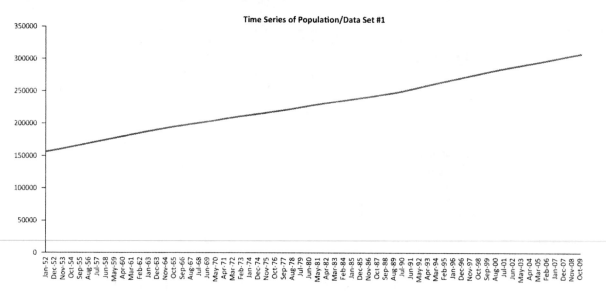

Solution

The graph in Figure 12.17 indicates a clear upward trend with little or no curvature. Therefore, a linear trend is certainly plausible. To estimate it with regression, a *numeric* time variable is needed—labels such as Jan-52 will not do. This time variable appears in column C of the data set, using the consecutive values 1 through 694. You can then run a simple regression of Population versus Time, with the results shown in Figure 12.18. The estimated linear trend line is

$$\text{Forecast Population} = 157003.69 + 211.55\,\text{Time}$$

Figure 12.18

Regression Output for Linear Trend

Summary	Multiple R	R-Square	Adjusted R-Square	StErr of Estimate		
	0.9982	0.9965	0.9965	2523.59		

ANOVA Table	Degrees of Freedom	Sum of Squares	Mean of Squares	F-Ratio	p-Value	
Explained	1	1.24664E+12	1.24664E+12	195750.8446	< 0.0001	
Unexplained	692	4406997370	6368493.309			

Regression Table	Coefficient	Standard Error	t-Value	p-Value	Confidence Interval 95% Lower	Upper
Constant	157003.69	191.80	818.6000	< 0.0001	156627.12	157380.26
Time	211.55	0.48	442.4374	< 0.0001	210.62	212.49

This equation implies that the population tends to increase by 211.55 thousand per month. (The 157003.69 value in this equation is the predicted population at time 0; that is, December 1951.) To use this equation to forecast future population values, substitute later values of Time into the regression equation, so that each future forecast is 211.55 larger than the previous forecast. For example, the forecast for January 2010 is

$$\text{Forecast Population Jan-2010} = 157003.69 + 211.55(697) = 304457$$

As described in Chapter 2, Excel provides an easier way to obtain this trend line. Once the graph in Figure 12.17 is constructed, you can use Excel's Trendline tool. To do so, right-click on any point on the chart and select Add Trendline. This provides several types of trend lines to choose from, and the linear option works well for this example. You can also check the options to show the regression equation and its R^2 value on the chart, as shown in Figure 12.19. This superimposed trend line indicates a very good fit.

Figure 12.19   Time Series Graph with Linear Trend Superimposed

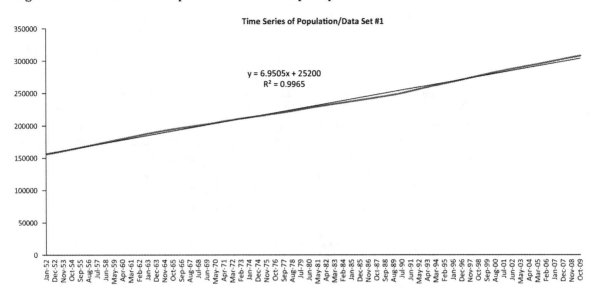

However, the fit is not perfect, as the plot of the residuals in Figure 12.20 indicates. These residuals tend to meander, staying negative for a while, then positive, then negative, and then positive. You can check that the runs test for these residuals produces a z-value of -26.13, with a corresponding p-value of 0.000, and that its first 32 autocorrelations are significantly positive. In short, these residuals are definitely *not* random noise, and they could be modeled further. However, we will not pursue this analysis here. In fact, it is not at all obvious how the autocorrelations of the residuals *could* be exploited to get a better forecast model.

Figure 12.20

Time Series Graph of Residuals

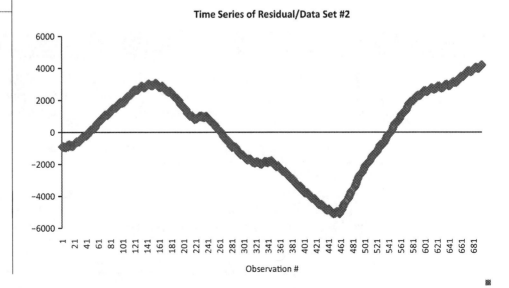

12.4.2 Exponential Trend

An exponential trend for Y is equivalent to a linear trend for the logarithm of Y.

In contrast to a linear trend, an exponential trend is appropriate when the time series changes by a constant *percentage* (as opposed to a constant dollar amount) each period. Then the appropriate regression equation is Equation (12.7), where c and b are constants, and u_t represents a *multiplicative* error term.

Exponential Trend Model

$$Y_t = ce^{bt}u_t \qquad\qquad (12.7)$$

Equation (12.7) is useful for understanding how an exponential trend works, as we will discuss, but it is not useful for estimation. For that, a *linear* equation is required. Fortunately, you can achieve linearity by taking natural logarithms of both sides of Equation (12.7). (The key, as usual, is that the logarithm of a product is the sum of the logarithms.) The result appears in Equation (12.8), where $a = \ln(c)$ and $e_t = \ln(u_t)$. This equation represents a *linear* trend, but the dependent variable is now the logarithm of the original Y_t. This implies the following important fact: If a time series exhibits an exponential trend, then a plot of its logarithm should be approximately linear.

Equivalent Linear Trend for Logarithm of Y

$$\ln(Y_t) = a + bt + e_t \qquad\qquad (12.8)$$

Because the software performs the calculations, your main responsibility is to interpret the final result. This is fairly easy. It can be shown that the coefficient b (expressed as a percentage) is approximately the percentage change per period. For example, if $b = 0.05$, the series is increasing by approximately 5% per period.[3] On the other hand, if $b = -0.05$, the series is decreasing by approximately 5% per period.

An exponential trend can be estimated with StatTools's Regression procedure, but only after the log transformation has been made on Y_t. We illustrate this in the following example.

EXAMPLE | **12.3 QUARTERLY PC DEVICE SALES**

The file PC Device Sales.xlsx contains quarterly sales data (in millions of dollars) for a large PC device manufacturer from the first quarter of 1995 through the fourth quarter of 2009. Are the company's sales growing exponentially through this entire period?

Objective   To estimate the company's exponential growth and to see whether it has been maintained during the entire period from 1995 until the end of 2009.

Solution

We first estimate and interpret an exponential trend for the years 1995 through 2005. Then we see how well the projection of this trend into the future fits the data after 2005. The

---

[3]More precisely, this percentage change is $e^b - 1$. For example, when $b = 0.05$, this is $e^b - 1 = 5.13\%$.

time series graph through 2005 appears in Figure 12.21. You can use Excel's Trendline tool, with the Exponential option, to superimpose an exponential trend line and the corresponding equation on this plot. The fit is evidently quite good. Equivalently, Figure 12.22 illustrates the time series of log sales for this same period, with a *linear* trend line superimposed. Its fit is equally good.

Figure 12.21   Time Series Graph of Sales with Exponential Trend Superimposed

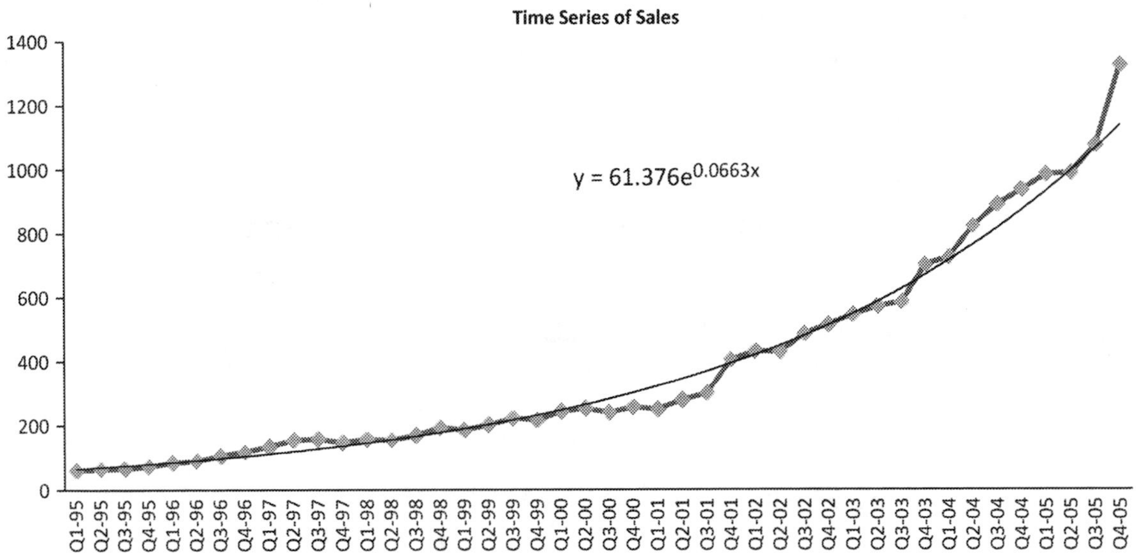

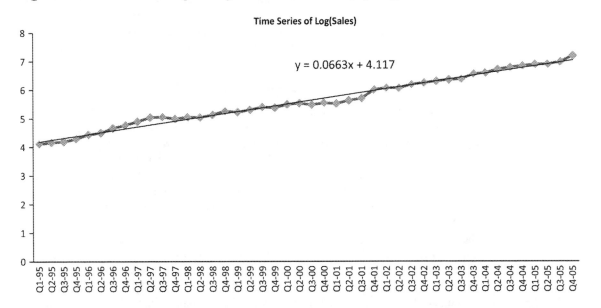

Figure 12.22   Time Series Graph of Log Sales with Linear Trend Superimposed

You can also use StatTools's Regression procedure to estimate this exponential trend, as shown in Figure 12.23. To produce this output, you must first add a time variable in column C (with values 1 through 44) and make a logarithmic transformation of Sales in column D.

Then you can regress Log(Sales) on Time (using the data through 2005 only) to obtain the regression output. Note that its two coefficients in cells B18 and B19 are the same as those shown for the linear trend in Figure 12.22. If you take the antilog of the constant 4.117 (with the formula = EXP(B18)), you will obtain the constant *multiple* shown in Figure 12.21. It corresponds to the constant c in Equation (12.7).

Figure 12.23 Regression Output for Estimating Exponential Trend

	A	B	C	D	E	F	G
7		Multiple	R-Square	Adjusted	StErr of		
8	*Summary*	R		R-Square	Estimate		
9		0.9922	0.9844	0.9840	0.1086		
10							
11		Degrees of	Sum of	Mean of	F-Ratio	p-Value	
12	*ANOVA Table*	Freedom	Squares	Squares			
13	Explained	1	31.21992793	31.21992793	2645.6403	< 0.0001	
14	Unexplained	42	0.495621782	0.011800519			
15							
16		Coefficient	Standard	t-Value	p-Value	Confidence Interval 95%	
17	*Regression Table*		Error			Lower	Upper
18	Constant	4.1170	0.0333	123.5616	< 0.0001	4.0498	4.1843
19	Time	0.0663	0.0013	51.4358	< 0.0001	0.0637	0.0689

What does it all mean? The estimated Equation (12.7) is

$$\text{Forecast Sales} = 61.376e^{0.0663t}$$

The most important constant in this equation is the coefficient of Time, $b = 0.0663$. Expressed as a percentage, this coefficient implies that the company's sales increased by approximately 6.63% per quarter throughout this 11-year period. (The constant multiple, $c = 61.376$, is the forecast of sales at time 0; that is, quarter 4 of 1994.) To use this equation for forecasting the future, substitute later values of Time into the regression equation, so that each future forecast is about 6.63% larger than the previous forecast. For example, the forecast of the second quarter of 2006 is

$$\text{Forecast Sales in Q2-06} = 61.376e^{0.0663(46)} = 1295.72$$

Has this exponential growth continued beyond 2005? It has *not*, due possibly to slumping sales in the computer industry or increased competition from other manufacturers. You can check this by creating the Forecast column in Figure 12.24 (by substituting into the regression equation for the entire period through Q4−09). You can then use StatTools to create a time series graph of the two series Sales and Forecast, shown in Figure 12.25. It is clear that sales in the forecast period did not exhibit nearly the 6.63% growth observed in the estimation period. As the company clearly realizes, nothing this good lasts forever.

Before leaving this example, we comment briefly on the standard error of estimate shown in cell E9 of Figure 12.23. This value, 0.1086, is in *log* units, not original dollar units. Therefore, it is a totally misleading indicator of the forecast errors that might be made from the exponential trend equation. To obtain more meaningful measures, you should first obtain the forecasts of sales, as explained previously. Then you can easily obtain any of the three forecast error measures discussed previously. The results appear in Figure 12.26. The squared errors, absolute errors, and absolute percentage errors are first calculated with the formulas =(B2-E2)^2, =ABS(B2-E2), and =G2/B2 in cells F2, G2, and H2, which are then copied down. The error measures (for the data through 2005 only)

Figure 12.24
Creating Forecasts of Sales

	A	B	C	D
1	Quarter	Sales	Time	Log(Sales)
2	Q1-95	61.14	1	4.1131663
3	Q2-95	64.07	2	4.1599762
4	Q3-95	66.18	3	4.1923783
5	Q4-95	72.76	4	4.2871664
6	Q1-96	84.70	5	4.4391156
7	Q2-96	90.05	6	4.5003651
8	Q3-96	106.06	7	4.664005
9	Q4-96	118.21	8	4.7724627
10	Q1-97	134.38	9	4.9006716
11	Q2-97	154.67	10	5.0412938
12	Q3-97	157.41	11	5.0588539
13	Q4-97	147.16	12	4.9915204

Figure 12.25

Time Series Graph
of Forecasts
Superimposed on
Sales for the Entire
Period

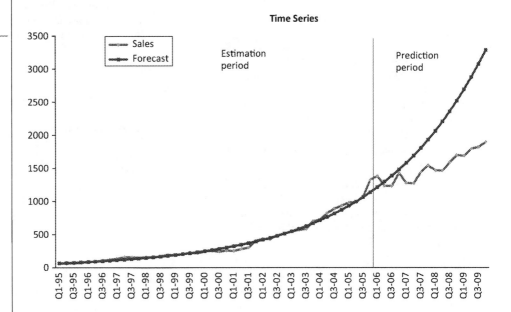

then appear in cells K2, K3, and K4. The corresponding formulas for RMSE, MAE, and MAPE are straightforward. RMSE is the square root of the average of the squared errors in column F, and MAE and MAPE are the averages of the values in columns G and H, respectively. The latter is particularly simple to interpret. Forecasts for the 11-year estimation period were off, on average, by 7.86%. (Of course, as you can check, forecasts for the quarters *after* 2005 were off by much more.)

Figure 12.26   Measures of Forecast Errors

	A	B	C	D	E	F	G	H	I	J	K	L
1	Quarter	Sales	Time	Log(Sales)	Forecast	SqError	AbsError	AbsPctError		Measures of forecast error		
2	Q1-95	61.14	1	4.1131663	65.58583	19.76541	4.445831	0.07271559		RMSE	41.86	
3	Q2-95	64.07	2	4.1599762	70.08398	36.16795	6.013979	0.09386576		MAE	25.44	
4	Q3-95	66.18	3	4.1923783	74.89063	75.87506	8.710629	0.13162027		MAPE	7.86%	
5	Q4-95	72.76	4	4.2871664	80.02694	52.8084	7.266939	0.09987547				
6	Q1-96	84.70	5	4.4391156	85.51552	0.66507	0.815518	0.00962831				
7	Q2-96	90.05	6	4.5003651	91.38053	1.770302	1.330527	0.01477542				
8	Q3-96	106.06	7	4.664005	97.64778	70.7654	8.412218	0.07931565				

Whenever you observe a time series that is increasing at an increasing rate (or decreasing at a decreasing rate), an exponential trend model is worth trying. The key to the analysis is to regress the *logarithm* of the time series variable versus time (or use Excel's Trendline tool). The coefficient of time, written as a percentage, is then the approximate percentage increase (if positive) or decrease (if negative) per period. ∎

PROBLEMS

Level A

9. The file P12_01.xlsx contains the monthly number of airline tickets sold by a travel agency.
   a. Does a linear trend appear to fit these data well? If so, estimate and interpret the linear trend model for this time series. Also, interpret the R^2 and s_e values.
   b. Provide an indication of the typical forecast error generated by the estimated model in part **a**.
   c. Is there evidence of some seasonal pattern in these sales data? If so, characterize the seasonal pattern.

10. The file P12_10.xlsx contains the daily closing prices of Walmart stock for a one-year period. Does a linear or exponential trend fit these data well? If so, estimate and interpret the best trend model for this time series. Also, interpret the R^2 and s_e values.

11. The file P12_11.xlsx contains monthly values of the U.S. national debt (in dollars) from 1993 to early 2010. Fit an exponential growth curve to these data. Write a short report to summarize your findings. If the U.S. national debt continues to rise at the exponential rate you find, approximately what will its value be at the end of 2020?

12. The file P12_12.xlsx contains five years of monthly data on sales (number of units sold) for a particular company. The company suspects that except for random noise, its sales are growing by a constant *percentage* each month and will continue to do so for at least the near future.
   a. Explain briefly whether the plot of the series visually supports the company's suspicion.
   b. Fit the appropriate regression model to the data. Report the resulting equation and state explicitly what it says about the percentage growth per month.
   c. What are the RMSE and MAPE for the forecast model in part **b**? In words, what do they measure? Considering their magnitudes, does the model seem to be doing a good job?

   d. In words, how does the model make forecasts for future months? Specifically, given the forecast value for the last month in the data set, what simple arithmetic could you use to obtain forecasts for the next few months?

13. The file P12_13.xlsx contains quarterly data on GDP. (The data are expressed as an index where 2005 = 100, and they are seasonally adjusted.)
   a. Look at a time series plot of GDP. Does it suggest a linear relationship; an exponential relationship?
   b. Use regression to estimate a linear relationship between GDP and Time (starting with 1 for Q1-1966). Interpret the associated constant term and the slope term. Would you say that the fit is good?

Level B

14. The file P03_30.xlsx gives monthly exchange rates (units of local currency per U.S. dollar) for nine currencies. Technical analysts believe that by charting past changes in exchange rates, it is possible to predict future changes of exchange rates. After analyzing the autocorrelations for these data, do you believe that technical analysis has potential?

15. The unit sales of a new drug for the first 25 months after its introduction to the marketplace are recorded in the file P12_15.xlsx.
   a. Estimate a linear trend equation using the given data. How well does the linear trend fit these data? Are the residuals from this linear trend model *random*?
   b. If the residuals from this linear trend model are *not* random, propose another regression-based trend model that more adequately explains the long-term trend in this time series. Estimate the alternative model(s) using the given data. Check the residuals from the model(s) for randomness. Summarize your findings.
   c. Given the best estimated model of the trend in this time series, interpret R^2 and s_e.

12.5 THE RANDOM WALK MODEL

Random series are sometimes building blocks for other time series models. The model we now discuss, the **random walk model**, is an example of this. In a random walk model, the series itself is not random. However, its *differences*—that is, the changes from one period to the next—are random. This type of behavior is typical of stock price data (as well as various other time series data). For example, the graph in Figure 12.27 shows monthly closing prices for a tractor manufactor's stock from January 2003 through April 2009. (See the file Tractor Closing Prices.xlsx.) This series is not random, as can be seen from its gradual upward trend at the beginning and the general meandering behavior throughout. (Although the runs test and autocorrelations are not shown for the series itself, they confirm that the series is not random. There are significantly *fewer* runs than expected, and the autocorrelations are significantly *positive* for many lags.)

Figure 12.27   **Time Series Graph of Tractor Stock Prices**

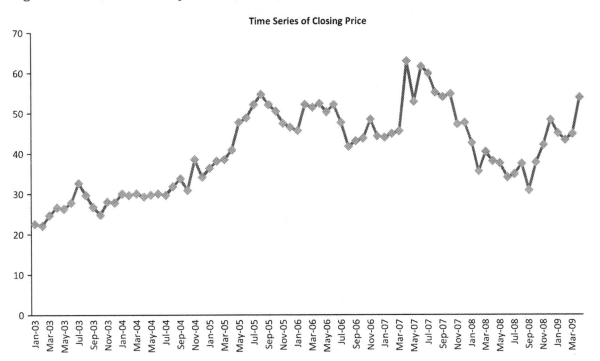

If it were April 2009, and you were asked to forecast the company's prices for the next few months, it is intuitive that you would not use the average of the historical values as your forecast. This forecast would tend to be too low because of the upward trend. Instead, you might base your forecast on the most recent observation. This is exactly what the random walk model does.

Equation (12.9) for the random walk model is given as follows, where m (for mean difference) is a constant and e_t is a random series (noise) with mean 0 and a standard deviation that remains *constant* through time.

> *Random Walk Model*
>
> $$Y_t = Y_{t-1} + m + e_t \qquad (12.9)$$

If we let $DY_t = Y_t - Y_{t-1}$, the change in the series from time t to time $t-1$ (where D stands for difference), then the random walk model can be rewritten as in Equation (12.10). This implies that the differences form a random series with mean m and a constant standard deviation. An estimate of m is the average of the differences, labeled $\overline{Y}_D$, and an estimate of the standard deviation is the sample standard deviation of the differences, labeled s_D.

> *Difference Form of Random Walk Model*
>
> $$DY_t = m + e_t \qquad (12.10)$$

In words, a series that behaves according to this random walk model has random differences, and the series tends to trend upward (if $m > 0$) or downward (if $m < 0$) by an amount m each period. If you are standing in period t and want to forecast Y_{t+1}, then a reasonable forecast is given by Equation (12.11). That is, you add the estimated trend to the current observation to forecast the next observation.

> *One-Step-Ahead Forecast for Random Walk Model*
>
> $$F_{t+1} = Y_t + \overline{Y}_D \qquad (12.11)$$

We illustrate this method in the following example.

EXAMPLE | **12.4 RANDOM WALK MODEL OF STOCK PRICES**

The monthly closing prices of the tractor company's stock from January 2003 through April 2009, shown in Figure 12.27, indicate some upward trend. (See the file Tractor Sales.xlsx.) Does this series follow a random walk model with an upward trend? If so, how should future values of these stock prices be forecast?

Objective To check whether the company's monthly closing prices follow a random walk model with an upward trend and to see how future prices can be forecast.

Solution

We have already seen that the closing price series itself is not random, due to the upward trend. To check for the adequacy of a random walk model, a series of *differences* is required. Each value in the differenced series is that month's closing price minus the previous month's closing price. You can calculate this series easily with an Excel formula, or you can generate it automatically with the Difference item on the StatTools Data Utilities dropdown menu. (When asked for the *number* of difference variables, accept the default value of 1.) This differenced series appears in column C of Figure 12.28. This figure also shows the mean and standard deviation of the differences, 0.418 and 4.245, which are used in forecasting. Finally, this figure shows several autocorrelations of the differences, only one of which is (barely) significant. A runs test for the differences, not shown here, has a large *p*-value, which supports the conclusion that the differences are random.

Figure 12.28

Differences of
Closing Prices

	A	B	C	D	E	F
1	Month	Closing Price	Diff1(Closing Price)			Diff1(Closing Price)
2	Jan-03	22.595			*One Variable Summary*	Data Set #1
3	Feb-03	22.134	-0.461		Mean	0.418
4	Mar-03	24.655	2.521		Std. Dev.	4.245
5	Apr-03	26.649	1.994		Count	75
6	May-03	26.303	-0.346			
7	Jun-03	27.787	1.484			Diff1(Closing Price)
8	Jul-03	32.705	4.918		*Autocorrelation Table*	Data Set #1
9	Aug-03	29.745	-2.96		Number of Values	75
10	Sep-03	26.741	-3.004		Standard Error	0.1155
11	Oct-03	24.852	-1.889		Lag #1	**-0.2435**
12	Nov-03	28.050	3.198		Lag #2	0.1348
13	Dec-03	27.847	-0.203		Lag #3	-0.0049
14	Jan-04	30.040	2.193		Lag #4	-0.0507
15	Feb-04	29.680	-0.36		Lag #5	0.0696
16	Mar-04	30.139	0.459		Lag #6	0.0009
17	Apr-04	29.276	-0.863		Lag #7	-0.0630
18	May-04	29.703	0.427		Lag #8	-0.0295
19	Jun-04	30.017	0.314		Lag #9	0.0496
20	Jul-04	29.687	-0.33		Lag #10	-0.1728
21	Aug-04	31.765	2.078		Lag #11	-0.0334
22	Sep-04	33.788	2.023		Lag #12	-0.0554
23	Oct-04	30.942	-2.846			

The plot of the differences appears in Figure 12.29. A visual inspection of the plot also supports the conclusion of random differences, although these differences do not vary

Figure 12.29   Time Series Graph of Differences

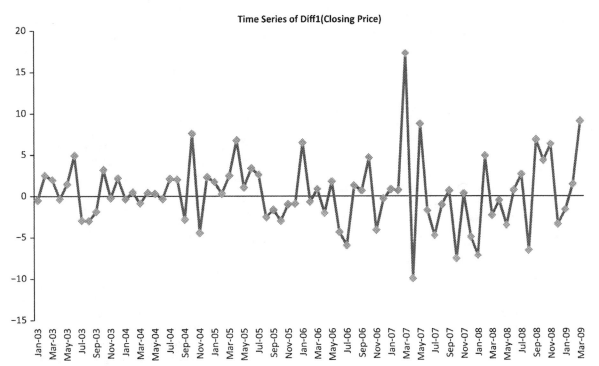

around a mean of 0. Rather, they vary around a mean of 0.418. This positive value measures the upward trend—the closing prices increase, on average, by 0.418 per month. Finally, the variability in this figure is fairly constant (except for the two wide swings in 2007). Specifically, the zigzags do not tend to get appreciably wider through time. Therefore, it is reasonable to conclude that the random walk model with an upward drift fits this series fairly well.

To forecast future closing prices, simply multiply the mean difference by the number of periods ahead, and add this to the final closing price (53.947 in April 2009). For example, a forecast of the closing price for September 2009 is:

$$\text{Forecast Closing Price for 9/09} = 53.947 + 0.418(5) = 56.037$$

As a rough measure of the accuracy of this forecast, you can use the standard deviation of the differences, 4.245. Specifically, it can be shown that the standard error for forecasting k periods ahead is the standard deviation of the differences multiplied by the square root of k. In this case, the standard error is 9.492. As usual, you can be 95% confident that the actual closing price in September will be no more than two standard errors from the forecast. Unfortunately, this results in a wide interval—from about 37 to 75. This reflects the fact that it is very difficult to make accurate forecasts, especially long-range forecasts, for a series with this much variability. ■

PROBLEMS

Level A

16. The file P12_16.xlsx contains the daily closing prices of American Express stock for a one-year period.
  a. Use the random walk model to forecast the closing price of this stock on the next trading day.
  b. You can be about 95% certain that the forecast made in part **a** will be off by no more than how many dollars?

17. The closing value of the AMEX Airline Index for each trading day during a one-year period is given in the file P12_17.xlsx.
  a. Use the random walk model to forecast the closing price of this stock on the next trading day.
  b. You can be about 68% certain that the forecast made in part **a** will be off by no more than how many dollars?

18. The file P12_18.xlsx contains the daily closing prices of Chevron stock for a one-year period.
  a. Use the random walk model to forecast the closing price of this stock on the next trading day.
  b. You can be about 99.7% certain that the forecast made in part **a** will be off by no more than how many dollars?

19. The closing value of the Dow Jones Industrial Average for each trading day for a one-year period is provided in the file P12_19.xlsx.
  a. Use the random walk model to forecast the closing price of this index on the next trading day.

  b. Would it be wise to use the random walk model to forecast the closing price of this index for a trading day approximately *one month* after the next trading day? Explain why or why not.

20. Continuing the previous problem, consider the differences between consecutive closing values of the Dow Jones Industrial Average for the given set of trading days. Do these differences form a random series? Demonstrate why or why not.

21. The closing price of a share of J.P. Morgan's stock for each trading day during a one-year period is recorded in the file P12_21.xlsx.
  a. Use the random walk model to forecast the closing price of this stock on the next trading day.
  b. You can be about 68% certain that the forecast made in part **a** will be off by no more than how many dollars?

22. The purpose of this problem is to get you used to the concept of autocorrelation in a time series. You could do this with any time series, but here you should use the series of Walmart daily stock prices in the file P12_10.xlsx.
  a. First, do it the quick way. Use the Autocorrelation procedure in StatTools to get a list of autocorrelations and a corresponding correlogram of the closing prices. You can choose the number of lags.
  b. Now do it the more time-consuming way. Create columns of lagged versions of the Close variable—3 or 4 lags will suffice. Next, look at scatterplots of

Close versus its first few lags. If the autocorrelations are large, you should see fairly tight scatters—that's what autocorrelation is all about. Also, generate a correlation matrix to see the correlations between Close and its first few lags. These should be approximately the same as the autocorrelations from part **a**. (Autocorrelations are calculated slightly differently than regular correlations, which accounts for any slight discrepancies you might notice, but these discrepancies should be minor.)

c. Create the first differences of Close in a new column. (You can do this manually with formulas, or you can use StatTools's Difference procedure on the Data Utilities menu.) Now repeat parts **a** and **b** with the differences instead of the original closing prices—that is, examine the autocorrelations of the differences. They should be small, and the scatterplots of the differences versus lags of the differences should be shapeless swarms. This illustrates what happens when the differences of a time series variable have insignificant autocorrelations.

d. Write a short report of your findings.

23. Consider a random walk model with the following equation: $Y_t = Y_{t-1} + 500 + e_t$, where e_t is a normally distributed random series with mean 0 and standard deviation 10.

a. Use Excel to simulate a time series that behaves according to this random walk model.

b. Use the time series you constructed in part **a** to forecast the next observation.

24. The file P12_24.xlsx contains the daily closing prices of Procter & Gamble stock for a one-year period. Use only the 2003 data to estimate the trend component of the random walk model. Next, use the estimated random walk model to forecast the behavior of the time series for the 2004 dates in the series. Comment on the accuracy of the generated forecasts over this period. How could you improve the forecasts as you progress through the 2004 trading days?

12.6 AUTOREGRESSION MODELS[4]

We now discuss a regression-based extrapolation method that regresses the current value of the time series on past (lagged) values. This is called **autoregression**, where the *auto-* means that the explanatory variables in the equation are lagged values of the dependent variable, so that the dependent variable is regressed on lagged versions of *itself*. This procedure is fairly straightforward in Excel. You first create lags of the dependent variable and then use a regression procedure to regress the original series on the lagged series. Some trial and error is generally required to determine the appropriate number of lags in the regression equation. The following example illustrates the procedure.

EXAMPLE | 12.5 FORECASTING HAMMER SALES

A retailer has recorded its weekly sales of hammers (units purchased) for the past 42 weeks. (See the file Hammer Sales.xlsx.) A graph of this time series appears in Figure 12.30. It reveals a meandering pattern of behavior. The values begin high and stay high awhile, then get lower and stay lower awhile, then get higher again. (This behavior could be caused by any number of things, including the weather, increases and decreases in building projects, and possibly others.) How useful is autoregression for modeling these data and how can it be used for forecasting?

Objective To use autoregression, with an appropriate number of lagged terms, to forecast hammer sales.

[4]This section can be omitted without any loss of continuity.

Figure 12.30   Time Series Graph of Sales of Hammers

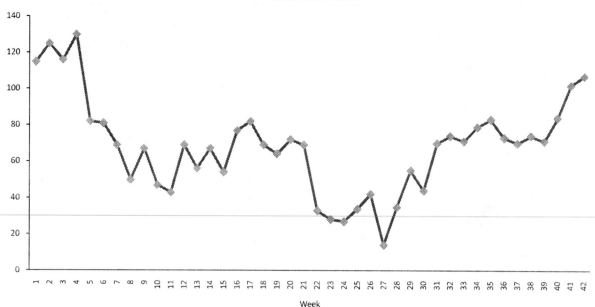

Solution

It is generally best to begin with plenty of lags and then delete the higher numbered lags that aren't necessary.

A good place to start is with the autocorrelations of the series. These indicate whether the Sales variable is linearly related to any of its lags. The first six autocorrelations are shown in Figure 12.31. The first three of them are significantly positive, and then they decrease. Based on this information, create three lags of Sales and run a regression of Sales versus these three lags. The output from this regression appears in Figure 12.32. You can see that R^2 is fairly high, about 57%, and that s_e is about 15.7. However, the p-values for lags 2 and 3 are both quite large. It appears that once the first lag is included in the regression equation, the other two are not really needed.

Figure 12.31

Autocorrelations for Hammer Sales Data

	A	B
27		Sales
28	*Autocorrelation Table*	Data Set #1
29	Number of Values	42
30	Standard Error	0.1543
31	Lag #1	**0.7523**
32	Lag #2	**0.5780**
33	Lag #3	**0.4328**
34	Lag #4	0.2042
35	Lag #5	0.1093
36	Lag #6	-0.0502

This suggests running another regression with only the first lag included. (Actually, we first omitted only the third lag. But the resulting output showed that the second lag was still insignificant, so we then deleted it.) The regression output with only the first lag

Figure 12.32   Autoregression Output with Three Lagged Variables

	A	B	C	D	E	F	G
7		Multiple	R-Square	Adjusted	StErr of		
8	Summary	R		R-Square	Estimate		
9		0.7573	0.5736	0.5370	15.7202		
10							
11		Degrees of	Sum of	Mean of	F-Ratio	p-Value	
12	ANOVA Table	Freedom	Squares	Squares			
13	Explained	3	11634.19978	3878.066594	15.6927	< 0.0001	
14	Unexplained	35	8649.38996	247.1254274			
15							
16		Coefficient	Standard	t-Value	p-Value	Confidence Interval 95%	
17	Regression Table		Error			Lower	Upper
18	Constant	15.4986	7.8820	1.9663	0.0572	-0.5027	31.5000
19	Lag1(Sales)	0.6398	0.1712	3.7364	0.0007	0.2922	0.9874
20	Lag2(Sales)	0.1523	0.1987	0.7665	0.4485	-0.2510	0.5556
21	Lag3(Sales)	-0.0354	0.1641	-0.2159	0.8303	-0.3686	0.2977

The two curves in this figure look pretty close to one another. However, a comparison of the vertical distances between pairs of points indicates that they are not that close after all.

included appears in Figure 12.33. In addition, a graph of the dependent and fitted variables, that is, the original Sales variable and its forecasts, appears in Figure 12.34. (This latter graph was formed from the Week, Sales, and Fitted columns.) The estimated regression equation is

$$\text{Forecast Sales}_t = 13.763 + 0.793\text{Sales}_{t-1}$$

The associated R^2 and s_e values are approximately 65% and 15.4. The R^2 value is a measure of the reasonably good fit evident in Figure 12.34, whereas s_e is a measure of the likely forecast error for short-term forecasts.[5] It implies that a short-term forecast could easily be off by as much as two standard errors, or about 31 hammers.

Figure 12.33   Autoregression Output with a Single Lagged Variable

	A	B	C	D	E	F	G
7		Multiple	R-Square	Adjusted	StErr of		
8	Summary	R		R-Square	Estimate		
9		0.8036	0.6458	0.6367	15.4476		
10							
11		Degrees of	Sum of	Mean of	F-Ratio	p-Value	
12	ANOVA Table	Freedom	Squares	Squares			
13	Explained	1	16969.97657	16969.97657	71.1146	< 0.0001	
14	Unexplained	39	9306.511237	238.6284932			
15							
16		Coefficient	Standard	t-Value	p-Value	Confidence Interval 95%	
17	Regression Table		Error			Lower	Upper
18	Constant	13.7634	6.7906	2.0268	0.0496	0.0281	27.4988
19	Lag1(Sales)	0.7932	0.0941	8.4329	< 0.0001	0.6029	0.9834

[5]If you are very observant, you may have noticed that R^2 increased when the two lag variables were omitted from the equation. Isn't R^2 always supposed to decrease when variables are omitted? Yes it is, but in this case the two equations are based on different data. When the second and third lags were included, weeks 1−3 of the data set were omitted because of missing data in the lag columns. But when these lags were omitted, only the week 1 row had to be omitted because of missing data.

Figure 12.34   Forecasts from Autoregression

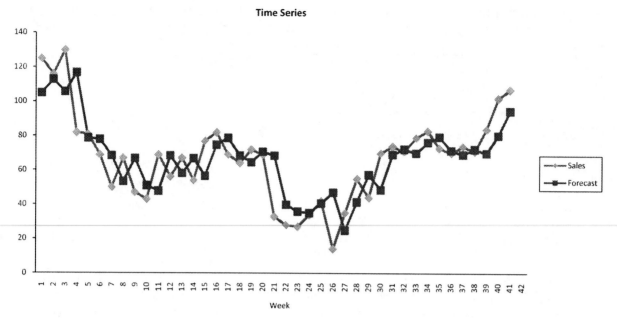

To forecast, substitute known values of Y into the regression equation if they are available. Otherwise, substitute forecast values.

To use the regression equation for forecasting *future* sales values, you can substitute known or forecast sales values in the right-hand side of the equation. Specifically, the forecast for week 43, the first week after the data period, is

$$\text{Forecast Sales}_{43} = 13.763 + 0.793\text{Sales}_{42} = 13.763 + 0.793(107) \simeq 98.6$$

Here the *known* value of sales in week 42 is used. However, the forecast for week 44 requires the *forecast* value of sales in week 43:

$$\text{Forecast Sales}_{44} = 13.763 + 0.793\text{Forecast Sales}_{43}$$
$$= 13.763 + 0.793(98.6) \simeq 92.0$$

Perhaps these two forecasts of future sales values are on the mark, and perhaps they are not. The only way to know for certain is to observe future sales values. However, it is interesting that in spite of the *upward* movement in the series in the last three weeks, the forecasts for weeks 43 and 44 are for *downward* movements. This is a combination of two properties of the regression equation. First, the coefficient of Sales_{t-1}, 0.793, is positive. Therefore, the equation forecasts that large sales will be followed by large sales, that is, positive autocorrelation. Second, however, this coefficient is less than 1, and this provides a dampening effect. The equation forecasts that a large will follow a large, but not *that* large. ▪

Sometimes an autoregression model is virtually equivalent to another forecasting model. As an example, suppose you find that the following equation adequately models a time series variable *Y*:

$$Y_t = 75.65 + 0.976Y_{t-1}$$

The coefficient of the lagged term, 0.976, is nearly equal to 1. If this coefficient were 1, you could subtract the lagged term from both sides of the equation and write that the *difference* series is a constant—that is, a random walk model. As you can see, a random walk model is a special case of an autoregression model. However, autoregression models are much more general. Unfortunately, a more thorough study of them would take us into the realm of econometrics, which is well beyond the level of this book.

PROBLEMS

Level A

25. Consider the Consumer Price Index (CPI), which provides the annual percentage change in consumer prices. The data are in the file P02_19.xlsx.
  a. Find the first six autocorrelations of this time series.
  b. Use the results of part **a** to specify one or more promising autoregression models. Estimate each model with the available data. Which model provides the best fit to the data?
  c. Use the best autoregression model from part **b** to produce a forecast of the CPI in the next year. Also, provide a measure of the likely forecast error.

26. The Consumer Confidence Index (CCI) attempts to measure people's feelings about general business conditions, employment opportunities, and their own income prospects. The file P02_20.xlsx contains the annual average values of the CCI.
  a. Find the first six autocorrelations of this time series.
  b. Use the results of part **a** to specify one or more promising autoregression models. Estimate each model with the available data. Which model provides the best fit to the data?
  c. Use the best autoregression model from part **b** to produce a forecast of the CCI in the next year. Also, provide a measure of the likely forecast error.

27. Consider the proportion of Americans under the age of 18 living below the poverty level. The data are in the file P02_44.xlsx.
  a. Find the first six autocorrelations of this time series.
  b. Use the results of part **a** to specify one or more promising autoregression models. Estimate each model with the available data. Which model provides the best fit to the data?
  c. Use the best autoregression model from part **b** to produce a forecast of the proportion of American children living below the poverty level in the next year. Also, provide a measure of the likely forecast error.

28. The file P02_25.xlsx contains monthly values of two key interest rates, the federal funds rate and the prime rate.
  a. Specify one or more promising autoregression models based on autocorrelations of the federal funds rate series. Estimate each model with the available data. Which model provides the best fit to data?
  b. Use the best autoregression model from part **a** to produce forecasts of the federal funds rate in the next two years.
  c. Repeat parts **a** and **b** for the prime rate series.

29. The file P02_24.xlsx contains time series data on the percentage of the resident population in the United States who completed four or more years of college.
  a. Specify one or more promising autoregression models based on autocorrelations of this time series. Estimate each model with the available data. Which model provides the best fit to the data?
  b. Use the best autoregression model from part **a** to produce forecasts of higher education attainment (i.e., completion of four or more years of college) in the United States in the next three years.

30. Consider the average annual interest rates on 30-year fixed mortgages in the United States. The data are recorded in the file P02_21.xlsx.
  a. Specify one or more promising autoregression models based on autocorrelations of this time series. Estimate each model with the available data. Which model provides the best fit to the data?
  b. Use the best autoregression model from part **a** to produce forecasts of the average annual interest rates on 30-year fixed mortgages in the next three years.

31. The file P12_31.xlsx lists the monthly unemployment rates for several years. A common way to forecast time series is by using regression with lagged variables.
  a. Predict future monthly unemployment rates using some combination of the unemployment rates for the last four months. For example, you might use last month's unemployment rate and the unemployment rate from three months ago as explanatory variables. Make sure all variables that you decide to keep in your final equation are significant at the 15% significance level.
  b. Do the residuals in your equation exhibit any autocorrelation?
  c. Predict the next month's unemployment rate.
  d. There is a 5% chance that the next month's unemployment rate will be less than what value?
  e. What is the probability the next month's unemployment rate will be less than 6%, assuming normally distributed residuals?

Level B

32. The unit sales of a new drug for the first 25 months after its introduction to the marketplace are recorded in the file P12_15.xlsx. Specify one or more promising autoregression models based on autocorrelations of this time series. Estimate each model with the available data. Which model provides the best fit to the data? Use the best autoregression model you found to forecast the sales of this new drug in the 26th month.

33. The file P12_02.xlsx contains the weekly sales at a local bookstore for each of the past 25 weeks.

  a. Specify one or more promising autoregression models based on autocorrelations of this time series. Estimate each model with the available data. Which model provides the best fit to the data?

  b. What general result emerges from your analysis in part **a**? In other words, what is the most appropriate autoregression model for any given *random* time series?

  c. Use the best autoregression model from part **a** to forecast weekly sales at this bookstore for the next three weeks.

34. The file P12_24.xlsx contains the daily closing prices of Procter & Gamble stock for a one-year period.

  a. Use only the 2003 data to estimate an appropriate autoregression model.

  b. Next, use the estimated autoregression model from part **a** to forecast the behavior of this time series for the 2004 dates of the series. Comment on the accuracy of the forecasts over this period.

  c. How well does the autoregression model perform in comparison to the random walk model with respect to the accuracy of these forecasts? Explain any observed differences between the forecasting abilities of the two models.

12.7 MOVING AVERAGES

Perhaps the simplest and one of the most frequently used extrapolation methods is the **moving averages** method. To implement this method, you first choose a **span**, the number of terms in each moving average. Let's say the data are monthly and you choose a span of six months. Then the forecast of next month's value is the average of the values of the last six months. For example, you average January to June to forecast July, you average February to July to forecast August, and so on. This procedure is the reason for the term *moving* averages.

> A **moving average** is the average of the observations in the past few periods, where the number of terms in the average is the **span**.

A moving averages model with a span of 1 is a random walk model with a mean trend of 0.

The role of the span is important. If the span is large—say, 12 months—then many observations go into each average, and extreme values have relatively little effect on the forecasts. The resulting series of forecasts will be much smoother than the original series. (For this reason, the moving average method is called a *smoothing* method.) In contrast, if the span is small—say, three months—then extreme observations have a larger effect on the forecasts, and the forecast series will be much less smooth. In the extreme, if the span is 1, there is no smoothing effect at all. The method simply forecasts next month's value to be the same as the current month's value. This is often called the *naive* forecasting model. It is a special case of the random walk model with the mean difference equal to 0.

What span should you use? This requires some judgment. If you believe the ups and downs in the series are random noise, then you don't want future forecasts to react too quickly to these ups and downs, and you should use a relatively large span. But if you want to track every little zigzag—under the belief that each up or down is predictable—then you should use a smaller span. You shouldn't be fooled, however, by a plot of the (smoothed) forecast series superimposed on the original series. This graph will almost always look better when a small span is used, because the forecast series will appear to track the original series better. Does this mean it will always provide better future forecasts? Not necessarily. There is little point in tracking random ups and downs closely if they represent unpredictable noise.

The following example illustrates the use of moving averages.

EXAMPLE | **12.6 Houses Sold in the United States**

The file House Sales.xlsx contains monthly data on the number of new one-family houses sold in the U.S. (in thousands) from January 1991 through September 2009. (These data, available from the U.S. Census Bureau Web site, are listed as SAAR, seasonally adjusted at an annual rate.)[6] A time series graph of the data appears in Figure 12.35. Housing sales were steadily trending upward until about the beginning of 2006, but then the bottom fell out of the housing market. Does a moving averages model fit this series well? What span should be used?

Figure 12.35 Time Series Plot of Monthly House Sales

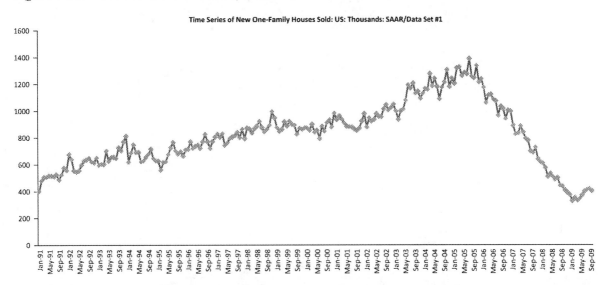

Time Series of New One-Family Houses Sold: US: Thousands: SAAR/Data Set #1

Objective To see whether a moving averages model with an appropriate span fits the housing sales data and to see how StatTools implements this method.

Solution

Although the moving averages method is quite easy to implement in Excel—you just form an average of the appropriate span and copy it down—it can be tedious. It is much easier to implement with StatTools. Actually, the StatTools forecasting procedure is fairly general in that it allows you to forecast with several methods, either with or without taking seasonality into account. Because this is your first exposure to this procedure, we will go through it in some detail in this example. In later examples, we will mention some of its other capabilities.

To use the StatTools Forecasting procedure, select Forecast from the StatTools Time Series and Forecasting dropdown list. This brings up the dialog box in Figure 12.36, which has three tabs in its bottom section. The Time Scale tab, shown in Figure 12.36, allows you to select the time period. The Forecast Settings tab, shown in Figure 12.37, allows you to select a forecasting method. Finally, the Graphs to Display tab, not shown here, allows you to select several optional time series graphs. For now, fill out the dialog box sections as

---

[6]We discuss seasonal adjustment in section 12.9. Government data are often reported in seasonally adjusted form, with the seasonality removed, to make any trends more apparent.

shown and select the Forecast Overlay option in the Graphs to Display tab. In particular, note from Figure 12.37 that the moving averages method is being used with a span of 3, and it will generate forecasts for the next 12 months.

Figure 12.36

Forecast Dialog Box with Time Scale Tab Visible

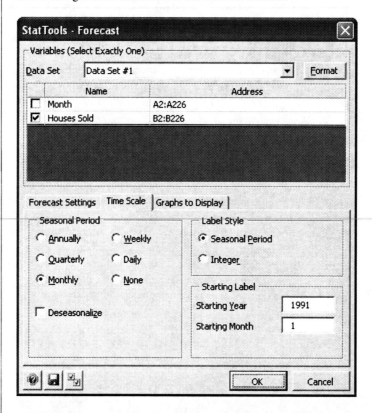

Figure 12.37

Forecast Dialog Box with Forecast Settings Tab Visible

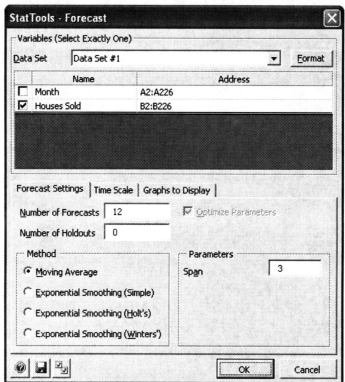

Another option in Figure 12.37 is that you can elect to "hold out" a subset of the series for validation purposes. If you hold out several periods at the end of the series for validation, any model that is built is estimated only for the non-holdout observations, and summary measures are reported for the non-holdout and holdout subsets separately. For now, don't use a holdout period.

The output consists of several parts, as shown in Figures 12.38 through 12.41. We actually ran the analysis twice, once for a span of 3 and once for a span of 12. These figures show the comparison. (We also obtained output for a span of 6, with results fairly similar to those for a span of 3.) First, the summary measures MAE, RMSE, and MAPE of the forecast errors are shown in Figure 12.38. As you can see, the forecasts using a span of 3 are considerably more accurate. For example, they are off by about 5.4% on average, whereas the similar measure with a span of 12 is 8.88%.

Figure 12.38   Moving Averages Summary Output

	A	B	C	D	E	F	G	H
8	*Forecasting Constant*						*Forecasting Constant*	
9	Span	3					Span	12
10								
11								
12	*Moving Averages*						*Moving Averages*	
13	Mean Abs Err	41.88					Mean Abs Err	66.29
14	Root Mean Sq Err	53.64					Root Mean Sq Err	85.45
15	Mean Abs Per% Err	5.37%					Mean Abs Per% Err	8.88%

Figure 12.39   Moving Averages Detailed Output

	A	B	C	D	E	F	G	H	I	J
40	*Forecasting Data*	*Houses Sold*	*Forecast*	*Error*			*Forecasting Data*	*Houses Sold*	*Forecast*	*Error*
41	Jan-1991	401.00					Jan-1991	401.00		
42	Feb-1991	482.00					Feb-1991	482.00		
43	Mar-1991	507.00					Mar-1991	507.00		
44	Apr-1991	508.00	463.33	44.67			Apr-1991	508.00		
45	May-1991	517.00	499.00	18.00			May-1991	517.00		
46	Jun-1991	516.00	510.67	5.33			Jun-1991	516.00		
47	Jul-1991	511.00	513.67	-2.67			Jul-1991	511.00		
48	Aug-1991	526.00	514.67	11.33			Aug-1991	526.00		
49	Sep-1991	487.00	517.67	-30.67			Sep-1991	487.00		
50	Oct-1991	524.00	508.00	16.00			Oct-1991	524.00		
51	Nov-1991	575.00	512.33	62.67			Nov-1991	575.00		
52	Dec-1991	558.00	528.67	29.33			Dec-1991	558.00		
53	Jan-1992	676.00	552.33	123.67			Jan-1992	676.00	509.33	166.67
54	Feb-1992	639.00	603.00	36.00			Feb-1992	639.00	532.25	106.75
55	Mar-1992	554.00	624.33	-70.33			Mar-1992	554.00	545.33	8.67
265	Sep-2009	402.00	409.67	-7.67			Sep-2009	402.00	380.75	21.25
266	Oct-2009		410.67				Oct-2009		377.92	
267	Nov-2009		409.89				Nov-2009		375.33	
268	Dec-2009		407.52				Dec-2009		374.10	
269	Jan-2010		409.36				Jan-2010		374.11	
270	Feb-2010		408.92				Feb-2010		377.87	
271	Mar-2010		408.60				Mar-2010		379.86	
272	Apr-2010		408.96				Apr-2010		383.85	
273	May-2010		408.83				May-2010		387.09	
274	Jun-2010		408.80				Jun-2010		388.43	
275	Jul-2010		408.86				Jul-2010		387.55	
276	Aug-2010		408.83				Aug-2010		385.43	
277	Sep-2010		408.83				Sep-2010		382.79	

The essence of the forecasting method is very simple and is captured in column C of Figure 12.39 for a span of 3 (with many hidden rows). Each value in the historical period in this column is an average of the three preceding values in column B. The forecast errors are then just the differences between columns B and C. For the future periods, the forecast

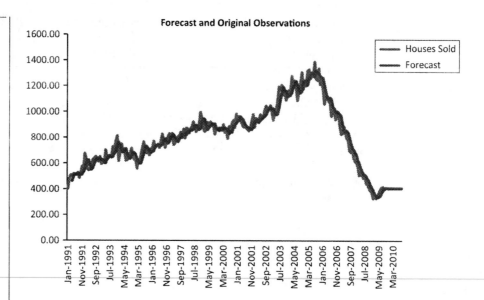

Figure 12.40

Moving Averages Forecasts with Span 3

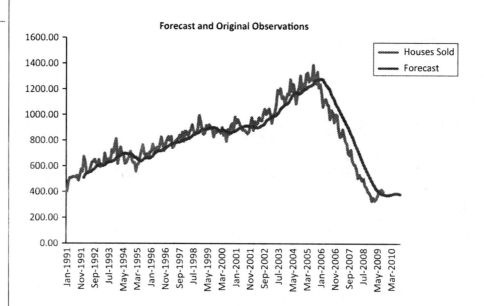

Figure 12.41

Moving Averages Forecasts with Span 12

formulas in column C use observations when they are available. If they are not available, previous forecasts are used. For example, the value in cell C267, the forecast for November 2009, is the average of the *observed* values in August and September and the *forecast* value in October.

The graphs in Figures 12.40 and 12.41 show the behavior of the forecasts. The forecast series with span 3 follows the ups and downs of the actual series fairly closely, and when the series starts going down, the moving averages track the turnaround fairly well. In contrast, the 12-month moving average series is much smoother. This is probably a good feature when the series is trending upward—there is no sense in tracking the noise—but when the series suddenly starts downward, the moving averages consistently lag behind. That is, the forecasts in this latter period are consistently too high. (This same behavior occurs for a span of 6, but the forecasts are not as biased in the latter part of the series as with a span of 12.)

One interesting feature of the moving average method is that *future* forecasts tend to be quite flat. This is apparent in the last two figures, but you can check that if we had used only the data through 2008, where the series was still trending downward, the forecasts for 2009 would still be fairly constant; they would *not* continue to decrease. This is a basic property of moving average forecasts: *future* forecasts tend to be close to the last few values of the series. ■

The moving average method we have presented is the simplest of a group of moving average methods used by professional forecasters. We *smoothed* exactly once; that is, we took moving averages of several observations at a time and used these as forecasts. More complex methods smooth more than once, basically to get rid of random noise. They take moving averages, then moving averages of these moving averages, and so on for several stages. This can become quite complex, but the objective is quite simple—to smooth the data so that underlying patterns are easier to see.

PROBLEMS

Level A

35. The file P12_16.xlsx contains the daily closing prices of American Express stock for a one-year period.
   a. Using a span of 3, forecast the price of this stock for the next trading day with the moving average method. How well does this method with span 3 forecast the known observations in this series?
   b. Repeat part **a** with a span of 10.
   c. Which of these two spans appears to be more appropriate? Justify your choice.

36. The closing value of the AMEX Airline Index for each trading day during a one-year period is given in the file P12_17.xlsx.
   a. How well does the moving average method track this series when the span is 4; when the span is 12?
   b. Using the more appropriate span, forecast the closing value of this index on the next trading day with the moving average method.

37. The closing value of the Dow Jones Industrial Average for each trading day during a one-year period is provided in the file P12_19.xlsx.
   a. Using a span of 2, forecast the price of this index on the next trading day with the moving average method. How well does the moving average method with span 2 forecast the known observations in this series?
   b. Repeat part **a** with a span of 5; with a span of 15.
   c. Which of these three spans appears to be most appropriate? Justify your choice.

38. The file P12_10.xlsx contains the daily closing prices of Walmart stock during a one-year period. Use the moving average method with a carefully chosen span to forecast this time series for the next three trading days. Defend your choice of the span used.

39. The Consumer Confidence Index (CCI) attempts to measure people's feelings about general business conditions, employment opportunities, and their own income prospects. The file P02_20.xlsx contains the annual average values of the CCI. Use the moving average method with a carefully chosen span to forecast this time series in the next two years. Defend your choice of the span used.

Level B

40. The file P02_28.xlsx contains total monthly U.S. retail sales data. While holding out the final six months of observations for validation purposes, use the method of moving averages with a carefully chosen span to forecast U.S. retail sales in the next year. Comment on the performance of your model. What makes this time series more challenging to forecast?

41. Consider a random walk model with the following equation: $Y_t = Y_{t-1} + e_t$, where e_t is a random series with mean 0 and standard deviation 1. Specify a moving average model that is equivalent to this random walk model. In particular, what is the appropriate span in the equivalent moving average model? What is the smoothing effect of this span?

12.8 EXPONENTIAL SMOOTHING

There are two possible criticisms of the moving averages method. First, it puts equal weight on each value in a typical moving average. Many analysts would argue that if next month's forecast is to be based on the previous 12 months' observations, more weight should be placed on the more recent observations. The second criticism is that the moving averages method requires a lot of data storage. This is particularly true for companies that routinely make forecasts of hundreds or even thousands of items. If 12-month moving averages are used for 1000 items, then 12,000 values are needed for next month's forecasts. This may or may not be a concern, given today's inexpensive computer storage.

Exponential smoothing is a method that addresses both of these criticisms. It bases its forecasts on a weighted average of past observations, with more weight on the more recent observations, and it requires very little data storage. In addition, it is not difficult for most business people to understand, at least conceptually. Therefore, this method is used widely in the business world, particularly when frequent and automatic forecasts of many items are required.

There are many variations of exponential smoothing. The simplest is appropriately called *simple* exponential smoothing. It is relevant when there is no pronounced trend or seasonality in the series. If there is a trend but no seasonality, *Holt's* method is applicable. If, in addition, there is seasonality, *Winters'* method can be used. This does not exhaust the types of exponential smoothing models—researchers have invented many other variations—but these three models will suffice for us.

Exponential Smoothing Models

Simple exponential smoothing is appropriate for a series with no pronounced trend or seasonality. **Holt's** method is appropriate for a series with trend but no seasonality. **Winters'** method is appropriate for a series with seasonality (and possibly trend).

In this section we examine simple exponential smoothing and Holt's model for trend. Then in the next section we examine Winters' model for seasonal models.

12.8.1 Simple Exponential Smoothing

The level is an estimate of where the series would be if it were not for random noise.

We now examine simple exponential smoothing in some detail. We first introduce two new terms. Every exponential model has at least one **smoothing constant**, which is always a number between 0 and 1. Simple exponential smoothing has a single smoothing constant denoted by α. (Its role is discussed shortly.) The second new term is L_t, called the *level* of the series at time t. This value is not observable but can only be estimated. Essentially, it is an estimate of where the series would be at time t if there were no random noise. Then the simple exponential smoothing method is defined by the following two equations, where F_{t+k} is the forecast of Y_{t+k} made at time t:

Simple Exponential Smoothing Formulas

$$L_t = \alpha Y_t + (1 - \alpha)L_{t-1} \tag{12.12}$$

$$F_{t+k} = L_t \tag{12.13}$$

Even though you usually don't have to substitute into these equations manually, you should understand what they say. Equation (12.12) shows how to update the estimate of the level. It is a weighted average of the current observation, Y_t, and the previous level, L_{t-1}, with respective weights α and $1 - \alpha$. Equation (12.13) shows how forecasts are made. It says that the k-period-ahead forecast, F_{t+k}, made of Y_{t+k} in period t is the most recently estimated level, L_t. This is the *same* for any value of $k \geq 1$. The idea is that in simple exponential smoothing, you believe that the series is not really going anywhere. So as soon as you estimate where the series ought to be in period t (if it weren't for random noise), you forecast that this is where it will be in any future period.

The smoothing constant α is analogous to the span in moving averages. There are two ways to see this. The first way is to rewrite Equation (12.12), using the fact that the forecast error, E_t, made in forecasting Y_t at time $t - 1$ is $Y_t - F_t = Y_t - L_{t-1}$. Using algebra, Equation (12.12) can be rewritten as Equation (12.14).

Equivalent Formula for Simple Exponential Smoothing

$$L_t = L_{t-1} + \alpha E_t \qquad \textbf{(12.14)}$$

This equation says that the next estimate of the level is adjusted from the previous estimate by adding a multiple of the most recent forecast error. This makes sense. If the previous forecast was too high, then E_t is negative, and the estimate of the level is adjusted downward. The opposite is true if the previous forecast was too low. However, Equation (12.14) says that the method does not adjust by the entire magnitude of E_t, but only by a fraction of it. If α is small, say, $\alpha = 0.1$, the adjustment is minor; if α is close to 1, the adjustment is large. So if you want the method to react quickly to movements in the series, you should choose a large α; otherwise, you should choose a small α.

Another way to see the effect of α is to substitute recursively into the equation for L_t. By performing some algebra, you can verify that L_t satisfies Equation (12.15), where the sum extends back to the first observation at time $t = 1$.

Another Equivalent Formula for Simple Exponential Smoothing

$$L_t = \alpha Y_t + \alpha(1 - \alpha)Y_{t-1} + \alpha(1 - \alpha)^2 Y_{t-2} + \alpha(1 - \alpha)^3 Y_{t-3} + \cdots \qquad \textbf{(12.15)}$$

Equation (12.15) shows how the exponentially smoothed forecast is a weighted average of previous observations. Furthermore, because $1 - \alpha$ is less than 1, the weights on the Ys decrease from time t backward. Therefore, if α is close to 0, then $1 - \alpha$ is close to 1 and the weights decrease very slowly. In other words, observations from the distant past continue to have a large influence on the next forecast. This means that the graph of the forecasts will be relatively smooth, just as with a large span in the moving averages method. But when α is close to 1, the weights decrease rapidly, and only very recent observations have much influence on the next forecast. In this case forecasts react quickly to sudden changes in the series. This is equivalent to a small span in moving averages.

Small smoothing constants provide forecasts that respond slowly to changes in the series. Large smoothing constants do the opposite.

What value of α should you use? There is no universally accepted answer to this question. Some practitioners recommend always using a value around 0.1 or 0.2. Others recommend experimenting with different values of α until a measure such as RMSE or MAPE is minimized. Some packages even have an optimization feature to find this optimal value of α. (This is the case with StatTools.) But just as we discussed in the moving averages section, the value of α that tracks the historical series most closely does not necessarily guarantee the most accurate *future* forecasts.

Smoothing Constants in Exponential Smoothing

All versions of exponential smoothing—and there are more than are discussed here—use one or more smoothing constants between 0 and 1. To make any such method produce smoother forecasts, and hence react less quickly to noise, use smaller smoothing constants, such as 0.1 or 0.2. When larger smoothing constants are used, the historical forecasts might appear to track the actual series fairly closely, but they might just be tracking random noise.

EXAMPLE | **12.6 HOUSES SOLD IN THE UNITED STATES (CONTINUED)**

Previously, we used the moving averages method to forecast monthly housing sales in the U.S. (See the House Sales.xlsx file.) How well does simple exponential smoothing work with this data set? What smoothing constant should be used?

Objective To see how well a simple exponential smoothing model, with an appropriate smoothing constant, fits the housing sales data, and to see how StatTools implements this method.

Solution

You can use StatTools to implement the simple exponential smoothing model, specifically equations (12.12) and (12.13). You do this again with the Forecast item from the StatTools Time Series and Forecasting dropdown list. Specifically, you fill in the forecast dialog box essentially as with moving averages, except that you select the simple exponential smoothing option in the Forecast Settings tab (see Figure 12.42). You should also choose a

Figure 12.42

Forecast Settings for Exponential Smoothing

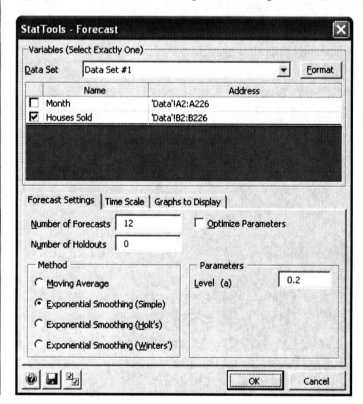

smoothing constant (0.2 was chosen here, but any other value could be chosen) or you can elect to find an optimal smoothing constant (we didn't optimize for this example, at least not yet).

The results appear in Figures 12.43 (with many hidden rows) and 12.44. The heart of the method takes place in columns C, D, and E of Figure 12.43. Column C calculates the smoothed levels (L_t) from Equation (12.12), column D calculates the forecasts (F_t) from Equation (12.13), and column E calculates the forecast errors (E_t) as the observed values minus the forecasts. Although the Excel formulas do not appear in the figure, you can examine them in the StatTools output.

	A	B	C	D	E
8	*Forecasting Constant*				
9	Level (Alpha)	0.200			
10					
11					
12	*Simple Exponential*				
13	Mean Abs Err	54.81			
14	Root Mean Sq Err	69.91			
15	Mean Abs Per% Err	7.45%			
38					
39					
40	*Forecasting Data*	Houses Sold	Level	Forecast	Error
41	Jan-1991	401.00	401.00		
42	Feb-1991	482.00	417.20	401.00	81.00
43	Mar-1991	507.00	435.16	417.20	89.80
44	Apr-1991	508.00	449.73	435.16	72.84
45	May-1991	517.00	463.18	449.73	67.27
46	Jun-1991	516.00	473.75	463.18	52.82
47	Jul-1991	511.00	481.20	473.75	37.25
48	Aug-1991	526.00	490.16	481.20	44.80
263	Jul-2009	413.00	392.29	387.12	25.88
264	Aug-2009	417.00	397.24	392.29	24.71
265	Sep-2009	402.00	398.19	397.24	4.76
266	Oct-2009			398.19	
267	Nov-2009			398.19	
268	Dec-2009			398.19	
269	Jan-2010			398.19	
270	Feb-2010			398.19	
271	Mar-2010			398.19	
272	Apr-2010			398.19	
273	May-2010			398.19	
274	Jun-2010			398.19	
275	Jul-2010			398.19	
276	Aug-2010			398.19	
277	Sep-2010			398.19	

Every exponential smoothing method requires *initial* values, in this case the initial smoothed level in cell C41. There is no way to calculate this value, L_1, from Equation (12.12) because the *previous* value, L_0, is unknown. Different implementations of exponential smoothing initialize in different ways. StatTools initializes by setting L_1 equal to Y_1 (in cell B41). The effect of initializing in different ways is usually minimal because any effect of early data is usually washed out as forecast are made into the future. In the present example, values from 1991 have little effect on forecasts for 2009 and beyond.

Note that the 12 future forecasts (rows 266 down) are all equal to the last calculated smoothed level, the one for September 2009 in cell C265. The fact that these remain con-

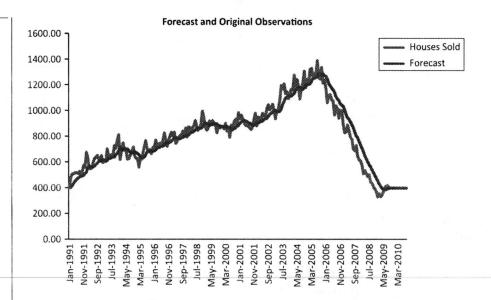

Figure 12.44

Graph of Forecasts
from Simple
Exponential
Smoothing

stant is a consequence of the assumption behind *simple* exponential smoothing, namely, that the series is not really going anywhere. Therefore, the last smoothed level is the best available indication of future values of the series.

Figure 12.44 shows the forecast series superimposed on the original series. You can see the obvious smoothing effect of a relatively small α level. The forecasts don't track the series very well, but if the various zigzags in the original series are really random noise, then perhaps the forecasts shouldn't try to track these random ups and downs too closely. That is, perhaps a forecast series that emphasizes the basic underlying pattern is preferred. However, notice that once the series starts going downhill, the forecasts never quite catch up. This is the same behavior you saw with a span of 12 for moving averages.

You can see several summary measures of the forecast errors in Figure 12.43. The RMSE and MAE indicate that the forecasts from this model are typically off by a magnitude of about 55 to 70 thousand, and the MAPE indicates that they are off by about 7.5%. (These are similar to the errors obtained earlier with moving averages with span 12.) These are fairly sizable errors. One way to reduce the errors is to use a different smoothing method. We will try this in the next subsection with Holt's method. Another way to reduce the errors is to use a different smoothing constant. There are two methods you can use. First, you can simply enter different values in the smoothing constant cell in the Forecast sheet. All formulas, including those for MAE, RMSE, and MAPE, will update automatically.

Second, you can check the Optimize Parameters option in the Forecast dialog box shown in Figure 12.42. This automatically runs an optimization algorithm (not Solver, by the way) to find the smoothing constant that minimizes RMSE. (StatTools is programmed to minimize RMSE. However, you could try minimizing MAPE, say, by using Excel's Solver add-in.) When this optimization option is used for the housing data, the results in Figure 12.45 are obtained (from a smoothing constant of 0.691). The corresponding MAE, RMSE, and MAPE are 39.6, 50.1, and 5.01%, respectively—better than before. This larger smoothing constant produces a less smooth forecast curve and slightly better error measures. However, there is no guarantee that *future* forecasts made with this optimal smoothing constant will be any better than with a smoothing constant of 0.2.

Figure 12.45

Graph of Forecasts
with an Optimal
Smoothing Constant

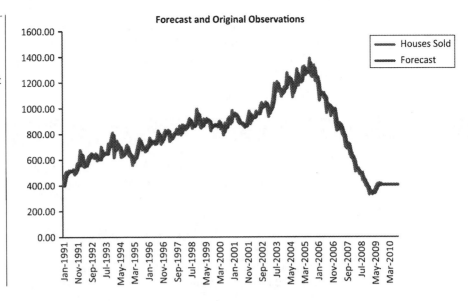

Forecast and Original Observations

12.8.2 Holt's Model for Trend

The trend term in Holt's method estimates the change from one period to the next.

The simple exponential smoothing model generally works well if there is no obvious trend in the series. But if there is a trend, this method consistently lags behind it. For example, if the series is constantly increasing, simple exponential smoothing forecasts will be consistently low. Holt's method rectifies this by dealing with trend explicitly. In addition to the level of the series, L_t, Holt's method includes a trend term, T_t, and a corresponding smoothing constant β. The interpretation of L_t is exactly as before. The interpretation of T_t is that it represents an estimate of the *change* in the series from one period to the next. The equations for Holt's model are as follows.

Formulas for Holt's Exponential Smoothing Method

$$L_t = \alpha Y_t + (1 - \alpha)(L_{t-1} + T_{t-1}) \tag{12.16}$$

$$T_t = \beta(L_t - L_{t-1}) + (1 - \beta)T_{t-1} \tag{12.17}$$

$$F_{t+k} = L_t + kT_t \tag{12.18}$$

These equations are not as bad as they look. (And don't forget that the software does all of the calculations for you.) Equation (12.16) says that the updated level is a weighted average of the current observation and the previous level plus the estimated change. Equation (12.17) says that the updated trend is a weighted average of the difference between two consecutive levels and the previous trend. Finally, Equation (12.18) says that the *k*-period-ahead forecast made in period *t* is the estimated level plus *k* times the estimated change per period.

Everything we said about α for simple exponential smoothing applies to both α and β in Holt's model. The new smoothing constant β controls how quickly the method reacts to observed changes in the trend. If β is small, the method reacts slowly. If it is large, the method reacts more quickly. Of course, there are now two smoothing constants to select.

Some practitioners suggest using a small value of α (0.1 to 0.2, say) and setting β equal to α. Others suggest using an optimization option (available in StatTools) to select the optimal smoothing constants. We illustrate the possibilities in the following continuation of the housing sales example.

EXAMPLE

12.6 HOUSES SOLD IN THE UNITED STATES (CONTINUED)

We again examine the monthly data on housing sales in the U.S. In the previous subsection, we saw that simple exponential smoothing, even with an optimal smoothing constant, does only a fair job of forecasting housing sales. Given that there is an upward trend and then a downward trend in housing sales over this period, Holt's method might be expected to perform better. Does it? What smoothing constants are appropriate?

Objective   To see whether Holt's method, with appropriate smoothing constants, captures the trends in the housing sales data better than simple exponential smoothing (or moving averages).

Solution

You implement Holt's method in StatTools almost exactly as you did for simple exponential smoothing. The only difference is that you can now choose *two* smoothing constants, as shown in Figure 12.46. They can have different values, but they have both been chosen to be 0.2 for this example.

Figure 12.46

Dialog Box for
Holt's Method

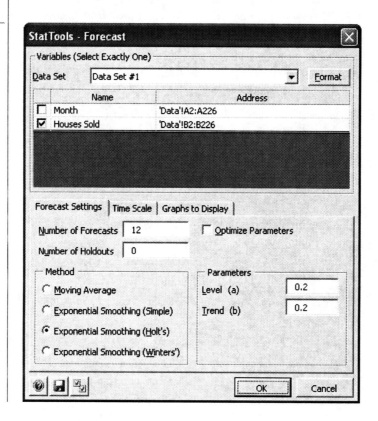

The StatTools outputs in Figures 12.47 and 12.48 are also very similar to the simple exponential smoothing outputs. The only difference is that there is now a trend column, column D, in the numerical output. You can check that the formulas in columns C, D, and E implement equations (12.16), (12.17), and (12.18). As before, an initialization is required in row 42. These require values of L_1 and T_1 to get the method started. Different implementations of Holt's method obtain these initial values in slightly different ways, but the effect is fairly minimal in most cases. (You can check cells C42 and D42 to see how StatTools does it.[7])

Figure 12.47

Output from Holt's Method

	A	B	C	D	E	F
8	Forecasting Constants					
9	Level (Alpha)	0.200				
10	Trend (Beta)	0.200				
11						
12						
13	Holt's Exponential					
14	Mean Abs Err	42.59				
15	Root Mean Sq Err	54.85				
16	Mean Abs Per% Err	5.57%				
40						
41	Forecasting Data	Houses Sold	Level	Trend	Forecast	Error
42	Jan-1991	401.00	401.00	0.00		
43	Feb-1991	482.00	417.20	3.24	401.00	81.00
44	Mar-1991	507.00	437.76	6.71	420.45	86.55
45	Apr-1991	508.00	457.17	9.25	444.46	63.54
46	May-1991	517.00	476.54	11.27	466.42	50.58
47	Jun-1991	516.00	493.45	12.40	487.81	28.19
48	Jul-1991	511.00	506.88	12.60	505.84	5.16
49	Aug-1991	526.00	520.78	12.87	519.48	6.52
50	Sep-1991	487.00	524.32	11.00	533.65	-46.65
264	Jul-2009	413.00	325.12	-4.21	303.15	109.85
265	Aug-2009	417.00	340.12	-0.37	320.91	96.09
266	Sep-2009	402.00	352.20	2.12	339.75	62.25
267	Oct-2009				354.32	
268	Nov-2009				356.44	
269	Dec-2009				358.56	
270	Jan-2010				360.68	
271	Feb-2010				362.80	
272	Mar-2010				364.92	
273	Apr-2010				367.03	
274	May-2010				369.15	
275	Jun-2010				371.27	
276	Jul-2010				373.39	
277	Aug-2010				375.51	
278	Sep-2010				377.63	

The error measures for this implementation of Holt's method are slightly better than for simple exponential smoothing, but these measures are fairly sensitive to the smoothing constants. Therefore, a second run of Holt's method was performed, using the Optimize Parameters option. This resulted in somewhat better results and the forecasts shown in Figure 12.49. The optimal smoothing constants are $\alpha = 0.691$ and $\beta = 0.000$, and the MAE, RMSE, and MAPE values are identical to those from simple exponential smoothing with an optimal smoothing constant. Note that the zero smoothing constant for trend

[7]The initial trend in cell D42 (the first period) is the final observation minus the initial observation, all divided by the number of observations. This is the average change over the entire time period. This is probably not the best way to initialize, as suggested by the literature, and StatTools will probably be rewritten in a future version to initialize with the average change over the first two years. This will give it a better chance to *learn* how a trend changes over time.

Figure 12.48

Forecasts from
Holt's Method with
Nonoptimal
Smoothing
Constants

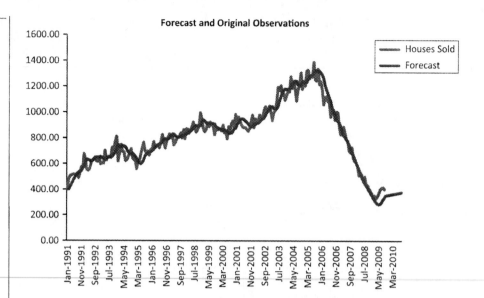

doesn't mean that there is no trend. It just means that the *initial* estimate of trend, the average change from the first time period to the last, is kept throughout. For this particular time series, despite the upward trend and the downward trend, the series ends very close to where it started. Therefore, the initial trend estimate is about zero, and future forecasts with the optimal smoothing constants are essentially flat. However, you can check that if a larger smoothing constant for trend is used, say 0.4, future forecasts will exhibit the same upward trend evident in the first nine months of 2009. Based on a look at the graph and common sense, we would suggest smoothing constants of about 0.2 for this series.

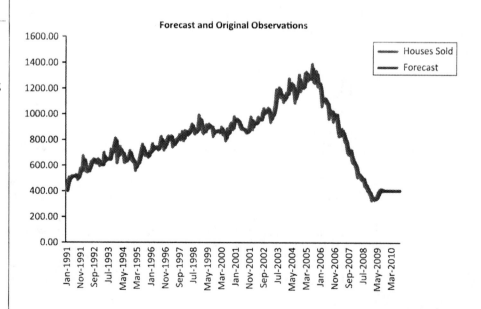

You should not conclude from this example that Holt's method is never superior to simple exponential smoothing. Holt's method is often able to react quickly to a sudden upswing or downswing in the data, whereas simple exponential smoothing typically has a delayed reaction to such a change. ∎

PROBLEMS

Level A

42. Consider the airline ticket data in the file P12_01.xlsx.
    a. Create a time series chart of the data. Based on what you see, which of the exponential smoothing models do you think should be used for forecasting? Why?
    b. Use simple exponential smoothing to forecast these data, using no holdout period and requesting 12 months of future forecasts. Use the default smoothing constant of 0.1.
    c. Repeat part b, optimizing the smoothing constant. Does it make much of an improvement?
    d. Write a short report to summarize your results.

43. Consider the applications for home mortgages data in the file P12_04.xlsx.
    a. Create a time series chart of the data. Based on what you see, which of the exponential smoothing models do you think should be used for forecasting? Why?
    b. Use simple exponential smoothing to forecast these data, using no holdout period and requesting four quarters of future forecasts. Use the default smoothing constant of 0.1.
    c. Repeat part b, optimizing the smoothing constant. Does it make much of an improvement?
    d. Write a short report to summarize your results.

44. Consider the American Express closing price data in the file P12_16.xlsx. Focus only on the closing prices.
    a. Create a time series chart of the data. Based on what you see, which of the exponential smoothing models do you think should be used for forecasting? Why?
    b. Use Holt's exponential smoothing to forecast these data, using no holdout period and requesting 20 days of future forecasts. Use the default smoothing constants of 0.1.
    c. Repeat part b, optimizing the smoothing constants. Does it make much of an improvement?
    d. Repeat parts a and b, this time using a holdout period of 50 days.
    e. Write a short report to summarize your results.

45. Consider the poverty level data in the file P02_44.xlsx.
    a. Create a time series chart of the data. Based on what you see, which of the exponential smoothing models do you think should be used for forecasting? Why?
    b. Use simple exponential smoothing to forecast these data, using no holdout period and requesting three years of future forecasts. Use the default smoothing constant of 0.1.

    c. Repeat part b, optimizing the smoothing constant. Make sure you request a chart of the series with the forecasts superimposed. Does the Optimize Parameters option make much of an improvement?
    d. Write a short report to summarize your results. Considering the chart in part c, would you say the forecasts are adequate?

Problems 46 through 48 ask you to apply the exponential smoothing formulas. These do not require StatTools. In fact, they do not even require Excel. You can do them with a calculator (or with Excel).

46. An automobile dealer is using Holt's method to forecast weekly car sales. Currently, the level is estimated to be 50 cars per week, and the trend is estimated to be six cars per week. During the current week, 30 cars are sold. After observing the current week's sales, forecast the number of cars three weeks from now. Use $\alpha = \beta = 0.3$.

47. You have been assigned to forecast the number of aircraft engines ordered each month from an engine manufacturing company. At the end of February, the forecast is that 100 engines will be ordered during April. Then during March, 120 engines are actually ordered.
    a. Using $\alpha = 0.3$, determine a forecast (at the end of March) for the number of orders placed during April and during May. Use simple exponential smoothing.
    b. Suppose that MAE = 16 at the end of March. At the end of March, the company can be 68% sure that April orders will be between what two values, assuming normally distributed forecast errors? (*Hint*: It can be shown that the standard deviation of forecast errors is approximately 1.25 times MAE.)

48. Simple exponential smoothing with $\alpha = 0.3$ is being used to forecast sales of SLR (single lens reflex) cameras at an appliance store. Forecasts are made on a monthly basis. After August camera sales are observed, the forecast for September is 100 cameras.
    a. During September, 120 cameras are sold. After observing September sales, what is the forecast for October camera sales? What is the forecast for November camera sales?
    b. It turns out that June sales were recorded as 10 cameras. Actually, however, 100 cameras were sold in June. After correcting for this error, what is the forecast for October camera sales?

Level B

49. Holt's method assumes an *additive* trend. For example, a trend of five means that the level will increase by five units per period. Suppose that there is actually a

multiplicative trend. For example, if the current estimate of the level is 50 and the current estimate of the trend is 1.2, the forecast of demand increases by 20% per period. So the forecast demand for next period is 50(1.2) and forecast demand for two periods in the future is $50(1.2)^2$. If you want to use a multiplicative trend in Holt's method, you should use equations of the form:

$$L_t = \alpha Y_t + (1 - \alpha)(I)$$
$$T_t = \beta(II) + (1 - \beta)T_{t-1}$$

a. What should (*I*) and (*II*) be?
b. Suppose you are working with monthly data and month 12 is December, month 13 is January, and so on. Also suppose that $L_{12} = 100$ and $T_{12} = 1.2$, and you observe $Y_{13} = 200$. At the end of month 13, what is the forecast for Y_{15}? Assume $\alpha = \beta = 0.5$ and a multiplicative trend.

50. A version of simple exponential smoothing can be used to predict the outcome of sporting events. To illustrate, consider pro football. Assume for simplicity that all games are played on a neutral field. Before each day of play, assume that each team has a rating. For example, if the rating for the Bears is +10 and the rating for the Bengals is +6, the Bears are predicted to beat the Bengals by 10 − 6 = 4 points. Suppose that the Bears

play the Bengals and win by 20 points. For this game, the model underpredicted the Bears' performance by 20 − 4 = 16 points. Assuming that the best α for pro football is 0.10, the Bears' rating will increase by 16(0.1) = 1.6 points and the Bengals' rating will decrease by 1.6 points. In a rematch, the Bears will then be favored by (10 + 1.6) − (6 − 1.6) = 7.2 points.

a. How does this approach relate to the equation $L_t = L_{t-1} + \alpha E_t$?
b. Suppose that the home field advantage in pro football is three points; that is, home teams tend to outscore equally rated visiting teams by an average of three points a game. How could the home field advantage be incorporated into this system?
c. How might you determine the *best* α for pro football?
d. How could the ratings for each team at the beginning of the season be chosen?
e. Suppose this method is used to predict pro football (16-game schedule), college football (11-game schedule), college basketball (30-game schedule), and pro basketball (82-game schedule). Which sport do you think will have the smallest optimal α? Which will have the largest optimal α? Why?
f. Why might this approach yield poor forecasts for major league baseball?

12.9 SEASONAL MODELS

Some time series software packages have special types of graphs for spotting seasonality, but we won't discuss these here.

So far we have said practically nothing about seasonality. Seasonality is the consistent month-to-month (or quarter-to-quarter) differences that occur each year. (It could also be the day-to-day differences that occur each week.) For example, there is seasonality in beer sales—high in the summer months, lower in other months. Toy sales are also seasonal, with a huge peak in the months preceding Christmas. In fact, if you start thinking about time series variables that you are familiar with, the majority of them probably have some degree of seasonality.

How can you tell whether there is seasonality in a time series? The easiest way is to check whether a graph of the time series has a *regular* pattern of ups and/or downs in particular months or quarters. Although random noise can sometimes mask such a pattern, the seasonal pattern is usually fairly obvious.

As you saw with the housing sales data, government agencies often perform part of the second method for us—that is, they deseasonalize the data.

There are basically three methods for dealing with seasonality. First, you can use Winters' exponential smoothing model. It is similar to simple exponential smoothing and Holt's method, except that it includes another component (and smoothing constant) to capture seasonality. Second, you can *deseasonalize* the data, then use any forecasting method to model the deseasonalized data, and finally "reseasonalize" these forecasts. Finally, you can use multiple regression with dummy variables for the seasons. We discuss all three of these methods in this section.

Seasonal models are usually classified as *additive* or *multiplicative*. Suppose that the series contains monthly data, and that the average of the 12 monthly values for a typical year is 150. An **additive** model finds seasonal indexes, one for each month, that are *added* to the monthly average, 150, to get a particular month's value. For example, if the index for March is 22, then a typical March value is 150 + 22 = 172. If the seasonal index for

September is -12, then a typical September value is $150 - 12 = 138$. A **multiplicative** model also finds seasonal indexes, but they are *multiplied* by the monthly average to get a particular month's value. Now if the index for March is 1.3, a typical March value is $150(1.3) = 195$. If the index for September is 0.9, then a typical September value is $150(0.9) = 135$.

In an **additive** seasonal model, an appropriate seasonal index is added to a base forecast. These indexes, one for each season, typically average to 0.

In a **multiplicative** seasonal model, a base forecast is multiplied by an appropriate seasonal index. These indexes, one for each season, typically average to 1.

Either an additive or a multiplicative model can be used to forecast seasonal data. However, because multiplicative models are somewhat easier to interpret (and have worked well in applications), we focus on them. Note that the seasonal index in a multiplicative model can be interpreted as a percentage. Using the figures in the previous paragraph as an example, March tends to be 30% above the monthly average, whereas September tends to be 10% below it. Also, the seasonal indexes in a multiplicative model typically average to 1. Software packages usually ensure that this happens.

12.9.1 Winters' Exponential Smoothing Model

We now turn to Winters' exponential smoothing model. It is very similar to Holt's model—it again has level and trend terms and corresponding smoothing constants α and β—but it also has seasonal indexes and a corresponding smoothing constant γ (gamma). This new smoothing constant controls how quickly the method reacts to observed changes in the seasonality pattern. If γ is small, the method reacts slowly. If it is large, the method reacts more quickly. As with Holt's model, there are equations for updating the level and trend terms, and there is one extra equation for updating the seasonal indexes. For completeness, we list these equations, but they are clearly too complex for hand calculation and are best left to the software. In Equation (12.21), S_t refers to the multiplicative seasonal index for period t. In equations (12.19), (12.21), and (12.22), M refers to the number of seasons ($M = 4$ for quarterly data, $M = 12$ for monthly data).

Formulas for Winters' Exponential Smoothing Model

$$L_t = \alpha \frac{Y_t}{S_{t-M}} + (1 - \alpha)(L_{t-1} + T_{t-1}) \qquad (13.19)$$

$$T_t = \beta(L_t - L_{t-1}) + (1 - \beta)T_{t-1} \qquad (13.20)$$

$$S_t = \gamma \frac{Y_t}{L_t} + (1 - \gamma)S_{t-M} \qquad (13.21)$$

$$F_{t+k} = (L_t + kT_t)S_{t+k-M} \qquad (13.22)$$

To see how the forecasting in Equation (12.22) works, suppose you have observed data through June and you want a forecast for the coming September, that is, a three-month-ahead forecast. (In this case t refers to June and $t + k = t + 3$ refers to September.) The method first adds 3 times the current trend term to the current level. This gives a forecast for September that would be appropriate if there were no seasonality. Next, it multiplies this forecast by the most recent estimate of September's seasonal index (the one from the previous September) to get the forecast for September. Of course, the software does all of the arithmetic, but this is basically what it is doing. We illustrate the method in the following example.

EXAMPLE | **12.7 QUARTERLY SOFT DRINK SALES**

The data in the Soft Drink Sales.xlsx file represent quarterly sales (in millions of dollars) for a large soft drink company from quarter 1 of 1994 through quarter 4 of 2009. There has been an upward trend in sales during this period, and there is also a fairly regular seasonal pattern, as shown in Figure 12.50. Sales in the warmer quarters, 2 and 3, are consistently higher than in the colder quarters, 1 and 4. How well can Winters' method track this upward trend and seasonal pattern?

Figure 12.50

Time Series Graph of Soft Drink Sales

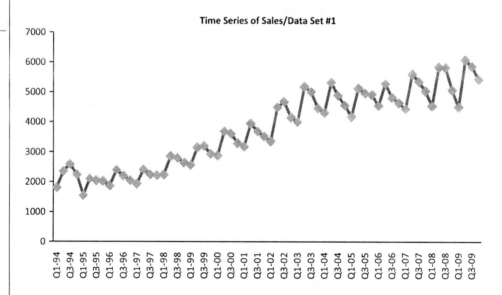

Objective To see how well Winters' method, with appropriate smoothing constants, can forecast the company's seasonal soft drink sales.

Solution

To use Winters' method with StatTools, you proceed exactly as with any of the other exponential smoothing methods. However, for a change (and because there are so many years of data), you can use StatTools's option of holding out some of the data for validation. Specifically, fill out the Time Scale tab in the Forecast dialog box as shown in Figure 12.51. Then fill in the Forecast Settings tab of this dialog box as shown in Figure 12.52, selecting Winters' method, basing the model on the data through Q4-2007, holding out eight quarters of data (Q1-2008 through Q4-2009), and forecasting four quarters into the future (all of 2010). Note that when you choose Winters' method in Figure 12.52, the Deseasonalize option in Figure 12.51 is automatically disabled. It wouldn't make sense to deseasonalize *and* use Winters' method; you do one or the other. Also, you can optimize the smoothing constants as is done here, but this is optional.

Figure 12.51

Time Scale Settings for Soft Drink Sales

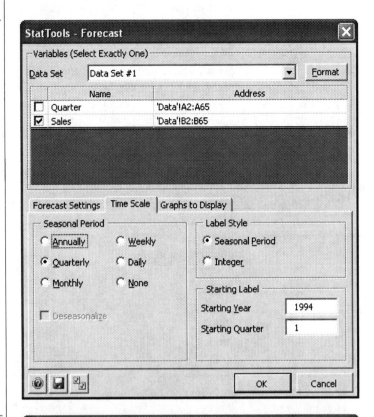

Figure 12.52

Forecast Settings for Soft Drink Sales

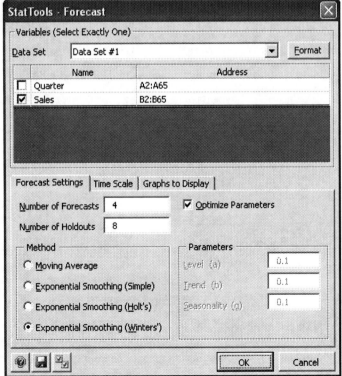

You can check that if three years of data are held out, the MAPE for the holdout period increases quite a lot. It is common for the fit to be considerably better in the estim-ation period than in the holdout period.

Parts of the output are shown in Figure 12.53. The following points are worth noting: (1) The optimal smoothing constants (those that minimize RMSE) are $\alpha = 1.0$, $\beta = 0.0$, and $\gamma = 0.0$. Intuitively, these mean that the method reacts immediately to changes in level, but it never reacts to changes in the trend or the seasonal pattern. (2) Aside from seasonality, the series is trending upward at a rate of 56.65 per quarter (see column D). This is the initial esti-mate of trend and, because β is 0, it never changes. (3) The seasonal pattern stays constant throughout this 14-year period. The seasonal indexes, shown in column E, are 0.88, 1.10, 1.05, and 0.96. For example, quarter 1 is 12% below the yearly average, and quarter 2 is 10% above the yearly average. (4) The forecast series tracks the actual series quite well during the non-holdout period. For example, MAPE is 3.86%, meaning that the forecasts are off by about 4% on average. Surprisingly, MAPE for the holdout period is even lower, at 2.48%.

Figure 12.53   Output from Winters' Method for Soft Drink Sales

	A	B	C	D	E	F	G
8	**Forecasting Constants (Optimized)**						
9	Level (Alpha)	1.000					
10	Trend (Beta)	0.000					
11	Season (Gamma)	0.000					
12							
13		Estimation	Holdouts				
14	**Winters' Exponential**	Period	Period				
15	Mean Abs Err	123.23	123.65				
16	Root Mean Sq Err	166.71	158.65				
17	Mean Abs Per% Err	3.86%	2.48%				
41							
42	**Forecasting Data**	Sales	Level	Trend	Season	Forecast	Error
43	Q1-1994	1807.37	2052.06	56.65	0.88		
44	Q2-1994	2355.32	2136.61	56.65	1.10	2324.57	30.75
45	Q3-1994	2591.83	2461.52	56.65	1.05	2309.37	282.46
46	Q4-1994	2236.39	2320.05	56.65	0.96	2427.36	-190.97
47	Q1-1995	1549.14	1758.87	56.65	0.88	2093.30	-544.16
48	Q2-1995	2105.79	1910.25	56.65	1.10	2001.37	104.42
49	Q3-1995	2041.32	1938.69	56.65	1.05	2071.03	-29.71
50	Q4-1995	2021.01	2096.62	56.65	0.96	1923.38	97.63
92	Q2-2006	5284.71	4793.98	56.65	1.10	5748.01	-463.30
93	Q3-2006	4817.43	4575.22	56.65	1.05	5107.42	-289.99
94	Q4-2006	4634.50	4807.88	56.65	0.96	4464.83	169.67
95	Q1-2007	4431.36	5031.31	56.65	0.88	4284.47	146.89
96	Q2-2007	5602.21	5082.00	56.65	1.10	5608.78	-6.57
97	Q3-2007	5349.85	5080.87	56.65	1.05	5410.69	-60.84
98	Q4-2007	5036.00	5224.40	56.65	0.96	4952.25	83.75
99	Q1-2008	4534.61				4651.32	-116.71
100	Q2-2008	5836.17				5884.09	-47.92
101	Q3-2008	5818.28				5679.93	138.35
102	Q4-2008	5070.42				5254.42	-184.00
103	Q1-2009	4497.47				4850.90	-353.43
104	Q2-2009	6075.52				6133.88	-58.36
105	Q3-2009	5868.67				5918.52	-49.85
106	Q4-2009	5432.24				5472.85	-40.61
107	Q1-2010					5050.47	
108	Q2-2010					6383.67	
109	Q3-2010					6157.11	
110	Q4-2010					5691.27	

The plot of the forecasts superimposed on the original series, shown in Figure 12.54, indicates that Winters' method clearly picks up the seasonal pattern and the upward trend and projects both of these into the future. In later examples, we will investigate whether other seasonal forecasting methods can do this well.

Figure 12.54

Graph of Forecasts
from Winters'
Method

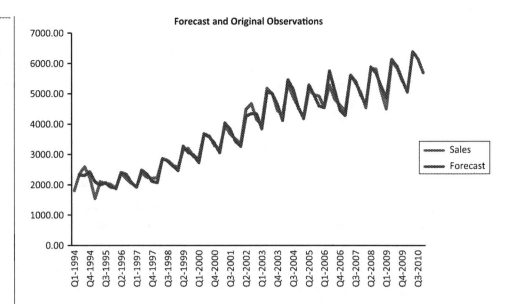

Forecast and Original Observations

One final comment is that you are not obligated to find the *optimal* smoothing constants. Some analysts suggest using more "typical" values such as $\alpha = \beta = 0.2$ and $\gamma = 0.5$. (It is customary to choose γ larger than α and β because each season's seasonal index gets updated only once per year.) To see how these smoothing constants affect the results, you can substitute their values in the range B9:B11 of Figure 12.53. As expected, MAE, RMSE, and MAPE all get somewhat worse (they increase to 185, 236, and 5.78%, respectively, for the estimation period), but a plot of the forecasts superimposed on the original sales data still indicates a very good fit. ▪

The three exponential smoothing methods we have examined are not the only ones available. For example, there are linear and quadratic models available in some software packages. These are somewhat similar to Holt's model except that they use only a single smoothing constant. There are also adaptive exponential smoothing models, where the smoothing constants themselves are allowed to change over time. Although these more complex models have been studied thoroughly in the academic literature and are used by some practitioners, they typically offer only marginal gains in forecast accuracy over the models we have examined.

12.9.2 Deseasonalizing: The Ratio-to-Moving-Averages Method

You have probably seen references to time series data that have been **deseasonalized**. (Web sites often use the abbreviations SA and NSA for seasonally adjusted and nonseasonally adjusted.) The reason why data are often published in deseasonalized form is that readers can then spot trends more easily. For example, if you see a time series of sales that has not been deseasonalized, and it shows a large increase from November to December, you might not be sure whether this represents a real increase in sales or a seasonal phenomenon (Christmas sales). However, if this increase is really just a seasonal effect, the deseasonalized version of the series will show no such increase in sales.

Government economists and statisticians have a variety of sophisticated methods for deseasonalizing time series data, but they are typically variations of the **ratio-to-moving-averages** method described here. This method is applicable when seasonality is multiplicative, as described in the previous section. The goal is to find the seasonal indexes, which can then be used to deseasonalize the data. For example, if the estimated index for June is 1.3, this means that June's values are typically about 30% larger than the average for all months. Therefore, June's value is *divided* by 1.3 to obtain the (smaller) deseasonalized value. Similarly, if February's index is 0.85, then February's values are 15% below the average for all months, so February's value is divided by 0.85 to obtain the (larger) deseasonalized value.

> To **deseasonalize** an observation (assuming a multiplicative model of seasonality), *divide* it by the appropriate seasonal index.

To find the seasonal index for June 2009 (or any other month) in the first place, you essentially divide June's observation by the average of the 12 observations surrounding June. (This is the reason for the term *ratio* in the name of the method.) There is one minor problem with this approach. June 2009 is not exactly in the middle of any 12-month sequence. If you use the 12 months from January 2009 to December 2009, June 2009 is in the *first* half of the sequence; if you use the 12 months from December 2008 to November 2009, June 2009 is in the *last* half of the sequence. Therefore, you can compromise by averaging the January-to-December and December-to-November averages. This is called a *centered* average. Then the seasonal index for June is June's observation divided by this centered average. The following equation shows more specifically how it works.

$$\text{Jun2009 index} = \frac{\text{June2009}}{\left(\dfrac{\text{Dec2010} + \cdots + \text{Nov2009}}{12} + \dfrac{\text{Jan2009} + \cdots + \text{Dec2009}}{12} \right)/2}$$

The only remaining question is how to combine all of the indexes for any specific month such as June. After all, if the series covers several years, the procedure produces several June indexes, one for each year. The usual way to combine them is to average them. This single average index for June is then used to deseasonalize *all* of the June observations.

Once the seasonal indexes are obtained, each observation is divided by its seasonal index to deseasonalize the data. The deseasonalized data can then be forecast by *any* of the methods we have described (other than Winters' method, which wouldn't make much sense). For example, Holt's method or the moving averages method could be used to forecast the deseasonalized data. Finally, the forecasts are "reseasonalized" by *multiplying* them by the seasonal indexes.

As this description suggests, the method is not meant for hand calculations. However, it is straightforward to implement in StatTools, as we illustrate in the following example.

EXAMPLE | **12.7 QUARTERLY SOFT DRINK SALES (CONTINUED)**

We return to the soft drink sales data. (See the file Soft Drink Sales.xlsx.) Is it possible to obtain the same forecast accuracy with the ratio-to-moving-averages method as with Winters' method?

Objective   To use the ratio-to-moving-averages method to deseasonalize the soft drink data and then forecast the deseasonalized data.

Solution

The answer to this question depends on which forecasting method is used to forecast the *deseasonalized* data. The ratio-to-moving-averages method only provides a means for deseasonalizing the data and providing seasonal indexes. Beyond this, any method can be used to forecast the deseasonalized data, and some methods typically work better than others. For this example, we actually compared two possibilities: the moving averages method with a span of four quarters, and Holt's exponential smoothing method optimized, but the results are shown only for the latter. Because the deseasonalized series still has a clear upward trend, Holt's method should do well, and the moving averages forecasts should tend to lag behind the trend. This is exactly what occurred. For example, the values of MAPE for the two methods are 6.11% (moving averages) and 3.86% (Holt's). (To make a fair comparison with the Winters' method output for these data, an eight-quarter holdout period was again used). The MAPE values reported are for the non-holdout period.)

To implement this latter method in StatTools, proceed exactly as before, but this time check the Deseasonalize option in the Time Scale tab of the Forecast dialog box. (See Figure 12.55.) Note that when the Holt's option is checked, this Deseasonalize option is enabled. When you check this option, you get a larger selection of optional charts in the Graphs to Display tab. You can ask to see charts of the deseasonalized data and/or the original "reseasonalized" data.

Figure 12.55

Checking the Deseasonalizing Option

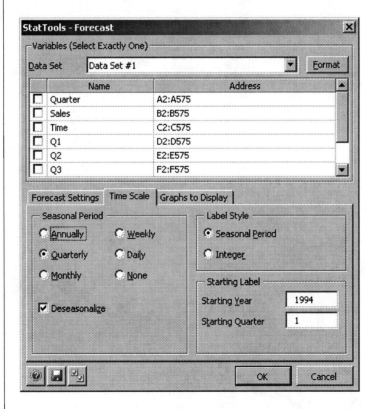

Selected outputs are shown in Figures 12.56 through 12.59. Figures 12.56 and 12.57 show the numerical output. In particular, Figure 12.57 shows the seasonal indexes from the ratio-to-moving averages method in column C. These are virtually identical to the seasonal indexes found with Winters' method, although the methods are mathematically different. Column D contains the deseasonalized sales (column B divided by column C), columns E through H implement Holt's method on the deseasonalized data, and columns I and J are the "reseasonalized" forecasts and errors.

Figure 12.56

Summary Measures for Forecast Errors

	A	B	C	D	E
8	**Forecasting Constants (Optimized)**				
9	Level (Alpha)	1.000			
10	Trend (Beta)	0.000			
11					
12		Estimation	Holdouts	Deseason	Deseason
13	**Holt's Exponential**	Period	Period	Estimate	Holdouts
14	Mean Abs Err	123.23	123.65	124.26	130.24
15	Root Mean Sq Err	166.71	158.65	169.38	173.56
16	Mean Abs Per% Err	3.86%	2.48%	3.86%	2.48%

Figure 12.57 Ratio-to-Moving-Averages Output

	A	B	C	D	E	F	G	H	I	J
61			Season	Deseason	Deseason	Deseason	Deseason	Deseason	Season	Season
62	Forecasting Data	Sales	Index	Sales	Level	Trend	Forecast	Errors	Forecast	Errors
63	Q1-1994	1807.37	0.88	2052.06	2052.06	56.65				
64	Q2-1994	2355.32	1.10	2136.61	2136.61	56.65	2108.71	27.89	2324.57	30.75
65	Q3-1994	2591.83	1.05	2461.52	2461.52	56.65	2193.26	268.26	2309.37	282.46
66	Q4-1994	2236.39	0.96	2320.05	2320.05	56.65	2518.17	-198.11	2427.36	-190.97
67	Q1-1995	1549.14	0.88	1758.87	1758.87	56.65	2376.70	-617.83	2093.30	-544.16
68	Q2-1995	2105.79	1.10	1910.25	1910.25	56.65	1815.52	94.73	2001.37	104.42
69	Q3-1995	2041.32	1.05	1938.69	1938.69	56.65	1966.90	-28.21	2071.03	-29.71
70	Q4-1995	2021.01	0.96	2096.62	2096.62	56.65	1995.33	101.28	1923.38	97.63
112	Q2-2006	5284.71	1.10	4793.98	4793.98	56.65	5214.26	-420.28	5748.01	-463.30
113	Q3-2006	4817.43	1.05	4575.22	4575.22	56.65	4850.63	-275.41	5107.42	-289.99
114	Q4-2006	4634.50	0.96	4807.88	4807.88	56.65	4631.86	176.01	4464.83	169.67
115	Q1-2007	4431.36	0.88	5031.31	5031.31	56.65	4864.53	166.78	4284.47	146.89
116	Q2-2007	5602.21	1.10	5082.00	5082.00	56.65	5087.96	-5.96	5608.78	-6.57
117	Q3-2007	5349.85	1.05	5080.87	5080.87	56.65	5138.64	-57.78	5410.69	-60.84
118	Q4-2007	5036.00	0.96	5224.40	5224.40	56.65	5137.52	86.88	4952.25	83.75
119	Q1-2008	4534.61	0.88	5148.54			5281.05	-132.51	4651.32	-116.71
120	Q2-2008	5836.17	1.10	5294.23			5337.70	-43.47	5884.09	-47.92
121	Q3-2008	5818.28	1.05	5525.74			5394.35	131.40	5679.93	138.35
122	Q4-2008	5070.42	0.96	5260.11			5451.00	-190.89	5254.42	-184.00
123	Q1-2009	4497.47	0.88	5106.37			5507.64	-401.27	4850.90	-353.43
124	Q2-2009	6075.52	1.10	5511.35			5564.29	-52.94	6133.88	-58.36
125	Q3-2009	5868.67	1.05	5573.60			5620.94	-47.34	5918.52	-49.85
126	Q4-2009	5432.24	0.96	5635.46			5677.59	-42.13	5472.85	-40.61
127	Q1-2010		0.88				5734.24		5050.47	
128	Q2-2010		1.10				5790.89		6383.67	
129	Q3-2010		1.05				5847.54		6157.11	
130	Q4-2010		0.96				5904.19		5691.27	

Figure 12.58

Forecast Graph of Deseasonalized Series

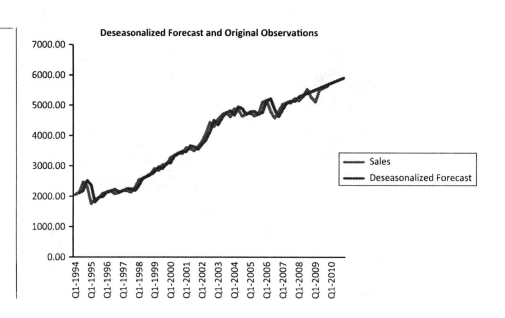

Deseasonalized Forecast and Original Observations

— Sales
— Deseasonalized Forecast

Figure 12.59

Forecast Graph of
Reseasonalized
(Original) Series

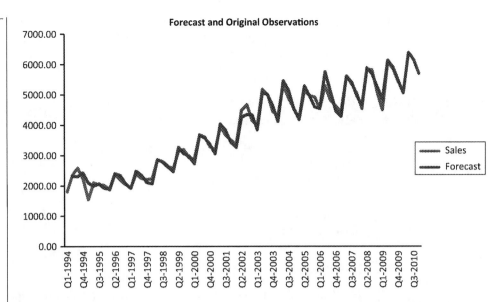

Forecast and Original Observations

The deseasonalized data, with forecasts superimposed, appear in Figure 12.58. Here you see only the smooth upward trend with no seasonality, which Holt's method is able to track very well. Then Figure 12.59 shows the results of reseasonalizing. Again, the forecasts track the actual sales data very well. In fact, you can see that the summary measures of forecast errors (in Figure 12.56, range B14:B16) are quite comparable to those from Winters' method. The reason is that both arrive at virtually the same seasonal pattern. ∎

12.9.3 Estimating Seasonality with Regression

We now examine a regression approach to forecasting seasonal data that uses dummy variables for the seasons. Depending on how you write the regression equation, you can create either an additive or a multiplicative seasonal model.

As an example, suppose that the data are quarterly data with a possible linear trend. Then you can create dummy variables Q_1, Q_2, and Q_3 for the first three quarters (using quarter 4 as the reference quarter) and estimate the additive equation

$$\text{Forecast } Y_t = a + bt + b_1Q_1 + b_2Q_2 + b_3Q_3$$

Then the coefficients of the dummy variables, b_1, b_2 and b_3, indicate how much each quarter differs from the reference quarter, quarter 4, and the coefficient b represents the trend.

For example, if the estimated equation is

$$\text{Forecast } Y_t = 130 + 25t + 15Q_1 + 5Q_2 - 20Q_3$$

the average increase from one quarter to the next is 25 (the coefficient of t). This is the trend effect. However, quarter 1 averages 15 units higher than quarter 4, quarter 2 averages 5 units higher than quarter 4, and quarter 3 averages 20 units lower than quarter 4. These coefficients indicate the seasonality effect.

As discussed in Chapter 10, it is also possible to estimate a *multiplicative* model using dummy variables for seasonality (and possibly time for trend). Then you would estimate the equation

$$\text{Forecast } Y_t = ae^{bt}e^{b_1Q_1}e^{b_2Q_2}e^{b_3Q_3}$$

or, after taking logs,

$$\text{Forecast LN } Y_t = \text{LN } a + bt + b_1Q_1 + b_2Q_2 + b_3Q_3$$

One advantage of this approach is that it provides a model with *multiplicative* seasonal factors. It is also fairly easy to interpret the regression output, as illustrated in the following continuation of the soft drink sales example.

EXAMPLE | 12.7 QUARTERLY SOFT DRINK SALES (CONTINUED)

Returning to the soft drink sales data (see the file Soft Drink Sales.xlsx), does a regression approach provide forecasts that are as accurate as those provided by the other seasonal methods in this chapter?

Objective To use a multiplicative regression equation, with dummy variables for seasons and a time variable for trend, to forecast soft drink sales.

Solution

We illustrate the multiplicative approach, although an additive approach is also possible. Figure 12.60 illustrates the data setup. Besides the Sales and Time variables, you need to create dummy variables for three of the four quarters and a Log(Sales) variable. You can then use multiple regression, with Log(Sales) as the dependent variable, and Time, Q1, Q2, and Q3 as the explanatory variables.

Figure 12.60

Data Setup for Multiplicative Model with Dummies

	A	B	C	D	E	F	G
1	Quarter	Sales	Time	Q1	Q2	Q3	Log(Sales)
2	Q1-94	1807.37	1	1	0	0	7.499628
3	Q2-94	2355.32	2	0	1	0	7.7644319
4	Q3-94	2591.83	3	0	0	1	7.8601195
5	Q4-94	2236.39	4	0	0	0	7.7126182
6	Q1-95	1549.14	5	1	0	0	7.3454552
7	Q2-95	2105.79	6	0	1	0	7.652446
8	Q3-95	2041.32	7	0	0	1	7.6213519
9	Q4-95	2021.01	8	0	0	0	7.6113527
10	Q1-96	1870.46	9	1	0	0	7.5339397
11	Q2-96	2390.56	10	0	1	0	7.7792829
12	Q3-96	2198.03	11	0	0	1	7.6953168
13	Q4-96	2046.83	12	0	0	0	7.6240475
14	Q1-97	1934.19	13	1	0	0	7.5674439
15	Q2-97	2406.41	14	0	1	0	7.7858913

The regression output appears in Figure 12.61. (Again, to make a fair comparison with previous methods, the regression is based only on the data through quarter 4 of 2007. That is, the last eight quarters are again held out. This means that the StatTools data set should extend only through row 57.) Of particular interest are the coefficients of the explanatory variables. Recall that for a log-dependent variable, these coefficients can be interpreted as *percentage* changes in the original sales variable. Specifically, the coefficient of Time means that deseasonalized sales increase by about 1.9% per quarter. Also, the coefficients of Q1, Q2, and Q3 mean that sales in quarters 1, 2, and 3 are, respectively, about 9.0% below, 14.0% above, and 9.1% above sales in the reference quarter, quarter 4. This pattern is quite comparable to the pattern of seasonal indexes you saw in previous models for these data.

Figure 12.61 Regression Output for Multiplicative Model

	A	B	C	D	E	F	G
7		Multiple	R-Square	Adjusted	StErr of		
8	Summary	R		R-Square	Estimate		
9		0.9628	0.9270	0.9218	0.102		
10							
11		Degrees of	Sum of	Mean of	F-Ratio	p-Value	
12	ANOVA Table	Freedom	Squares	Squares			
13	Explained	4	7.465	1.866	177.8172	< 0.0001	
14	Unexplained	56	0.588	0.010			
15							
16		Coefficient	Standard	t-Value	p-Value	Confidence Interval 95%	
17	Regression Table		Error			Lower	Upper
18	Constant	7.510	0.036	210.8236	< 0.0001	7.439	7.581
19	Time	0.019	0.001	25.9232	< 0.0001	0.018	0.021
20	Q1	-0.090	0.037	-2.4548	0.0172	-0.164	-0.017
21	Q2	0.140	0.037	3.7289	0.0005	0.065	0.215
22	Q3	0.091	0.037	2.4449	0.0177	0.017	0.166

To compare the forecast accuracy of this method to earlier models, you must perform several steps manually. (See Figure 12.62 for reference.) First, calculate the forecasts in column H by entering the formula

=EXP(Regression!$B$18+MMULT(Data!C2:F2,Regression!$B$19:$B$22))

in cell H2 and copying it down. (This formula assumes the regression output is in a sheet named Regression. It uses Excel's MMULT function to sum the products of explanatory values and regression coefficients. You can replace this by "writing out" the sum of products if you like. The formula then takes EXP of the resulting sum to convert the log sales value back to the original sales units.) Next, calculate the absolute errors, squared errors, and absolute percentage errors in columns I, J, and K, and summarize them in the usual way, both for the estimation period and the holdout period, in columns N and O.

Figure 12.62 Forecast Errors and Summary Measures

	A	B	C	D	E	F	G	H	I	J	K	L	M	N	O
1	Quarter	Sales	Time	Q1	Q2	Q3	Log(Sales)	Forecast	SqError	AbsError	PctAbsError		Error measures		
2	Q1-94	1807.37	1	1	0	0	7.499628	1701.137	11285.37	106.2326	0.05877746			Estimation	Holdout
3	Q2-94	2355.32	2	0	1	0	7.7644319	2182.866	29740.49	172.4543	0.07321906		RMSE	337.09	754.57
4	Q3-94	2591.83	3	0	0	1	7.8601195	2120.895	221779.5	470.9347	0.18169969		MAE	276.40	732.28
5	Q4-94	2236.39	4	0	0	0	7.7126182	1973.262	69236.44	263.1282	0.11765755		MAPE	8.05%	13.74%
6	Q1-95	1549.14	5	1	0	0	7.3454552	1837.876	83368.58	288.7362	0.18638482				
7	Q2-95	2105.79	6	0	1	0	7.652446	2358.326	63774.52	252.5362	0.11992467				
8	Q3-95	2041.32	7	0	0	1	7.6213519	2291.375	62527.28	250.0545	0.1224965				
9	Q4-95	2021.01	8	0	0	0	7.6113527	2131.874	12290.87	110.8642	0.05485584				
10	Q1-96	1870.46	9	1	0	0	7.5339397	1985.606	13258.63	115.1461	0.06156034				
11	Q2-96	2390.56	10	0	1	0	7.7792829	2547.89	24752.83	157.3303	0.06581317				

Note that these summary measures are considerably larger for this regression model than for the previous seasonality models, especially in the holdout period. You can get some idea why the holdout period does so poorly by looking at the plot of observations versus forecasts in Figure 12.63. The multiplicative regression model with Time included really implies *exponential* growth (as in section 12.4.2), with seasonality superimposed. However, this company's sales growth tapered off in the last couple of years and did not keep up with the exponential growth curve. In short, the dummy variables do a good job of tracking seasonality, but the underlying exponential trend curve outpaces actual sales. It is reasonable to conclude that this regression model is *not* as good for forecasting this company's sales as Winters' method or Holt's method on the deseasonalized data.

Figure 12.63

Graph of Forecasts for Multiplicative Model

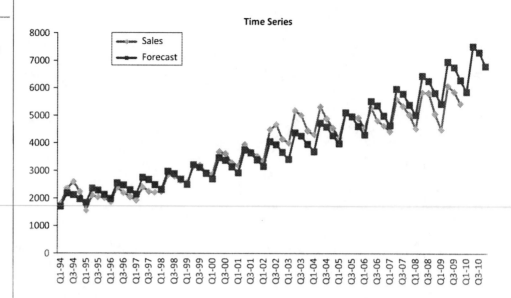

This method of detecting seasonality by using dummy variables in a regression equation is always an option. The other variables included in the regression equation could be time t, lagged versions of Y_t, and/or current or lagged versions of other explanatory variables. These variables would capture any time series behavior other than seasonality. Just remember that there is always one less dummy variable than the number of seasons. If the data are quarterly, then three dummies are needed; if the data are monthly, then 11 dummies are needed. If the coefficients of any of these dummies turn out to be statistically insignificant, they can be omitted from the equation. Then the omitted terms are effectively combined with the reference season. For example, if the Q_1 term were omitted, then quarters 1 and 4 would essentially be combined and treated as the reference season, and the other two seasons would be compared to them through their dummy variable coefficients. ∎

PROBLEMS

Level A

51. The University Credit Union is open Monday through Saturday. Winters' method is being used (with $\alpha = \beta = \gamma = 0.5$) to predict the number of customers entering the bank each day. After incorporating the arrivals on Monday, October 16, the seasonal indexes are: Monday, 0.90; Tuesday, 0.70; Wednesday, 0.80; Thursday, 1.1; Friday, 1.2; Saturday, 1.3. Also, the current estimates of level and trend are 200 and 1. On Tuesday, October 17, 182 customers enter the bank. At the close of business on October 17, forecast the number of customers who will enter the bank on each of the next six business days.

52. A local bank is using Winters' method with $\alpha = 0.2$, $\beta = 0.1$, and $\gamma = 0.5$ to forecast the number of customers served each day. The bank is open Monday through Friday. At the end of the previous week, the following seasonal indexes have been estimated: Monday, 0.80; Tuesday, 0.90; Wednesday, 0.95; Thursday, 1.10; Friday, 1.25. Also, the current estimates of level and trend are 20 and 1. After observing that 30 customers are served by the bank on this Monday, forecast the number of customers who will be served on each of the next five business days.

53. Suppose that Winters' method is used to forecast quarterly U.S. retail sales (in billions of dollars). At the end of the first quarter of 2010, the seasonal indexes are: quarter 1, 0.90; quarter 2, 0.95; quarter 3, 0.95; quarter 4, 1.20. Also, the current estimates of level and trend are 300 and 30. During the second quarter of 2010, retail sales are $360 billion. Assume $\alpha = 0.2$, $\beta = 0.4$, and $\gamma = 0.5$.

   a. At the end of the second quarter of 2010, develop a forecast for retail sales during the third and fourth quarters of 2010.

   b. At the end of the second quarter of 2010, develop a forecast for the first and second quarter of 2011.

54. The file P02_55.xlsx contains monthly retail sales of beer, wine, and liquor at U.S. liquor stores.

   a. Is seasonality present in these data? If so, characterize the seasonality pattern and then deseasonalize this time series using the ratio-to-moving-average method.

   b. If you decided to deseasonalize this time series in part **a**, forecast the deseasonalized data for each month of the next year using the moving average method with an appropriate span.

   c. Does Holt's exponential smoothing method, with optimal smoothing constants, outperform the moving average method employed in part **b**? Demonstrate why or why not.

55. Continuing the previous problem, how do your responses to the questions change if you employ Winters' method to handle seasonality in this time series? Explain. Which forecasting method do you prefer, Winters' method or one of the methods used in the previous problem? Defend your choice.

56. The file P12_56.xlsx contains monthly time series data for total U.S. retail sales of building materials (which includes retail sales of building materials, hardware and garden supply stores, and mobile home dealers).

   a. Is seasonality present in these data? If so, characterize the seasonality pattern and then deseasonalize this time series using the ratio-to-moving-average method.

   b. If you decided to deseasonalize this time series in part **a**, forecast the deseasonalized data for each month of the next year using the moving average method with an appropriate span.

   c. Does Holt's exponential smoothing method, with optimal smoothing constants, outperform the moving average method employed in part **b**? Demonstrate why or why not.

57. The file P12_57.xlsx consists of the monthly retail sales levels of U.S. gasoline service stations.

   a. Is there a seasonal pattern in these data? If so, how do you explain this seasonal pattern? Also, if necessary, deseasonalize these data using the ratio-to-moving-average method.

   b. Forecast this time series for the first four months of the next year using the most appropriate method for these data. Defend your choice of forecasting method.

58. The number of employees on the payroll at a food processing plant is recorded at the start of each month. These data are provided in the file P12_03.xlsx.

   a. Is there a seasonal pattern in these data? If so, how do you explain this seasonal pattern? Also, if necessary, deseasonalize these data using the ratio-to-moving-average method.

   b. Forecast this time series for the first four months of the next year using the most appropriate method. Defend your choice of forecasting method.

59. The file P12_59.xlsx contains total monthly U.S. retail sales data. Compare the effectiveness of Winters' method with that of the ratio-to-moving-average method in deseasonalizing this time series. Using the deseasonalized time series generated by each of these two methods, forecast U.S. retail sales with the most appropriate method. Defend your choice of forecasting method.

60. Suppose that a time series consisting of six years $(2005-2010)$ of quarterly data exhibits obvious seasonality. In fact, assume that the seasonal indexes turn out to be 0.75, 1.45, 1.25, and 0.55.

   a. If the last four observations of the series (the four quarters of 2010) are 2502, 4872, 4269, and 1924, calculate the deseasonalized values for the four quarters of 2010.

   b. Suppose that a plot of the deseasonalized series shows an upward linear trend, except for some random noise. Therefore, you estimate a linear regression equation for this series versus time and obtain the following equation:

Predicted deseasonalized value $= 2250 + 51$Quarter

   Here the time variable Quarter is coded so that Quarter $= 1$ corresponds to first quarter 2005, Quarter $= 24$ corresponds to fourth quarter 2010, and the others fall in between. Forecast the actual (not deseasonalized) values for the four quarters of 2011.

61. The file P12_61.xlsx contains monthly data on the number of nonfarm hires in the U.S. since 2000.

   a. What evidence is there that seasonality is important in this series? Find seasonal indexes (by any method you like) and state briefly what they mean.

   b. Forecast the next 12 months by using a linear trend on the seasonally adjusted data. State briefly the steps you use to obtain this type of forecast. Then give the final RMSE, MAPE, and forecast for the next month. Show numerically how you could replicate this forecast (i.e., explain in words how the package uses its estimated model to get the next month's forecast).

62. Quarterly sales for a department store over a six-year period are given in the file P12_62.xlsx.

  a. Use multiple regression to develop an equation that can be used to predict future quarterly sales. (*Hint:* Use dummy variables for the quarters and a time variable for the quarter number, 1 to 24.)

  b. Letting Y_t be the sales during quarter t, discuss how to estimate the following equation for this series.

$$Y_t = ab_1^t b_2^{X_1} b_3^{X_2} b_4^{X_3}$$

Here X_1 is a dummy for first quarters, X_2 is a dummy for second quarters, and X_3 is a dummy for third quarters.

  c. Interpret the results from part **b**.

  d. Which model appears to yield better predictions for sales, the one in part **a** or the one in part **b**?

63. A shipping company is attempting to determine how its shipping costs for a month depend on the number of units shipped during a month. The number of units shipped and total shipping cost for the last 15 months are given in the file P12_63.xlsx.

  a. Determine a relationship between units shipped and monthly shipping cost.

  b. Plot the errors for the predictions in order of time sequence. Is there any unusual pattern?

  c. It turns out that there was a trucking strike during months 11 through 15, and you believe that this might have influenced shipping costs. How can the answer to part **a** be modified to account for the effect of the strike? After accounting for this effect, does the unusual pattern in part **b** disappear?

Level B

64. Consider a monthly series of air conditioner (AC) sales. In the discussion of Winters' method, a monthly seasonality of 0.80 for January, for example, means that during January, AC sales are expected to be 80% of the sales during an average month. An alternative approach to modeling seasonality, called an *additive model*, is to let the seasonality factor for each month represent how far above average AC sales are during the current month. For instance, if $S_{Jan} = -50$, then AC sales during January are expected to be 50 fewer than AC sales during an average month. (This is 50 ACs, not 50%.) Similarly, if $S_{July} = 90$, then AC sales during July are expected to be 90 more than AC sales during an average month. Let

S_t = Seasonality for month t after observing month t demand

L_t = Estimate of level after observing month t demand

T_t = Estimate of trend after observing month t demand

Then the Winters' method equations given in the text should be modified as follows:

$$L_t = \alpha(I) + (1 - \alpha)(L_{t-1} + T_{t-1})$$
$$T_t = \beta(L_t - L_{t-1}) + (1 - \beta)T_{t-1}$$
$$S_t = \gamma(II) + (1 - \gamma)S_{t-12}$$

  a. What should (*I*) and (*II*) be?

  b. Suppose that month 13 is January, $L_{12} = 30$, $T_{12} = -3$, $S_1 = -50$, and $S_2 = -20$. Let $\alpha = \gamma = \beta = 0.5$. Suppose 12 ACs are sold during month 13. At the end of month 13, what is the forecast for AC sales during month 14 using this additive model?

65. Winters' method assumes a multiplicative seasonality but an additive trend. For example, a trend of 5 means that the level will increase by five units per period. Suppose that there is actually a *multiplicative* trend. Then (ignoring seasonality) if the current estimate of the level is 50 and the current estimate of the trend is 1.2, the forecast of demand increases by 20% per period. So the forecast demand for the next period is $50(1.2)$ and forecast demand for two periods in the future is $50(1.2)^2$. If you want to use a multiplicative trend in Winters' method, you should use the following equations (assuming a period is a month):

$$L_t = \alpha\left(\frac{Y_t}{S_{t-12}}\right) + (1 - \alpha)(I)$$
$$T_t = \beta(II) + (I - \beta)T_{t-1}$$
$$S_t = \gamma\left(\frac{Y_t}{L_t}\right) + (1 - \gamma)S_{t-12}$$

  a. What should (*I*) and (*II*) be?

  b. Suppose that you are working with monthly data and month 12 is December, month 13 is January, and so on. Also, suppose that $L_{12} = 100$, $T_{12} = 1.2$, $S_1 = 0.90$, $S_2 = 0.70$, and $S_3 = 0.95$. If you have just observed $Y_{13} = 200$, what is the forecast for Y_{15} using $\alpha = \beta = \gamma = 0.5$ and a multiplicative trend?

66. Consider the file P12_59.xlsx, which contains total monthly U.S. retail sales data. Does a regression approach for estimating seasonality provide forecasts that are as accurate as those provided by (a) Winters' method and (b) the ratio-to-moving-average method? Compare the summary measures of forecast errors associated with each method for deseasonalizing this time series. Summarize the results of these comparisons.

67. The file P12_56.xlsx contains monthly time series data for total U.S. retail sales of building materials (which includes retail sales of building materials, hardware and garden supply stores, and mobile home dealers). Does a regression approach for estimating seasonality provide forecasts that are as accurate as those provided by (a) Winters' method and (b) the ratio-to-moving-average method? Compare the summary measures of forecast errors associated with each method for deseasonalizing the given time series. Summarize the results of these comparisons.

12.10 CONCLUSION

We have covered a lot of ground in this chapter. Because forecasting is such an important activity in business, it has received a tremendous amount of attention by both academics and practitioners. All of the methods discussed in this chapter—and more—are actually used, often on a day-to-day basis. There is really no point in arguing which of these methods is best. All of them have their strengths and weaknesses. The most important point is that when they are applied properly, they have all been found to be useful in real business situations.

Summary of Key Terms

Term	Explanation	Excel	Page	Equation
Extrapolation methods	Forecasting methods where only past values of a variable (and possibly time itself) are used to forecast future values		672	
Causal (or econometric) methods	Forecasting methods based on regression, where other time series variables are used as explanatory variables		672	
Trend	A systematic increase or decrease of a time series variable through time		674	
Seasonality	A regular pattern of ups and downs based onthe season of the year, typically months or quarters		675	
Cyclic variation	An irregular pattern of ups and downs caused by business cycles		675	
Noise (or random variation)	The unpredictable ups and downs of a time series variable		676	
Forecast error	The difference between the actual value and the forecast		677	
Mean absolute error (MAE)	The average of the absolute forecast errors	StatTools/ Time Series & Forecasting/ Forecast	677	12.2
Root mean square error (RMSE)	The square root of the average of the squared forecast errors	StatTools/ Time Series & Forecasting/ Forecast	677	12.3
Mean absolute percentage error (MAPE)	The average of the absolute percentage forecast errors	StatTools/ Time Series& Forecasting/ Forecast	677	12.4
Runs test	A test of whether the forecast errors are random noise	StatTools/ Time Series& Forecasting/ Runs Test for Randomness	681	
Autocorrelations	Correlations of a time series variable with lagged versions of itself	StatTools/ Time Series & Forecasting/ Autocorrelation	683	
Correlogram	A bar chart of autocorrelations at different lags	StatTools/ Time Series & Forecasting/ Autocorrelation	684	

(continued)

Summary of Key Terms   *(Continued)*

Term	Explanation	Excel	Page	Equation
Linear trend model	A regression model where a time series variable changes by a constant amount each time period	StatTools/Regression & Classification/ Regression	687	12.6
Exponential trend model	A regression model where a time series variable changes by a constant percentage each time period	StatTools/ Regression & Classification/ Regression	690	12.7
Random walk model	A model indicating that the differences between adjacent observations of a time series variable are constant except for random noise		695	2.9 − 12.11
Autoregression model	A regression model where the only explanatory variables are lagged values of the dependent variable (and possibly other time series variables or their lags)	StatTools/ Regression & Classification/ Regression	699	
Moving averages model	A forecasting model where the average of several past observations is used to forecast the next observation	StatTools/ Time Series & Forecasting/ Forecast	704	
Span	The number of observations in each average of a moving averages model	StatTools/ Time Series & Forecasting/ Forecast	704	
Exponential smoothing models	A class of forecasting models where forecasts are based on weighted averages of previous observations, giving more weight to more recent observations	StatTools/ Time Series & Forecasting/ Forecast	710	
Smoothing constants	Constants between 0 and 1 that prescribe the weight attached to previous observations and hence the smoothness of the series of forecasts	StatTools/ Time Series & Forecasting/ Forecast	710	
Simple exponential smoothing	An exponential smoothing model useful for time series with no prominent trend or seasonality	StatTools/ Time Series & Forecasting/ Forecast	711	12.12 − 12.15
Holt's method	An exponential smoothing model useful for time series with trend but no seasonality	StatTools/ Time Series & Forecasting/ Forecast	715	12.16 − 12.18
Winters' method	An exponential smoothing model useful for time series with seasonality (and possibly trend)	StatTools/ Time Series & Forecasting/ Forecast	721	12.19 − 12.22
Deseasonalizing	A method for removing the seasonal component from a time series	StatTools/ Time Series& Forecasting/ Forecast	725	
Ratio-to-moving-averages method	A method for deseasonalizing a time series, so that some other method can then be used to forecast the deseasonalized series	StatTools/ Time Series & Forecasting/ Forecast	725	
Dummy variables for seasonality	A regression-based method for forecasting seasonality, where dummy variables are used for the seasons	StatTools/ Regression & Classification/ Regression	729	

PROBLEMS

Conceptual Questions

C.1. "A truly random series will likely have a very small number of runs." Is this statement true or false? Explain your choice.

C.2. Distinguish between a *correlation* and an *autocorrelation*. How are these measures similar? How are they different?

C.3. What is the relationship between the random walk model and an autoregression model, if any?

C.4. Under what conditions would you prefer a simple exponential smoothing model to the moving averages method for forecasting a time series?

C.5. Is it more appropriate to use an *additive* or a *multiplicative* model to forecast seasonal data? Summarize the difference(s) between these two types of seasonal models.

C.6. Explain why autocorrelations are so important in time series analysis. (Note that more advanced books on time series analysis investigate autocorrelations much more than we have done here.)

C.7. Suppose that monthly data on some time series variable exhibits a clear upward trend but no seasonality. You decide to use moving averages, with any appropriate span. Will there tend to be a systematic bias in your forecasts? Explain why or why not.

C.8. Suppose that monthly data on some time series variable exhibits obvious seasonality. Can you use moving averages, with any appropriate span, to track the seasonality well? Explain why or why not.

C.9. Suppose that quarterly data on some time series variable exhibits obvious seasonality, although the seasonal pattern varies somewhat from year to year. Which method do you believe will work best: Winters' method or regression with dummy variables for quarter (and possibly a time variable for trend)? Why?

C.10. Suppose you have three times series variables and you want to forecast the third one with an appropriate regression equation. You think that lagged values of all three variables might be useful explanatory variables in the regression equation. Explain how you could check the plausibility of this with appropriate correlations. If you find any fairly large correlations, explain how you would perform the appropriate regression with StatTools.

C.11. Most companies that use (any version of) exponential smoothing use fairly small smoothing constants such as 0.1 or 0.2. Explain why they don't tend to use larger values.

Level A

68. The file P12_68.xlsx contains monthly data on consumer revolving credit (in millions of dollars) through credit unions.
   a. Use these data to forecast consumer revolving credit through credit unions for the next 12 months. Do it in two ways. First, fit an exponential trend to the series. Second, use Holt's method with optimized smoothing constants.
   b. Which of these two methods appears to provide the best forecasts? Answer by comparing their MAPE values.

69. The file P12_69.xlsx contains net sales (in millions of dollars) for Procter & Gamble.
   a. Use these data to predict Procter & Gamble net sales for each of the next two years. You need consider only a linear and exponential trend, but you should justify the equation you choose.
   b. Use your answer from part **a** to explain how your predictions of Procter & Gamble net sales increase from year to year.
   c. Are there any outliers?
   d. You can be approximately 95% sure that Procter & Gamble net sales in the year following next year will be between what two values?

70. The file P12_70.xlsx lists annual revenues (in millions of dollars) for Nike. Forecast the company's revenue in each of the next two years with a linear or exponential trend. Are there any outliers in your predictions for the observed period?

71. The file P11_44.xlsx contains data on pork sales. Price is in dollars per hundred pounds sold, quantity sold is in billions of pounds, per capita income is in dollars, U.S. population is in millions, and GDP is in billions of dollars.
   a. Use these data to develop a regression equation that can be used to predict the quantity of pork sold during future periods. Is autocorrelation of residuals a problem?
   b. Suppose that during each of the next two quarters, price is $45, U.S. population is 240, GDP is 2620, and per capita income is $10,000. (All of these are expressed in the units described above.) Predict the quantity of pork sold during each of the next two quarters.
   c. Use Winters' method to develop a forecast of pork sales during the next two quarters. Does it appear to provide better (or different) predictions than the multiple regression in part **a**?

72. The file P12_72.xlsx contains data on a motel chain's revenue and advertising.
   a. Use these data and multiple regression to make predictions of the motel chain's revenues during

the next four quarters. Assume that advertising during each of the next four quarters is $50,000. (*Hint*: Try using advertising, lagged by one quarter, as an explanatory variable.)

  b. Use simple exponential smoothing to make predictions for the motel chain's revenues during the next four quarters.
  c. Use Holt's method to make forecasts for the motel chain's revenues during the next four quarters.
  d. Use Winters' method to determine predictions for the motel chain's revenues during the next four quarters.
  e. Which of these forecasting methods would you expect to be the most accurate for these data?

73. The file P12_73.xlsx contains data on monthly U.S. permits for new housing units (in thousands of houses).
  a. Using Winters' method, find values of α, β, and γ that yield an RMSE as small as possible. Does this method track the housing crash in recent years?
  b. Although we have not discussed autocorrelation for smoothing methods, good forecasts derived from smoothing methods should exhibit no substantial autocorrelation in their forecast errors. Is this true for the forecasts in part **a**?
  c. At the end of the observed period, what is the forecast of housing sales during the next few months?

74. Let Y_t be the sales during month t (in thousands of dollars) for a photography studio, and let P_t be the price charged for portraits during month t. The data are in the file P11_45.xlsx. Use regression to fit the following model to these data:

$$Y_t = a + b_1 Y_{t-1} + b_2 P_t + e_t$$

This equation indicates that last month's sales and the current month's price are explanatory variables. The last term, e_t, is an error term.
  a. If the price of a portrait during month 21 is $10, what would you predict for sales in month 21?
  b. Does there appear to be a problem with autocorrelation of the residuals?

Level B

75. The file P12_75.xlsx contains five years of monthly data for a particular company. The first variable is Time (1 to 60). The second variable, Sales1, contains data on sales of a product. Note that Sales1 increases linearly throughout the period, with only a minor amount of noise. (The third variable, Sales2, is discussed and used in the next problem.) For this problem use the Sales1 variable to see how the following forecasting methods are able to track a linear trend.
  a. Forecast this series with the moving average method with various spans such as 3, 6, and 12. What can you conclude?

  b. Forecast this series with simple exponential smoothing with various smoothing constants such as 0.1, 0.3, 0.5, and 0.7. What can you conclude?
  c. Now repeat part **b** with Holt's exponential smoothing method, again for various smoothing constants. Can you do significantly better than in parts **a** and **b**?
  d. What can you conclude from your findings in parts **a**, **b**, and **c** about forecasting this type of series?

76. The Sales2 variable in the file from the previous problem was created from the Sales1 variable by multiplying by monthly seasonal factors. Basically, the summer months are high and the winter months are low. This might represent the sales of a product that has a linear trend and seasonality.
  a. Repeat parts **a**, **b**, and **c** from the previous problem to see how well these forecasting methods can deal with trend *and* seasonality.
  b. Now use Winters' method, with various values of the three smoothing constants, to forecast the series. Can you do much better? Which smoothing constants work well?
  c. Use the ratio-to-moving-average method, where you first deseasonalize the series and then forecast (by any appropriate method) the deseasonalized series. Does this perform as well as, or better than, Winters' method?
  d. What can you conclude from your findings in parts **a**, **b**, and **c** about forecasting this type of series?

77. The file P12_77.xlsx contains monthly time series data on corporate bond yields. These are averages of daily figures, and each is expressed as an annual rate. The variables are:
  ■ Yield AAA: average yield on AAA bonds
  ■ Yield BAA: average yield on BAA bonds

If you examine either Yield variable, you will notice that the autocorrelations of the series are not only large for many lags, but that the lag 1 autocorrelation of the *differences* is significant. This is very common. It means that the series is not a random walk and that it is probably possible to provide a better forecast than the naive forecast from the random walk model. Here is the idea. The large lag 1 autocorrelation of the differences means that the differences are related to the first lag of the differences. This relationship can be estimated by creating the difference variable and a lag of it, then regressing the former on the latter, and finally using this information to forecast the original Yield variable.
  a. Verify that the autocorrelations are as described, and form the difference variable and the first lag of it. Call these DYield and L1DYield (where D means difference and L1 means first lag).
  b. Run a regression with DYield as the dependent variable and L1DYield as the single explanatory

variable. In terms of the original variable Yield, this equation can be written as

$$\text{Yield}_t - \text{Yield}_{t-1} = a + b(\text{Yield}_{t-1} - \text{Yield}_{t-2})$$

Solving for Yield_t is equivalent to the following equation that can be used for forecasting:

$$\text{Yield}_t = a + (1 + b)\text{Yield}_{t-1} - b\text{Yield}_{t-2}$$

Try it—that is, try forecasting the next month from the known last two months' values. How might you forecast values two or three months from the last observed month? (*Hint*: If you do not have an *observed* value to use in the right side of the equation, use a forecast value.)

c. The autocorrelation structure led us to the equation in part **b**. That is, the autocorrelations of the original series took a long time to die down, so we looked at the autocorrelations of the differences, and the large spike at lag 1 led to regressing DYield on L1DYield. In turn, this ultimately led to an equation for Yield_t in terms of its first two lags. Now see what you would have obtained if you had tried regressing Yield_t on its first two lags in the first place—that is, if you had used regression to estimate the equation

$$\text{Yield}_t = a + b_1\text{Yield}_{t-1} + b_2\text{Yield}_{t-2}$$

When you use multiple regression to estimate this equation, do you get the same equation as in part **b**?

78. The file P12_78.xlsx lists monthly and annual values of the average surface air temperature of the earth (in degrees Celsius). (Actually, the data are indexes, relative to the period $1951-1980$ where the average temperature was about 14 degrees Celsius. So if you want the actual temperatures, you can add 14 to all values.) A look at the time series shows a gradual upward trend, starting with negative values and ending with (mostly) positive values. This might be used to support the claim of global warming. For this problem, use only the annual averages in column N.

a. Is this series a random walk? Explain.

b. Regardless of your answer in part **a**, use a random walk model to forecast the next value (2010) of the series. What is your forecast, and what is an approximate 95% forecast interval, assuming normally distributed forecast errors?

c. Forecast the series in three ways: (i) simple exponential smoothing ($\alpha = 0.35$), (ii) Holt's method ($\alpha = 0.5$, $\beta = 0.1$), and (iii) simple exponential smoothing ($\alpha = 0.3$) on trend-adjusted data, that is, the residuals from regressing linearly versus time. (These smoothing constants are close to optimal.) For each of these, list the MAPE, the RMSE, and the forecast for next year. Also, comment on any "problems" with forecast errors from any of these three approaches. Finally, compare the qualitative features of the three forecasting methods. For example, how do their short-run or longer-run forecasts differ? Is any one of the methods clearly superior to the others?

d. Does your analysis predict convincingly that global warming has been occurring? Explain.

79. The file P12_79.xlsx contains data on mass layoff events in all industries in the U.S. (See the file for an explanation of how mass layoff events are counted.) There are two versions of the data: nonseasonally adjusted and seasonally adjusted. Presumably, seasonal factors can be found by dividing the nonseasonally adjusted values by the seasonally adjusted values. For example, the seasonal factor for April 1995 is 1431/1492=0.959. How well can you replicate these seasonal factors with appropriate StatTools analyses?

The Eastland Plaza Branch of the Indiana University Credit Union was having trouble getting the correct staffing levels to match customer arrival patterns. On some days, the number of tellers was too high relative to the customer traffic, so that tellers were often idle. On other days, the opposite occurred. Long customer waiting lines formed because the relatively few tellers could not keep up with the number of customers. The credit union manager, James Chilton, knew that there was a problem, but he had little of the quantitative training he believed would be necessary to find a better staffing solution. James figured that the problem could be broken down into three parts. First, he needed a reliable forecast of each day's number of customer arrivals. Second, he needed to translate these forecasts into staffing levels that would make an adequate trade-off between teller idleness and customer waiting. Third, he needed to translate these staffing levels into individual teller work assignments—who should come to work when.

The last two parts of the problem require analysis tools (queueing and scheduling) that we have not covered. However, you can help James with the first part—forecasting. The file Credit Union Arrivals.xlsx lists the number of customers entering this credit union branch each day of the past year. It also lists other information: the day of the week, whether the day was a staff or faculty payday, and whether the day was the day before or after a holiday. Use this data set to develop one or more forecasting models that James could use to help solve his problem. Based on your model(s), make any recommendations about staffing that appear reasonable. ■

Amanta Appliances sells two styles of refrigerators at more than 50 locations in the Midwest. The first style is a relatively expensive model, whereas the second is a standard, less expensive model. Although weekly demand for these two products is fairly stable from week to week, there is enough variation to concern management at Amanta. There have been relatively unsophisticated attempts to forecast weekly demand, but they haven't been very successful. Sometimes demand (and the corresponding sales) are lower than forecast, so that inventory costs are high. Other times the forecasts are too low. When this happens and on-hand inventory is not sufficient to meet customer demand, Amanta requires expedited shipments to keep customers happy—and this nearly wipes out Amanta's profit margin on the expedited units.[8] Profits at Amanta would almost certainly increase if demand could be forecast more accurately.

Data on weekly sales of both products appear in the file Amanta Sales.xlsx. A time series chart of the two sales variables indicates what Amanta management expected—namely, there is no evidence of any upward or downward trends or of any seasonality. In fact, it might appear that each series is an unpredictable sequence of random ups and downs. But is this really true? Is it possible to forecast either series, with some degree of accuracy, with an extrapolation method (where only past values of *that* series are used to forecast current and future values)? Which method appears to be best? How accurate is it? Also, is it possible, when trying to forecast sales of one product, to somehow incorporate current or past sales of the *other* product in the forecast model? After all, these products might be "substitute" products, where high sales of one go with low sales of the other, or they might be complementary products, where sales of the two products tend to move in the *same* direction. ▪

[8]Because Amanta uses expediting when necessary, its sales each week are equal to its customer demands. Therefore, the terms "demand" and "sales" are used interchangeably.